Designed

FOR

KEVIN J. BROWN

Designed
FOR

GOOD

*Recovering the Idea, Language,
and Practice of Virtue*

HENDRICKSON
PUBLISHERS

Designed for Good:
Recovering the Idea, Language, and Practice of Virtue

© 2016 Hendrickson Publishers, LLC

Published by Hendrickson Publishers
an imprint of Hendrickson Publishing Group
P. O. Box 3473
Peabody, Massachusetts 01961-3473
www.hendricksonpublishinggroup.com

ISBN 978-1-61970-848-8

Printed in the United States of America

Second Printing — August 2022

Library of Congress Cataloging-in-Publication Data

Names: Brown, Kevin (Kevin J.), author.
Title: Designed for good : recovering the idea, language, and practice of
    virtue / Kevin J. Brown.
Description: Peabody, MA : Hendrickson Publishers, 2016. | Includes
bibliographical references.
Identifiers: LCCN 2016028543 | ISBN 9781619708488 (alk. paper)
Subjects: LCSH: Virtue.
Classification: LCC BV4630 .B76 2016 | DDC 241/.4--dc23
    LC record available at https://lccn.loc.gov/2016028543

This book is dedicated to Joe and Carolyn Brown, my parents. I have spent a lifetime watching them embody the very virtues this book aims to bring to light.

CONTENTS

ACKNOWLEDGMENTS

I would hesitate to claim a single thought in this book that was not implicitly or explicitly beholden to another source. A conversation. A book. A lecture. In that sense, it would be impossible to sufficiently acknowledge all of my debts.

Of course, some debts are more conspicuous than others. Specifically, I would like to thank my graduate school advisors, Dr. Eric Stoddart from St. Andrews University and Dr. Julie Clague and Gwilym Pryce from the University of Glasgow. If there is any rubbish in the book, I am most certainly to be credited—but I would like to think that if there is anything good in the book, their thumbprint can be found. Yet another thumbprint comes from Hannah Brown at Hendrickson Publishers. Given her skills as an editor in addition to her expertise in classical virtue ethics, I could not have been blessed with a more fortunate arrangement.

I am so thankful for working at an institution that fosters ideas and their dissemination. I owe a great debt to our Asbury lunch meetings, coffee conversations, book studies, and student gatherings. I also want to thank the folks at Anderson University's Falls School of Business for their investment in me as a person and an academic.

I am wonderfully fortunate to have a spouse who is committed to thinking carefully about faithful living and virtue. My wife, Maria, has produced an array of thoughts whose depth, quality, and insight meet or exceed those to be found in some of my most cherished books. In addition to Maria, my children, Cambel, Ada, and Oliver, are a perpetual source of inspiration.

I want to thank Hubert, Nate, and Adriel for a (rather caffeinated!) meeting at Starbucks years back in which we discussed the popular "Parable of the Sadhu" case. This launched me into a deeper articulation of agent-based ethical inquiry.

I am also very thankful to Jason Mitchell—pastor, author, but above all, friend. Jason has long been a source of insight, and he provided helpful direction in shaping some of the contours of this book and its arguments.

I am so grateful to Les Stobbe, my agent, for the effort and expertise he has provided on my behalf.

Finally, I want to thank my parents, Joe and Carolyn, and my sisters, Jenn and Laura. I can never know the full extent of the blessing they have been to me.

Introduction:
What Is Virtue?

Whatever the cross and the gospel are about, it is not a slap
on the hand for kids refusing to heed the rules of the cookie
jar. It is not mere advice to get you to clean up your life and
morals. It is not mere ideas to inform you about what it takes
to be nice. It is restoration and re-creation, a physician's
meditation; it is about human flourishing and discovering life.

—Stuart McAllister

One of the most critical battles in human history took place
over two thousand years ago. But you have probably never heard
of it. By today's standards, it might seem rather tame—or worse,
boring.

Why?

Well, to begin, the battle was not physical (no spears, swords,
gladiator fights, etc.); it was philosophical. Furthermore, the conflict was not historical; it was literary. The parties involved were not
military representatives, and the dispute had little to do with state
or culture. No kings were crowned, no enemies vanquished, no kin
avenged, and no damsels saved. Because this skirmish is stripped
of these seductive storytelling characteristics, we might be justified
in neglecting the details.

But we would be making a mistake.

In fact, this clash of beliefs may be one of the most important
confrontations ever recorded. It was—and is—a battle over the nature of human purpose, significance, meaning, and fulfillment. It is
about living well—what we tend to refer to as a "good" life. It speaks

to flourishing—being blessed or happy. Understood in these terms, everything is at stake, for everyone.

The confrontation is set in Plato's most famous work, *The Republic*. The book's main character is Socrates, who served as Plato's teacher in real life. After initiating a discussion about the meaning of justice, Socrates is challenged by a Greek teacher named Thrasymachus, who famously describes justice as "nothing other than the advantage of the stronger."[1] According to him, being a good and decent person actually holds one back from having a better life. It is an impediment to real satisfaction and contentment. The virtue exhibited by the just, so goes the argument, is a barrier to climbing up the social ladder, accumulating wealth, and ultimately attaining happiness. To summarize, Thrasymachus believes that in order to live a happy life, assuming that happiness is attained through status or wealth, one is better off being unjust than just.

Thrasymachus is not alone. Chiming in on the argument is one of Socrates's students, Glaucon. He affirms the belief that injustice is something of a necessary evil, "for the life of the unjust man is, after all, far better than that of the just man, as they say."[2] To prove it, Glaucon provides an argument in the form of a thought experiment, a familiar story called the "Ring of Gyges."

Here is a modern-day version of the story. Imagine that while on a solitary hike in the woods, you stumble upon an alluring gold ring lying on the ground. As you will soon learn, this is no ordinary ring. When you turn the ring half a rotation on your finger, those around you speak and act as if you were not there. But when you turn the ring back to its normal position, they recognize your presence. To your amazement, you have stumbled upon a ring that can make you disappear and reappear at will.

What would it mean if such power were granted to you? It would mean that you could do whatever you wanted without the threat of judgment, consequence, or retaliation. You might be tempted to steal desirable goods, fulfill all manner of lusts, or perhaps enact cruel revenge against your enemies.

So, knowing that you could take any action you desired without consequence, how would you live? What would you do? In what way would you harness the power of this ring?

Glaucon suggests that even a just and upright man would use the ring to fulfill every desire he possessed. Without fear of punishment, he would steal from, harm, or sexually violate those around him, acting "as an equal to a god among humans."[3] Therefore, Glaucon, in line with Thrasymachus, summarizes: "All men suppose injustice is far more to their private profit than justice."[4]

What are Thrasymachus and Glaucon ultimately saying? In essence, they are suggesting that the moral life is not necessarily the happy life. We can seek to be moral, just, upright, and virtuous— but this will likely exclude us from the opportunity to be happy and fulfilled. However, if we seek the things that make us happy, this inevitably means that we cannot be moral. As ethicist Thomas Jensen writes, the implication is that "we have a hankering to free ourselves from morality, as if it were a burden preventing us from achieving happiness."[5]

Glaucon's "Ring of Gyges" exercise is meant to suggest that if we possessed the power of the ring, then we would ultimately reveal our true desires and thus our true selves. In other words, putting on the ring and unleashing its power strips away all social, political, and economic constraints, liberating the ring-bearer to indulge his or her innermost appetites. To paraphrase Oscar Wilde, it is when given a mask that a man reveals his true self.

After this challenge, the rest of *The Republic* is committed— through the mouth of Socrates—to proving that the just life is the best life one can lead. Contrary to Thrasymachus's and Glaucon's arguments that the unjust life is better, Socrates aims to convince them that a moral and virtuous lifestyle is not only the greatest expression of human excellence, but it is a life of happiness, meaning, and fulfillment; it is indeed a state worthy of pursuit.

These arguments presented thousands of years ago are actually quite relevant to how we conceive of morality today. In fact, I would go so far as to say that the "Ring of Gyges" story contains one of the most pressing and significant questions for our contemporary culture.

Hence, the purpose of this book.

The aim of this book is not to regurgitate Socrates's counterargument in defense of justice. However, my goal is to make a similar

case for virtue. That is, *the virtuous life is the best life.* The compre-
hension, vocabulary, and practice of virtue lead to the best version
of ourselves we can aspire to. To be virtuous is to seek, and attain,
the good.

The chapters to come will suggest that the ordered universe
that we inhabit is not simply an arbitrary by-product of chance plus
matter plus time, but a well-ordered design created by a deliberate
designer. Furthermore, I will argue that disconnecting our human
activity (how we function) from our intended design (our form)
will inevitably lead to an incoherent existence. In contrast to this
disconnect, when we recognize and participate in the idea, language, and practice of virtue, we draw closer to living the "perfect"
life as Jesus described it in Matthew 5:48, in which we are doing
what we were meant to do (function aligned with form).

Before getting under way with this argument, it is first important to attend to the very idea of virtue and what is meant by
this particular term. A few quick notes are in order. The descriptions below are not exhaustive, nor are they meant to be. Moreover,
some readers may quibble with how I describe virtue—the term is
packed with nuance and has been subject to an array of different
expressions over time. But this is not a book about the meaning of
virtue—it is a book about why virtue is our most necessary pursuit.
To assist the reader in the chapters to come, the section below aims
to articulate what is meant when this term is used.

Finally, many trace the virtue ethics tradition back to Plato
and Aristotle (and I will reference them accordingly). That said,
the thrust of the book's argument originates not from the classical
philosophers, but from the Christian faith tradition. In some places,
these two traditions may be consonant, but in other places they are
not. Where they are not, my appeal rests upon the foundations of
the faith tradition.

Arriving at Virtue

To best attend to the meaning of the word *virtue*, it is helpful
to explore what it is and what it is not.

Not "Ethics"

First and foremost, virtue—as I describe it—is not the same thing as ethics. Though certainly related to virtue, ethics and ethical reflection primarily involve the determination of what is right and wrong. Although we often talk about acting ethically, ethics as a discipline seems almost entirely concerned with establishing our dos and don'ts for particular situations.

In this sense, ethics is an intellectual exercise. Unfortunately, ethical knowledge or even ethical sensitivity does not necessarily translate into ethical action. Take, for example, the work of philosopher Eric Schwitzgebel, who has undertaken considerable research into the ethical behavior of ethics professors. It seems reasonable to believe that the more someone knows and understands ethics and ethical reasoning, the more likely they will be to *act* ethically in a given situation. Not true, Schwitzgebel says. He offers a humorous picture of what this gap looks like:

> An ethicist philosopher considers whether it's morally permissible to eat the meat of factory-farmed mammals. She reads Peter Singer. She reads objections and replies to Singer. She concludes that it is in fact morally bad to eat meat. She presents the material in her applied ethics class. Maybe she even writes on the issue. However, instead of changing her behavior to match her new moral opinions, she retains her old behavior. She teaches Singer's defense of vegetarianism, both outwardly and inwardly endorsing it, and then proceeds to the university cafeteria for a cheeseburger (perhaps feeling somewhat bad about doing so). To the student who sees her in the cafeteria, our philosopher says: Singer's arguments are sound. It is morally wrong of me to eat this delicious cheeseburger. But my role as a philosopher is only to discuss philosophical issues, to present and evaluate philosophical views and arguments, not to live accordingly.[6]

The hypocrisy is clear—the professor didn't "practice what she preached." Yet some simply do not see a problem with this disconnect. Schwitzgebel cites, for example, *New York Times* ethics writer Randy Cohen. In the final post of his long-running column, Cohen writes, "I wasn't hired to personify virtue, to be a role model for the kids, but to write about virtue in a way readers might find engaging."[7]

Or consider a rather puzzling exchange in an interview between philosopher Nigel Warburton and Marxist philosopher Gerry Cohen. After discussing Cohen's book *If You're an Egalitarian, How Come You're So Rich?*, Warburton points out that Cohen is an egalitarian who is rich. How does he reconcile this? Cohen responds, "I am not a morally exemplary person. That's all. That's the reconciliation."[8]

Here is the point: moral and ethical knowledge—while helpful, particularly as it relates to processing ethical situations—is different from moral and ethical performance. While a good nursing, accounting, or history class could conceivably produce a better nurse, accountant, or historian, we cannot claim that a good ethics class will make a student ethical. Deliberating over thorny ethical questions might be fodder for late-night dorm room discussions or dinner party conversations, but their application to our everyday life is another matter.

Virtue is altogether different. In fact, the difference can be found by looking at the word itself. The English word *virtue* derives from the Latin *virtus*, which can be translated as "manliness;" it can also mean "strength" or "vigor." As David Gill notes, the term "literally means something like power." That is, virtue is not simply knowledge about right action, but the *capacity* to act rightly. Gill writes, "Virtues are thus not just 'values' (traits that I feel are worthwhile) but 'powers' (real capabilities of achieving something good)."[9]

Furthermore, virtue is not simply knowing what is good, but desire for goodness. It connotes pursuit. It is striving to organize your life around the good, the right, and the true. Notice that virtue does not imply the abandonment of desire, but the cultivation of desire for what is truly desirable—that is, desiring well (more on this to come).

Thus, we may conclude that virtue is a strong disposition and a strong desire for good living (good thoughts, good language, and good actions). Given this, it is possible to have a robust sense of ethics, but to lack virtue.

Identity before Action

Often, we are tempted to think that virtue is a question of right or wrong action. This would be misleading. Virtue, and the larger "virtue ethics" tradition, has always been more concerned with who you are than with what you do. In other words, the analysis begins with the person doing the action (What kind of person should I be?) and then proceeds to the action (What should I do?), not the other way around.

Unfortunately, most "ethical" dilemmas are processed in a rigidly goal- or principle-based manner. There is nothing wrong with moral traditions that do this, but their primary concern relates to right *action*. For example, when students today are presented with an ethical question in a classroom setting, they are inevitably asked, "What should X do in Y situation?" In other words, what is the right activity? What is the optimal decision? What is the appropriate behavior for this situation? This implies that there is some magical ethics formula or decision-making matrix that allows the user to arrive at the morally appropriate answer. One is led to imagine something like a machine: you throw your ethical dilemma in the chute, churn the handle, and out comes the "right" solution.

Now, some may reasonably ask, "What is wrong with that?" First, such a mechanical approach to morality mistakes it for a science. This is wrong. Virtue is not a matter of testing falsifiable assertions; it is deliberating on, desiring, pursuing, and cultivating what it means to live well.

Second, and more importantly, virtue asks first about the good life, or what the nature and character of a person ought to be, and then determines the rightness or wrongness of specific actions based on that vision. This is not to dismiss the latter approach. Action-based ethical inquiry (i.e., inquiry about the *right* activity to do) is both important and necessary. However, this is different from an approach that focuses less on the isolated action, and more on the person performing the action. Virtue is about *being* over *doing*. That is to say, what kind of person should I be, and what right actions should I take as a function of who I am?

Jesus did not come simply to tell us what to do; he came to share and demonstrate who we should be, to confer an identity upon us, and to allow us think and act from this identity. As Skye Jethani writes, how we see will influence what we do in the world.[10] Unfortunately, many—if not most—do not regard virtue in this way.

As philosopher Alasdair Macintyre has stated, modern philosophy has a tendency to think atomistically about human action.[11] That is, we tend to divorce our activity (what we do) from other important dimensions of our life such as our identity (who we are). Virtue is not just about doing the right thing—it is about becoming the right kind of person. After accounting for what it means to live well, we can proceed to think carefully about the moral nature of our actions.

Wholeness vs. Right/Wrong

As the last section made clear, distilling ethics down to the study of isolated actions without considering the person doing the actions is problematic. In addition to this, we would be wrong to think that an action in itself can always be neatly parsed out as "right" or "wrong." As counterintuitive as it seems, this is actually an unaccommodating and misleading framework for understanding virtue.

To better think about this, it is helpful to borrow some statistical parlance commonly used to describe different kinds of variables. Some variables are *discrete*, meaning that the data can be grouped into distinct, "either/or" categories, or multiple categories that are all mutually exclusive. For example, either someone is pregnant or they are not pregnant. You can be either one or the other, but you cannot be both. It is an either/or category. Or consider a student's college rank: freshman, sophomore, junior, or senior. Here, there are several categories, but you cannot fall into two or more buckets (if you are a senior, then you aren't a junior, sophomore, or freshman).

Discrete variables are often contrasted with *continuous* variables. These variables can assume any value within a particular range. For example, when we talk about North Carolina's average temperature in July, our federal deficit, a firefighter's weight, the number of customers entering Starbucks each day, or foul balls at Wrigley per year, we are talking about continuous variables. If a variable is continuous, its values can be understood to fall within a range. Furthermore, movements along this range can reflect positions that are "better" or "worse." For example, if we asked how far along a project was relative to its completion date or whether someone who was sick is feeling better, the movement along the continuum reflects going from something undesirable to something desirable.

Here is why this matters: we often think (or like to think) of ethics and morality in discrete terms. Either an action is right or it is wrong. This may be appropriate for the field of theoretical ethics, but it is a poor paradigm for understanding what it means to be virtuous. Virtue is not simply about what we do, or our right and wrong actions (discrete); it is about attaining wholeness, being complete human beings. Moreover, note that this expression reflects attributes of being continuous. How? C. S. Lewis presents a helpful picture:

> People often think of Christian morality as a kind of bargain in which God says, "If you keep a lot of rules, I'll reward you, and if you don't I'll do the other thing." I do not think that is the best way of looking at it. I would much rather say that every time you make a choice you are turning the central part of you, the part of you that chooses, into something a little different from what it was before. . . . Each of us at each moment is progressing to the one state or the other.[12]

"Progressing to the one state or the other" implies that virtue, or its absence, is best understood as existing along a spectrum. If someone has a vacant, morally impoverished life, we would not simply say that he or she is "wrong"; a better description would be that such a person is incomplete. (Notice that this language is not merely relegated to the religious realm.) That is, people like this one are making decisions that fashion their characters into something less than whole. They are moving toward a kind of brokenness. They are organizing their lives in a way that stifles reason, short-circuits fulfillment, and impoverishes the human experience. In contrast, we have the capacity to make decisions that make us more whole—more aligned with our design. We can cultivate the disposition to think, speak, and act well. Though it is difficult to measure, we might say that virtue is a matter of degree.

For clarity, consider an example. I was once on a panel fielding questions from prospective students visiting our faith-based university. Toward the end, a young lady raised her hand and calmly said, "I have a controversial question." With everyone's attention, she continued, "I plan to be an English major in college—how do you feel about using literature that may possess questionable language such as cursing, etc.?"

I considered this, and answered that our desire is for all students to cultivate lifestyles that promote and foster the whole, or complete, life. In John 10:10, Jesus claimed that he had come that we may have life abundantly. Interestingly, the word for "abundantly," *perissós*, means equal distance, all over, or all around. In other words, Jesus is saying that the abundant life is the *complete* life ("life all around"). After explaining this, I ended by saying that we will pursue activities that will reasonably fulfill a student's opportunity to realize wholeness.

Now, some might say that this was an evasive answer, and to some degree that is a valid criticism. However, it is only evasive if you think that questions about cursing (or any other behavioral rules) are best understood in a simplified right-wrong matrix. Yet what if virtue was about "progressing toward something different," as Lewis suggests—about organizing our lives in a way so as to be complete? Here, actions no longer fall into discrete buckets or categories. Rather, they are bound up with larger questions of human purpose, wholeness, and design. Understood in these terms, the virtuous thing is the arrangement that best allows me to experience "life all around"; to develop into the person I was designed to be. The difference may be subtle, but it is an important one.

Therefore, we might say that virtue is a life of character. It is about organizing, prioritizing, and habituating ourselves to be fulfilled, whole, and complete. "This requires," writes virtue ethicist Julia Annas, "reflecting in a thoughtful way about your life as a whole and the kind of person you aspire to be."[13] This is very different from simply determining whether cursing (or fill in the blank) is "bad." As mentioned, concepts of "right" and "wrong" are logically dependent upon a larger conception of wholeness. Divorced from this, the binary categories of "right" and "wrong" are at best arbitrary and at worst incoherent.

More Than "Backseat Ethics"

Let's do an exercise. Suppose I were to ask you to articulate what is morally objectionable about the legalization of marijuana (or other drugs). What would you say? What moral reasons would you give to justify maintaining its illegal status in some states?

Next, suppose I were to change the question, and ask you what is morally objectionable about the criminalization of marijuana (or other drugs): What would you say? What moral reasons would you give to justify its legalization?

Most people's answer to the first scenario might appeal to the notion of "harm" in some way. In other words, something about the legalization of marijuana is *harmful*, and therefore its illegal status is morally justified. So, for example, answers might range from "Marijuana would have long-term adverse effects on cognitive capacity" or "There would be more car-related accidents or deaths" to "Open marijuana usage would undermine the moral foundations of civil society." Note that in all three responses, the concept of harm stands as the foundation for the moral appeal, whether it be harm to the individual, harm to others, or even harm to some larger idea of "civil society."

What about the second scenario? If someone had to morally justify the legalization of marijuana or other recreational drugs, they might appeal to "fairness" as a moral defense. For example, a common answer might be, "People have the right to put what they want in their body—including drugs. It's not my body, so I can't tell them otherwise." Or answers might even address both harm and fairness: "It is their body, and they have the right to put in it what they want so long as it doesn't harm me or anyone else."

In his book *The Righteous Mind*, Jonathan Haidt claims that people who fixate on harm or fairness as the primary basis for morality are "weird." Not weird as in strange, but WEIRD as in coming from a culture that is "Western, Educated, Industrialized, Rich, and

Democratic." Haidt claims that if you come from a WEIRD culture, you are much more likely to prize individuality and autonomy as social values. Moreover, the traditions that have arisen to govern societies that value these attributes have put forth moral systems "that are individualistic, rule-based, and universalist."[14] Such systems, naturally, emphasize avoiding harm and maintaining fairness. After all, if we are nothing but individual automatons with our own conceptions of what is good for us, then injury or inequity seem to pose the greatest threats to us.

I refer to this overemphasis on harm and fairness as *backseat ethics*. Why? Any parent who has ever travelled with children has suffered the frustration of siblings fighting in the backseat (I know my parents certainly did!). Interestingly, those backseat fights almost always originate from one of two problems: harm or lack of fairness. That is, the source of frustration will likely be attributed to some kind of harmful action ("He hit me!") or to some kind of unfair arrangement ("She got more than I did!").

In a general sense, it would be easy to collapse the larger notion of virtue into the more limited harm/fairness paradigm. Yet this would be a mistake. We have already discussed that virtue is associated with being (who you are), not simply doing (what you do). Virtue, however, fits awkwardly into a WEIRD culture. In other words, the term packs too many moral elements to fit into the otherwise limited suitcase of harm and fairness.

Here is the takeaway: to be virtuous and to live a virtuous life is to appeal to something greater than an ethic of autonomy. It is to draw from a deeper moral well that includes community, sacredness, divinity, purpose, meaning, significance, and destiny. It is the belief that there is an essence to reality, and that a good and virtuous life is intricately tied to this essence.

A person who is fair, compliant, and harmless is not likely to be labeled as bad. However, this does not by definition make them good or virtuous. Moreover, the ethic of harmlessness and fairness—and the individualistic, autonomous cloth it is cut from—are insufficient to capture the breadth, depth, and richness of moral excellence packed into the notion of virtue.

Happiness as a State of Mind?

Aristotle defined happiness as the "supreme good for man." In this sense, a good life—indeed, life's very purpose—is happiness. The term has a long history, but its place in the American lexicon was secured in 1776 in the Declaration of Independence. In it, Thomas Jefferson famously writes, "We hold these truths to be self-evident, that all men are created equal, that they are endowed by their Creator with certain unalienable Rights, that among these are Life, Liberty and the pursuit of Happiness." An "unalienable" (or "inalienable") right cannot be taken away. That is, in America, no one can take away our right to pursue a life of happiness.

Few will dispute this. However, there is less agreement on how we define the very term. What does it mean to be happy? One popular notion is that happiness is a state of mind. In other words, it relates to how one feels or perceives the world. Being happy is not so much about reality as it is about how you perceive reality. This was creatively illustrated in the popular 2010 movie *Inception*, in which the main character, Dominick Cobb (played by Leonardo DiCaprio), has the ability to traipse in and out of various dream worlds. Cobb is obsessed with what is real, but at the end of the movie, after trying to determine whether he is living in reality or in a dream, he finally ignores his pursuit of the truth and decides to inhabit the reality he finds himself in (not knowing whether it is the real world or a dream world). The point seems clear: if he is in a desirable state of mind (i.e., "happy"), is that not more important than determining what is real? What is reality, anyway? Better to live blissfully in an illusory world than to be miserable in a real one.

The idea isn't new. The famous political philosopher Robert Nozick described a hypothetical "experience machine" that enabled participants to have any experience they desired. For example, they could be made to believe that they had rich and fulfilling friendships, or perhaps even to live under the illusion that they were famous. All the while, however, they would be floating in a water tank with an array of electrodes connected to their body. "Of course," writes Nozick, "while in the tank you won't know that you're there;

you'll think it's all actually happening."[15] This naturally raises the question: If such a machine existed, would you use it? If life is indeed about feeling happy, would not such a machine be desirable?

On the surface, this may sound reasonable. Having a sense of pleasure, a grasp of power, or the perception of promise is, many believe, the secret sauce of happiness. However, we may not be as convinced as we think. Some have argued that happiness is not simply a state of mind, but rather a state of mind that is a logical function of a state of affairs. A life cannot be good in spite of how we live; it is good *because* it is lived well. That is, one's life is good when it functions the way it was meant to function.

Several years ago, a team of researchers from Yale conducted an experiment in which they pitched two similar scenarios to respondents about a hypothetical character, Maria. In each story, Maria is described as enjoying her day-to-day activities and, moreover, she feels like there isn't anything she would rather be doing with her life. However, her activities in the two stories are quite different. One describes Maria as a caring individual who nurtures her children, undertakes important work projects, and has a network of meaningful relationships. The other describes Maria as a shallow, sycophantic groveler with no meaningful friendships; otherwise aimless, her goal is to party and enhance her social status.

In the experiment, participants were randomly assigned to hear one of these two scenarios and were then asked, "Is Maria happy?" Now, if happiness were only about someone's emotional state, then we would expect all the respondents to answer that Maria was, in fact, happy. (Recall that both scenarios said she enjoyed her day-to-day activities and felt like there wasn't anything she would rather be doing with her life.) However, the researchers found that while participants who heard the first scenario overwhelmingly suggested that Maria was happy, those who heard the second scenario judged her to be unhappy.[16]

What are we to conclude from this? One implication is that our determinations about happiness are not simply relegated to judgments about a certain state of mind, but rather, they are judgments about the kind of life a person leads. Another way of putting it would be to say that our aim in life is not simply to "feel" a certain way (we have powerful drugs that can easily achieve that)—it is to live a certain way. We intuitively believe that how we feel should be consonant with how we live. We want a sense of achievement to be accompanied by the actual completion of an important task, not simply an artificial delusion that we have accomplished something significant. We believe happiness is rightfully derived from a life lived well.

The Greeks had a concept that captured this notion of happiness, *eudaemonia*. The term literally means "good demon." While *eudaemonia* is often translated with our modern-day word *happy*, it is an awkward translation at best. Rather, *eudaemonia* is supreme human excellence. It is flourishing. It is a blessed, righteous, fulfilling life. According to Aristotle, "what is most eudaemonistic is what is most lastingly admirable rather than most sensually and subjectively pleasurable."[17]

Though difficult to put in a box, notice that this idea of living well is not necessarily subjective. Once, while in a discussion with a friend, I was challenged for extolling virtue as a supreme human aim. My friend disagreed, suggesting that human aims are subjective experiences, and therefore one aim is no better than another. I said that I would accept the criticism if my friend could honestly say that an overweight recluse who spends his waking hours bingeing on whiskey and Doritos while watching television reruns could be described as living a "good life." Thankfully, my friend was not willing to make this concession.

Contrary to the philosophy of Thrasymachus and Glaucon mentioned earlier, one must possess virtue in order to attain *eudaemonia*—a life of fulfillment; flourishing. Moreover, as this chapter has sought to make clear, virtue is not a subjective idea; it is grounded in a larger conception of human meaning, purpose, and excellence. Rather, virtue is about being who I was created to be. In this sense, my welfare and well-being—my *happiness*—is not simply up to me.

Moving Forward—Why Virtue?

So, why virtue? I believe it is worth taking up the challenge posed by Thrasymachus and Glaucon centuries ago. The forthcoming chapters are an attempt to comprehensively answer this very question.

In his encyclical *Veritatis splendor*, Pope John Paul II writes, "This essential bond between Truth, the Good and Freedom has been largely lost sight of by present-day culture. As a result, helping man to rediscover it represents nowadays one of the specific requirements of the Church's mission, for the salvation of the world."[18] That was written over twenty years ago, but could easily be considered an appropriate, and perhaps urgent, challenge for our contemporary setting. I humbly invite the reader into this rediscovery: the idea, language, and practice of virtue. *The good.*

DISCUSSION QUESTIONS
FOR GROUP STUDY

1. The chapter begins by discussing the arguments of Thrasymachus and Glaucon found in Plato's famous work, *The Republic*. What is the point of their argument? In today's modern culture, where would their arguments find support?

2. The chapter talks about the etymological connection between the word *virtue* and the word *power*. What are the implications of this as we consider morality? Can you think of examples where you see ethics and morality that lack power today?

3. As mentioned, our actions do not occur in a vacuum, but are rather a function of identity or character. If you are willing, share where you may have "habituated immorality" in your life.

4. How does thinking of virtue and morality as something continuous—that is, moving on a scale toward wholeness—differ from thinking about it in binary categories of right and wrong? How might this metaphor for morality be helpful? Where do we need to be careful so that it does not become harmful?

5. Jonathan Haidt describes cultures that are WEIRD and notes their emphasis on harm or fairness as comprehensive moral foundations. Can you provide a reason for why recreational drugs should *not* be legalized that does not have harm, or perhaps fairness, as its moral basis?

6. Many countries attempt to measure the welfare and well-being of their citizens by conducting self-reported "happiness indices" (literally asking people how happy they are). Given the discussion of happiness in the chapter (and the findings from the Yale research team)—what are the implications of using "happiness" as a measure for well-being?

7. What would need to be different about your life today for you to experience *eudaemonia* as it was described in the chapter?

1

The Perfect Version of Ourselves

"How many of us ever know what it is to become the perfect version of ourselves?"

—"Eddie Morra" (Bradley Cooper), *Limitless*

An Intuition about Intuition

Consider two stories.

In fall of 1993, an otherwise uneventful train ride near Mobile, Alabama, turned disastrous. While the "Sunset Limited" Amtrak train passed over an unstable bridge in the middle of the night, the structure gave way, plunging the train into the dark bayou below. Over a hundred passengers were injured and over forty were killed. To this day, the wreck is still considered the worst in Amtrak's history. Amazingly, eleven-year-old Andrea Chauncey managed to live. Her survival, though, could not be attributed to her own physical strength; she was wheelchair-bound with cerebral palsy. In the brief moments before the train was completely engulfed in murky river water, Andrea's parents, Gary and Mary Jane Chauncey, managed to push their daughter through an opening in a nearby windowpane seconds before they drowned. Amidst the chaos and confusion, Andrea's parents committed their final earthly moments to her survival.[1]

Thirteen months later, and just a few hundred miles away, a somewhat similar tragedy occurred. On a late October evening in Union, South Carolina, a Mazda Protegé careened down the embankment of the John D. Long Lake, only to be submerged in water moments later. Sadly, two children, Michael Smith, who was three years old, and Alexander Smith, who was just one, were helplessly trapped in their car seats inside. Unlike Andrea Chauncey in the Amtrak wreck the year before, no heroic effort would be made to save them. Even darker, in the days that followed it was discovered that their mother, Susan Smith, had purposefully sent the two innocent children to their death. Why? So that she could continue an extramarital relationship with a wealthy businessman who made it clear that he did not want children in the equation.[2]

For different reasons, both stories evoke an intuitive reaction on the part of the reader. I use the word *intuitive* deliberately. A reaction that is intuitive is "based on what one feels to be true even without conscious reasoning."[3] In other words, I am assuming that upon hearing each story, the reader will not require a moment of rational reflection in order to determine the most appropriate response. Rather, it seems to work the other way around. We have an initial, visceral response and then use our rational resources to make sense of the intuition, or "gut reaction," that preceded it.

What does this gut reaction have to do with morality? If you have ever gotten into a heated argument with someone about a moral question or peered into the (often inflammatory) comments section of an online article, you may have come away with the idea that *all* moral judgments are derived from merely emotional reactions. Before we advance into a discussion of virtue, then, we first need to determine whether morality has any rational foundations in the first place.

The ordering between emotion and reason has been explored in the work of Jonathan Haidt, a professor of psychology at the University of Virginia (mentioned in the introduction). Haidt, who has dedicated a significant portion of his career to understanding moral reasoning in humans, has sought to answer the long-debated question: Which comes first, intuition or rationality? This question is important. For in answering, Haidt argues, we are also saying something about the origin of our moral and ethical reflection. In other words, do moral judgments originate from the heart (emotions), or from the head (reason)?

Haidt rightly points out that "Western philosophy has been worshipping reason and distrusting the passions for thousands of years."[4] Indeed, philosophers from Plato (who died 348/347 BC) to Immanuel Kant (1724–1804) urged that emotional reactions should be trained to accord with correct reasoning. Under this view, emotions may galvanize us to action, but they don't necessarily help us to discern the truth about what we ought to do. Instead, these philosophers asserted that correct moral judgments are a function of rational, calculated reflection.

In contrast, Scottish philosopher David Hume believed that reason was a servant to our "passions," or our emotions. Under this view, we have an intuitive reaction to a person, place, or thing, and then our reason sweeps in to justify our feelings. Rationality does not determine our belief; instead, our beliefs are justified with rational reasoning.

So, who has it right? The rationalists or the intuitionists?

Based upon his research, Haidt opts for the latter position. One way Haidt made this determination was to employ a unique survey method. It is unique because the surveyor, who normally plays a passive role (asks question, records answer), would provide a scenario to the respondent, ask them to react to it, and then proceed to aggressively inquire as to why they answered the way they did. The purpose of this was to determine if, by playing devil's advocate, they could get the respondent to change their initial judgment.

Here's an example. One experiment involved soliciting atheists to sell their soul in exchange for two dollars (they actually had to sign a contract agreeing to the exchange). One might assume that this would be a simple transaction since most atheists typically don't affirm the existence of the soul, or the devil. Amazingly, though, only 23 percent of subjects were willing to sell the very thing they didn't believe existed.[5] When atheists who were reluctant to sign the contract were pressed to articulate their reasons for hesitating, most subjects, writes Haidt, responded by saying, "I just don't want to do it, even though I can't give you a reason."[6] This experiment (and many others like it), led Haidt to conclude that Hume had it right: intuitions come first, reasoning second. Haidt writes: "You'll misunderstand moral reasoning if you think about it as something people do by themselves in order to figure out the truth."[7]

There are many implications to this claim. Haidt, an evolutionist, believes our intuitive reactions, passions, and even our moral judgments often reflect disgust. Disgust, he suggests, is an important evolutionary adaptation that prevents "contamination." In this view, human beings' lofty ideas about justice, freedom, sacredness, and the like are really just expressions of a "pre-wired," instinctive reaction that is designed to keep us alive. If this is true, there are considerable implications related to the nature of morality itself. According to one philosopher, Haidt's findings and other similar research provide strong evidence that there is no such thing as a moral truth:

> All the talk about ethical judgments and using reason to arrive at ethical judgments—it's a nice veneer on the basic fact that we really have inconsistent systems. [Our] emotions take over at some point or another, and therefore we simply make up these stories to explain to ourselves why we make judgments one way or the other.[8]

This would certainly make sense if, indeed, our deepest intuitions, emotional reactions, and moral judgments were simply a function of an evolutionarily developed sense of disgust that has assisted us in survival.

It is worth reflecting on the challenge Haidt poses. First, if Haidt's conclusion is true, then there is no such thing as morality that is rational. Rather, our moral judgments would boil down to an instinctual emotion rather than a consideration of an objective good.

But what if our intuition is telling us something else? Something more? What if our visceral, emotional reactions were not simply adapted survival instincts, but an impulse toward an order? An inclination toward the way things should be? An appeal to a standard outside of ourselves?

Further, let's test Haidt's theory from another direction: Are there any real moral goods that we can agree upon? Consider again the contrasting narratives of the Chaunceys and Susan Smith. The stories sting for different reasons. However, they share important attributes: love and sacrifice. It was love that made the Chaunceys instinctively force their disabled daughter through an opening to save her life rather than their own. Yet it was also love that motivated the troubled Smith to send her helpless children to their death so that she could sustain an affair. The difference, of course, is in the nature of the sacrifice. The Chaunceys sacrificed themselves so their daughter would live (love of other). Smith sacrificed her children so that she could pursue her desired lifestyle (love of self). It is the difference between sacrifice of self for another and the sacrifice of another for self.

At the very least, we have evidence that there may be rational moral goods that exist after all. Sacrificial love has an excellence to it. We admire the Chaunceys' demonstration of love as honorable, even sacred. Such stories humble us. Alternatively, the sacrifice of another for self, particularly the sacrifice of innocent children, is repulsive. In addition to our horror at the story, Smith's actions are objectively vile, cruel, and corrupt.

Are we really to believe that these judgments are arbitrary?

The Christian narrative suggests that our moral judgments need not be random emotional reactions, but rather, reflect an order that exists outside of us. According to this belief, our intuitions confirm the presence, not the absence, of a moral reality. They tell us that we are reacting to something real, present, and fixed when we take in the world around us. Moreover, the Christian narrative suggests that humans have an essence: intrinsic qualities far beyond the mere sum of our biological attributes. Simply put: we were designed. And if we were designed, then we have a purpose. The term "design" is etymologically connected to the word *designate*—we were *designated* for something.

If we accept this narrative and its claims, the implications are significant.

The Perfect Version of Myself

I have suggested that our moral reactions and judgments may not simply be arbitrary. Rather, they point to a kind of reality. This reality is not as visible as our physical and material reality, but it can just as easily be detected. It is a *stealth* reality. Like oxygen, it is not discernable to the naked eye. Although I cannot see oxygen, its presence is vital to me living and living well. C. S. Lewis referred to this reality as the *Tao*, or the "sole source of all value judgments."[9] Similarly, poet Antoine de Saint-Exupery writes, "It is only with the heart that one can see rightly; what is essential is invisible to the eye."[10] Or as Eugene Peterson tells us, though the existence of this reality is not visible, "Its character is known."[11]

This idea certainly isn't new. It was Plato who long ago suggested that there were two worlds. The first was the visible world. This world, which is the present one we occupy, can be understood through the senses: sight, sound, taste, smell, and touch.[12] This world is apprehended and known through observation and experience. The second world, contrastingly, contains everything that is changeless, undying, and perfect—what Plato referred to as the "Forms." This immaterial world, which cannot be understood through the senses, consists of the ideal, the true, and the real. According to Plato, the Forms are eternal and universal. They are thus more real than objects in the visible world, which are constantly changing and decaying.

For clarity, we might imagine a fictitious conversation with Plato himself. Suppose he were to ask you to define the essence of a cat. You might say, "Well, cats purr, claw, meow, and cuddle." True as this may be, Plato would likely respond by saying, "You have only described to me what a cat does, but this does not necessarily make a cat a cat. So, what gives a cat its cat-ness?" Here, Plato believed that there was a form of a cat that was common to all cats, providing us with a kind of *cat essence*. Whether he was discussing cats, circles, numbers, or even human laws and just decisions—these things, thought Plato, each depended on their own unchanging essence. Each had a perfect archetype in the universe of the forms. Therefore, the more each thing reflected its form, the closer it came to reality.

Beyond cats, there is a form—an *essence*—to a human. Again, it's important to note that for Plato, this human essence doesn't just correspond to the modern idea of a "species." On the one hand, as we saw with the cat, this human essence is already present in each of us. It's what makes us distinctively human. But because the essence of humanity is like the forms—perfect, complete, and unchanging—it's also something we can aspire to reflect more and more.

Plato's theory of the forms, while interesting, had little discussion of God or gods. St. Augustine, however, was different. Augustine recognized Plato's understanding of the "forms" but related them to God's eternal law. Specifically, he believed that the universe had a particular order to it. This order was not simply physical; it was moral as well. Therefore, for Augustine, to approach the perfect form of a human one had to participate in this moral and spiritual order. As Thomas Williams writes regarding Augustine's philosophy, "Moral uprightness . . . consists in submission to this eternal and immutable truth, which is not of our own making."[13] In other words, if I want to live right, I must live within the order laid out by the Creator. I must live the way the Designer designed me to live. I must fulfill my human purpose.

Even pop culture, in its own secularized way, has captured this idea. A helpful example can be found in the 2011 movie *Limitless*. The movie's main character, Eddie Morra (played by Bradley Cooper), is an aimless writer whose prospects are bleak. On the verge of losing his girlfriend and struggling to pay his rent, he is given special access to a pill that unlocks the full potential of his mind. His entire life is transformed. He writes his book in a matter of days, speaks multiple languages, amasses exorbitant wealth through day-trading, and transforms himself from a social misfit into an attractive socialite. He becomes *limitless*.

While the movie was interesting, my attention was captured in the film's preview. Eddie poses the question: "How many of us ever know what it is to become the perfect version of ourselves?" I was rather taken with this expression because it is, I believe, inherently Christian.

Jesus himself articulated a similar idea. During his Sermon on the Mount, Christ teaches the crowd to "be perfect, . . . as your heavenly Father is perfect" (Matt. 5:48). These days, the word *perfect* is not a very popular term. At face value, this text seems to suggest that we are expected to be perfect in the sense of being faultless or blameless. That is, "Don't ever do anything bad or wrong." Be flawless.

Such a reading, though, misses an important nuance in this term. The Greek word for "perfect" here is *teleioi*. This adjective (the singular form is *teleios*) describes something that has reached its end or its aim. The term originates from the word *telos*, which can mean "purpose," "end," or "good." For example, we might ask about the *telos* of a car, which is to transport people from one place to the next. Similarly, the *telos* of a chair is to allow me to sit, and sit comfortably, upon it. The *telos* of a flute is to produce beautiful music. In ancient Greek thought, a thing's *telos* is also closely related to its essence. A *telos* is not just any goal: it's the goal that each particular thing, whether a car, a chair, or a flute, is uniquely designed to accomplish.

So Jesus is not telling us to be faultless (there is another Greek word for that). He is telling us to be complete, to live the way we were meant to live. It is for this reason that Eugene Peterson translates this verse as saying, "Live out your God-created identity" (Matt. 5:48, *The Message*). We might say that Jesus is telling us to be "the perfect version of ourselves."

Implicit in Jesus' command to be "perfect" is the notion of design. In other words, to command us as followers to become complete is to suggest that there was intention behind our creation. Being "spiritual" is not simply about exhibiting spiritual traits such as humility, obedience, joy, or any other attribute you might hear in a classic hymn or a modern worship song. Rather, it is about becoming who I was meant to be. This, of course, raises some questions: How do I know who I am supposed to be? What "true self" should I be aiming toward?

Would the Real Mark Pierpont Please Stand Up?

Years ago, the prominent evangelical Mark Pierpont was working vigorously to promote a biblical view of sexuality and "cure" gay people of same-sex attraction. Pierpont had a problem, though. He was gay. In the 2007 documentary *Protagonist*, Pierpont openly discusses the dissonance he experienced between his beliefs against homosexual behavior and his own homosexual desires and actions.

In a 2011 *New York Times* article, philosopher Joshua Knobe explores Pierpont's story. Knobe was interested in the tension Pierpont experienced while attempting to harbor these two competing identities. When presented with Pierpont's dilemma, many might be quick to respond that he simply needs to be true to himself—a "distinctive ideal of modern life."[14] But, writes Knobe, which "self" should Pierpont be true to? Who is the real Mark Pierpont?

One perspective says that the true self can be found by reflecting on values. In other words, if you want to know who a person is, look at their beliefs. An alternative perspective is that the true self is observed in people's behaviors. Their suppressed urges, desires, and emotions are the more accurate indicator of who they are. Under this line of reasoning, if you want to know who a person is, look at their actions.

Knobe, who is not religious, is dissatisfied with both of these views. Believing that neither perspective fully captures the complexity of the "self," he points to the larger question of human purpose and design. He writes, "People's ordinary understanding of the true self appears to involve a kind of value judgment, a judgment about what sorts of lives are really worth living."[15] In other words, to answer Knobe's question (What is the true self?), we need an answer to an antecedent question: What are we designed to do? What is the purpose, or the *telos*, of a human?

We can think of human welfare and flourishing as encompassing two independent but highly related concepts: our design and our functioning. The idea of design suggests that there is meaning, purpose, and deliberation behind our existence. If we live in a world of design, then there is an aim or an objective to the human experience. In other words, we were meant to live a certain way. Separate, but highly related, is the notion of functioning. Functioning relates to how we live, act, behave, and operate. Functioning is about what we do.

An example may add clarity. Several years ago in Zambia there was a most unusual fishing crisis. Lake Tanganyika, one of the largest freshwater lakes in the world, was running out of fish. Contrary to what you might suspect, the problem was not that the lake was being overfished. Rather, it was the way the fishing occurred. Local fishermen were using mosquito nets instead of conventional fishing nets. These bed nets, which have a very fine mesh, caught small fish before they reached maturity, prohibiting them from spawning and producing new offspring.[16] The nets, clearly not used for their intended purpose, had been obtained through a government program to help prevent malaria. As a result of their misuse, the sustainability of fishing and the overall biodiversity of Lake Tanganyika have been severely threatened.

Returning to design and function, it is possible for a thing's design to make sense without it functioning accordingly. In the example above, the mosquito nets were designed to protect villagers in African countries from malaria. The design was a sound one. Their functional use, however, did not reflect that design. As opposed to being draped over beds, the nets were used for fishing which, in turn, harmed the conservation and future sustainability of one of East Africa's largest economic resources.

Here's the point: for the net to function correctly, there must be an antecedent notion of its intended purpose. Without this, the function of the net becomes a matter of how a person best sees fit to use it. This can have its benefits, as many items are repurposed for uses that deviate from their original design. However, as in the case of Lake Tanganyika, functioning without consideration for design can often lead to unnatural—and many times harmful—consequences.

The implications for the "real" self become clear. To relate this to the case of Mark Pierpont, his identity is not simply a matter of who he is; it is first and foremost a matter of who he should be. It is about determining his *telos*, or his end. Debating whether the real Mark Pierpont is the Bible-believing evangelical leader or the closet homosexual becomes a case of two ships passing in the night unless both of these identities are examined against an overarching reality.

In other words, when how we function is disconnected from a discussion about how we are meant to function, questions about identity (who we are) and action (what we do) become less about reality, and act more as a menu for us to choose from. Beliefs about the good life are relegated to the open marketplace of ideas. Given Haidt's findings that our intuitions tend to precede our reason, this arrangement conveniently allows us to believe whatever we like and justify our preference afterwards. The risk is a life that is incoherent. We want to be good, but we have only a vague sense of what "good" means. A 2015 Gallup poll found that when Americans were asked to rate the overall state of moral values in the United States, 42 percent of them provided a ranking of "poor." Even more troubling, 74 percent of those surveyed believed that the state of moral values is "getting worse" in our country.[17] Yet without an overarching sense of order, purpose, and design, it is unclear what "excellent" moral values would even look like. We lament the trajectory of our moral values, but when asked what moral excellence is, we shrug our shoulders. As C. S. Lewis wrote over half a century ago, "Such is the tragi-comedy of our situation. We continue to clamour for those very qualities we are rendering impossible."[18]

Unfortunately, it appears the divide between how we are functioning and how we were designed to function is widening.

"Not Into the Whole Design Thing"

Once while at a conference, I was excited to have a former student in the audience. When I had him in class, I deeply appreciated his personality, thoughts, and drive as a person. He would pull me aside after lectures and ask an array of questions relating to the material—a clear sign of interest. As a professor, such attentiveness was a delight (after all, it is nice to feel like what we're saying is important!).

My conference presentation related to preference theory in economics. One branch of welfare economics suggests that the most suitable arrangement is one in which people can best satisfy their preferences. This provides an array of benefits, but there is a problem: some have a preference for reading to children, while others have a preference for child pornography. However, both are given equal weight in the utilitarian calculus (in other words, individual morality is not a consideration even though the subject relates to human "welfare"). In response to this, I spent a considerable amount of time discussing Augustine, moral reality, and the idea of moral order. Without an overarching conception of design, I proposed, there is no standard by which to evaluate the moral significance of our various preferences.

Expecting some agreeable gesture or like-minded discussion from the student after the presentation, I was surprised to find a serious and concerned look on his face. After a few moments he addressed me: "You know I love these ideas and concepts: morality, order, meaning, purpose, and design. However, I think of my roommate. He just wants to do the very best he can do at his job and be an overall good guy. *He's not into the whole design thing.*"

The comment was an honest expression—but it's misguided. While I was much kinder, I would imagine that Augustine's reply could have sounded something like this: "Is your roommate also not into the whole *gravity* thing?" In other words, whether we choose to believe it or not, gravity exists. If I were to jump off the roof of my garage, completely sincere in my belief that gravity is fictitious, or at least convinced of its unimportance, my conviction would have no bearing whatsoever on the fact that I would break several bones seconds later. Is our moral reality any different from this physical reality? We can choose to say it doesn't exist. We can downplay its importance. We can be altogether unenthusiastic about "the whole design thing"—but this does not shield us from the effects of transgressing its laws.

I also noticed, however, his reference to his roommate's sincerity in wanting to be "good." This is not surprising in the least. After all, moral values are important to us. We desire moral and ethical uprightness in our president, our leaders, and our institutions. We desire it in ourselves. We believe moral and ethical sensibilities are necessary fixtures in our tool belt for success. A 2011 study found that the majority of people believe that character is what it takes for a young person to succeed in today's world.[19] Further, we express these beliefs to our offspring. A more recent study found that teaching children responsibility, hard work, and good manners were of utmost importance among the American general public when it comes to teaching values.[20] Part of having a good world, so goes the belief, is having a world of good people.

This detachment of design ("not into design") from morality ("I want to be good") is common today. We desire to be moral, but there is little agreement as to what "moral" really means. One Barna Research Group report summarizes the problem well:

American society has become more intrigued by moral issues in recent years, as evidenced by the fact that 55% of adults discuss moral issues with others during a typical week. But a nationwide survey . . . indicates that Americans have also redefined what it means to do the right thing in their own lives.[21]

Shortly after the September 11 attacks in 2001, another Barna study found that by a 3-to-1 margin, adults believed that truth is always relative to a person and their situation. The percentage of teenagers was even higher: 83 percent claimed that truth is relative to circumstance. The adults and teens had a common denominator: both groups believed that the most common justification for moral decisions was doing what "feels right" or what feels most comfortable in a given situation.[22]

Looking deeper, the question of moral absolutes is more complex than we might think. For example, a 2011 study sought to understand how ordinary people process questions of objective moral truth. Consistent with previous studies, they found that when presented with a straightforward moral case, most people hold to some form of objective morality. However, there is a twist. When respondents were presented with narratives involving individuals with different cultures or values, then "their intuitions move[d] steadily toward a kind of relativism."[23] For example, if told that the character in a given dilemma was from a much different culture or society, or a place that had a radically different way of life, participants were much less likely to say that murder, or even randomly stabbing another human being, was a violation of a fixed moral law.[24]

Christianity is not immune to these trends. In 2010, for example, Barna explored the proportion of adults claiming to have a "biblical worldview." Possessing a full biblical worldview, these people believe, involves orthodox beliefs about morality and truth, biblical authority, evil, salvation, the divinity of Jesus, and the nature of God. Of the adults surveyed, only 9 percent were found to hold orthodox beliefs across all of these areas. Furthermore, only 34 percent of all adults surveyed believed in the idea of a moral truth (some things are always right or wrong—i.e., moral laws). Moreover, when the sample was segmented by "born again adults," only 46 percent expressed belief in a moral reality.[25]

So we want to be good, but the idea of goodness has little connection to an overarching moral reality. Not surprisingly, as this schism has grown wider, Christianity and the church have grown less relevant. In 1992, Gallup asked people how important religion was in their own life. They found that 12 percent said it was not very important. Over twenty years later, that figure had nearly doubled to 22 percent.[26] More troubling, however, is the 76 percent of Americans who believe that religion as a whole is losing its influence within the United States.

Though written in the late 1990s, Rodney Clapp's book *A Peculiar People* captures the essence of this trend. He writes, "I would call this response to dying Christendom sentimental capitulation. It admits that in this modern (or postmodern), democratic, capitalistic world, the church has nothing distinctive to offer or to be. But it sentimentally hangs on to some Christian language or practice anyway."[27] Faith becomes nothing more than a scarf, hat, or purse to accent an otherwise humanistic outfit.

To recap: A person, place, or thing may rightfully be understood as having a design and a way of functioning (what it is meant to do, and what it actually does). Yet when applied to people, even people of faith, we have separated the idea of being "good" from being complete (*teleioi*) according to the way we were designed. We desire to be good people, have good kids, and create a good world. Moreover, we exhibit concern that morals and values are trending lower. Yet the possession of a biblical worldview and the belief in a moral reality cannot be found in the majority of people. Naturally, then, Christianity fades into the background in both relevance and practice.

Given this, how shall we then function? What are the current principles that people use to organize their lives?

Earlier I stated that a thing's design can make sense without it functioning accordingly. But what about the opposite? What does our functioning as humans look like without an overarching sense of design? How do we conceptualize the world if our thoughts have no connection to a robust sense of wholeness? What do we say when our words are not guided by an overarching sense of good? How do we act when there is no universal idea of reality, and specifically, of a moral reality?

I believe that without a common moral vision to aspire to—and against which to measure any and all thoughts, words, and actions—people use three primary guideposts to determine what is "good" as they navigate the world on a daily basis. I call this the E-3 paradigm: Efficiency, Equity, and Enforceability. Under the paradigm of efficiency, what is good is understood as the action that produces good consequences. Under equity, goodness means achieving equality, maintaining fairness, and protecting rights. Finally, enforceability relates to what is legal. It doesn't so much claim to be good as much as it defines what is *not* good (which is equated with what is *not* legal).

To be clear, these paradigms are not "bad" in themselves. In fact, we employ the kind of thinking that originates from these traditions every day. However, when they are disconnected from a larger moral vision of who we are and who we are meant to be, a close inspection will reveal considerable, and in some cases insurmountable, problems in each of these paradigms. It is not as if these guideposts can replace a sense of design and order; in fact, they are corrupted and inadequate in the absence of such an underlying design. To understand this better, these three guideposts will each be given serious attention in the coming chapters of this book.

Moving Forward

In 2009, Harvard University held a public conversation on justice at the John F. Kennedy School of Government. The event, which included a panel of contemporary thought leaders, explored issues of justice, morality, and virtue in our everyday life.[28] At the end of the evening, Professor Michael Sandel, whose course "Justice" has notched the highest attendance of any Harvard class in its history, was asked if simply discussing virtue was the goal of the course, or whether there are right answers when it comes to living a virtuous life. He responded:

> There was a famous political philosopher—Isaiah Berlin—who ended one of his essays by saying: "A wise man once wrote that 'to believe in the relative validity of one's convictions, and yet to stand for them unflinchingly, is what distinguishes a civilized man from a barbarian.'"[29] It's inspiring in a way, but I think it's wrong. Because if you really believed that your deepest convictions were only relatively valid—your personal opinions—it would not only be difficult to stand for them unflinchingly, it would also be foolish.

Sandel is right, but why?

He is right because our functioning (how we act, what we believe, what we say, what we desire) has an antecedent value: design. If you remove the latter, the former becomes arbitrary and, in many ways, unintelligible; we introduce incoherence into our lives.

In contrast, when what we do (function) aligns with what we were meant to do (design), we experience wholeness. This is not simply another formula that "works." It is, I humbly submit, the way we were meant to organize our lives.

In his book *The Quest*, Eugene Peterson writes: "One of the supreme tasks of the faith community is to announce to us early and clearly the kind of life into which we can grow, to help us set our sights on what it means to be a human being complete."[30] This is the aim of this book—to attempt to help us set our sights on what it means to be a "human being complete"; to fully comprehend and live out "the perfect version of ourselves."

This chapter began with the suggestion that we have an impulse, an *intuition*, to order. Many—including Plato, Augustine, and Jesus himself—have articulated some idea of what it means to be "the perfect version of ourselves." Jesus's call to "be perfect" suggests that we were designed to live a certain way, and that our decisions and actions should reflect, or cohere with, this reality. Yet how we function has been largely disconnected from this larger idea of how we have been designed to function. Without a clear sense of order and who we are supposed to be, our actions tend to be organized around matters of efficiency, equity, or enforceability.

The next chapter will explore these organizing guideposts in more detail. All of them show great promise. All "work" in some way. But without an overarching sense of our design and purpose, their coherence becomes nothing more than a mirage. The second half of the book will reconnect what we do (our functioning) to what we were meant to do (our design). We will explore the idea, language, and practice of virtue in chapters 3, 4, and 5.

DISCUSSION QUESTIONS
FOR GROUP STUDY

1. The chapter begins with a discussion of our impulse toward order. If someone asked you about order and design existing around us, what example(s) would you give to them?

2. This chapter discusses a different perspective on the word "perfect." How do we tend to think of perfection in today's culture, and how is this different from Jesus's use of the term in Matthew 5:48 ("Be perfect . . .")?

3. Most people buy into the maxim "To err is human." In other words, my humanity is defined by mistakes, poor decisions, and moral failure. How does the Christian narrative differ from this belief?

4. In discussing function (what something does) and design (what it was meant to do), the chapter mentioned mosquito nets used for fishing in Lake Tanganyika. Can you think of another example of an object whose function did not fit with its design? What was the result?

5. In Jeremiah 1, God says "I formed you in the [mother's] womb." Author and pastor Jason Mitchell points out that the noun "formed" is literally "potter." That is, "I *pottered* you." How does this idea connect with the chapter's discussion around *telos*?

6. The statistics reported in the chapter suggest that people want to be good, but each of us likes to define goodness in our own way. Where do you see this around you? If this is a problem, how do you—personally—contribute to this problem?

2

How Shall We Then Function?

Test everything; hold fast to what is good.

—1 Thessalonians 5:21

A Most Unique Auction

In early 2010, a young New Zealander logged into an online auction site and posted an unusual item for bidding. What was for sale? Her virginity. To help bid up the price, she described herself as attractive, fit, and healthy with a trim physique and no medical conditions. As long as the buyer was willing to adhere to some basic safety requests, "Unigirl"—as she referred to herself—was willing to sell her virginity to the highest bidder. After the auction, she assured a local newspaper that her decision was made with "full awareness of the circumstances and possible consequences."[1]

Like many students today, Unigirl was cash-strapped and looking to find a more efficient way to pay for her college expenses. Unlike many students, her idea of efficiency was unconventional to say the least. Nevertheless, given her desired goal, the auction strategy was successful. The online advertisement was viewed by over 30,000 people, and nearly 1,200 offers were made. The winning bid was $45,000 in New Zealand's currency (around $36,000 U.S. dollars).

With few exceptions, many will find this transaction strange or even gross. At worst, they will condemn it as morally reprehensible. But what, exactly, is objectionable about the sale of one's virginity? Each semester, I am deliberate about sharing this particular story with students across various classes. Predictably, they grimace or shake their heads in disgust as I describe Unigirl's auction. However, and what is of more interest, when I ask them to articulate to me what, exactly, is wrong with this particular exchange, there is typically less certainty than one would imagine given their initial reactions.

As bizarre as this story may be, I share it with students for two primary reasons. First, something visceral happens. They intuitively sense a problem with this arrangement. The story fits awkwardly into the typical right-wrong matrix used to process narratives with ethical implications. However, and secondly, when asked to articulate what, precisely, is morally wrong with the auction (or what moral reality has been transgressed in the selling of one's virginity), many conclude by virtue of their own reasoning that there is nothing morally objectionable about Unigirl's actions. Others determine that she did something wrong, but they are not sure how to articulate what it is.

As mentioned in chapter 1, my students' reactions reveal—I believe—an impulse toward an order. However, in the absence of a larger framework of design, meaning, and purpose, Unigirl's case is left to be processed by the guideposts of efficiency, equity, or enforceability. It is what I have referred to as the E-3 paradigm. Robert and Edward Skidelsky provide what I consider an utterly accurate and immeasurably important observation about this paradigm. In their 2012 book *How Much Is Enough?* they describe the loss of an overarching sense of "the good life" in Western culture. In its absence, our actions are understood in terms of what is efficient or what best protects our rights.[2] Life becomes less about aligning decisions to cohere with an overarching moral reality and more about choosing from a menu of "moral" standards. In other words, choosing what is right is less important than maintaining the right to choose, and the guideposts of efficiency, equity, and enforceability provide us with this ethical flexibility.

Before returning to Unigirl's auction, this chapter will explore these guideposts in more detail, and show why, on their own, they are insufficient to realize the good and virtuous life. I do not want to suggest that the descriptions below are exhaustive. Each guidepost has a nuanced history documented by volumes of scholarship. With that said, my aim is to provide enough information to at least communicate their flavor and point to the essence of each tradition and its particular claims. Furthermore, when highlighting some of the problems of each tradition, I have limited the discussion to problems that should be of particular concern for those within the Christian faith tradition.

Efficiency: Kill the Fat Man?

Over the last half-century, philosophers have given considerable attention to an interesting moral puzzle.[3] It goes something like this: Imagine that a runaway trolley is about to hit, and thus kill, five people who are somehow tied to the same train track the trolley occupies. To save them, you can press a button which will divert the trolley onto another track with one person tied to it. If you had only moments to decide how to act, what would you do? Most people agree that the "right" thing to do is to divert the trolley onto the track with one person. Why? Simple math. Killing one person, while traumatic, would not be as devastating as killing five. Or, put another way, it seems morally appropriate to sacrifice one person in order to save five.

Now imagine an alternative scenario. A runaway trolley is racing toward five people helplessly tied to the track. However, there is no button to push. Rather, there is an obese person nearby who, if pushed onto the track, could absorb the blow of the trolley, derail it from the track, and save the five people. This act, obviously, would require you—the decision-maker—to shove the obese person to their death. The calculus is still the same (one death to save five lives), but now the circumstances are different. So, if you are willing to press the button, should you also be willing to shove a person to their death? Or, as philosopher David Edmunds puts it, "Would you kill the fat man?"[4]

A common charge against similar "Trolley Puzzles" is that they are unrealistic.[5] However, contrary to this belief, history has produced several ethically troubling problems similar to the trolley quandary. One such situation, which occurred in the Arctic during the late nineteenth century, dealt with a similar question. In this case, the "fat man" was not so much fat as he was husky. Private Charles B. Henry of the Lady Franklin Bay Expedition and his fellow crew members found themselves in dire conditions out in the open Arctic. This American weather research expedition, later referred to as the Greely Expedition (named after its leader, First Lieutenant Adolphus Greely), had taken a terrible turn for the worse. After glaciers closed in around them, the men found themselves exposed to freezing temperatures with little hope of rescue in the near future. Worse yet, they were running desperately short on food.

Under these conditions, moral order was put to the test. On several occasions, Private Henry was caught stealing from their limited food provisions. Interestingly, when Henry was caught, he was open and honest about his transgressions. What, after all, were they going to do? Henry was the burliest member of the group and displayed no sign of fearing the other starved and emaciated group members (he was once described as the "biggest man and heaviest eater in the party").[6] Finally, after catching Henry stealing once again, Lt. Greely pulled aside three trusted men and ordered that he be shot to death. The logic was simple: if Henry continued stealing food, then all would surely die. It made little sense that one man satisfy himself with food and drink to the detriment of all the others.

The orders were obeyed, and Henry was confronted and executed on the spot. It was later said that of the ten men left, not one displayed any moral objection to the decision to execute a fellow member of the expedition. Later, describing the event, a Boston newspaper read: "Lieutenant Greely was therefore forced, in order to maintain military discipline and protect the lives of his other comrades, to issue a written order that Henry be shot."[7] That is, in order to ensure that everyone else survived, Greely had to "kill the fat man."

In a word, we can say that Greely acted "efficiently." Merriam-Webster defines this term as "effective operation as measured by a comparison of production with cost (as in energy, time, and money)."[8] In other words, to be efficient is for your output to exceed your input. It is the arrangement that produces the best consequence given one's initial resources. In the case of the Greely Expedition, the benefits of saving the most expedition members outweighed the cost of executing one of them.

Efficiency tends to be a guiding principle when it comes to decision making—particularly in organizations. It deals with using our time, talent, money, resources, and energy to achieve a desired outcome. Yet considerations of efficiency are not limited to economics or business. Many people organize their lives around being effective or efficient. But to properly understand the nature of efficiency and its role in our decisions and actions, it is important to understand the broader utilitarian cloth it is cut from.

Utilitarianism, as it is understood today, began with a certain conception of mankind that originated with eighteenth-century British philosopher Jeremy Bentham. Bentham believed that humans are motivated by two forces: pleasure and pain. More specifically, he believed humans seek to avoid pain and maximize their pleasure. While this was a description of human behavior, for Bentham it also became a prescription for how to live one's life. For him, the key to happiness was the maximization of pleasure and the minimization of pain.

Years later, this notion was adopted by another key thinker, John Stuart Mill. According to Mill, to have a large ratio of pleasure over pain was to have *utility* (or *satisfaction*). Therefore, the right or appropriate action to take was the one that produced the greatest degree of utility. However, Mill was not as hedonistic as Bentham was. He recognized that some pleasures are different from others (e.g., "higher" and "lower" pleasures) and that humans are different in their scope of pleasures than, say, animals.

Nevertheless, Mill was convinced that utility explains the actions of individuals. More importantly, Mill believed that utility is foundational for morality. In this way, determining what is morally right or wrong is based upon the consequence that an action will produce in terms of pleasure or pain. In ethical terms, this is called consequentialism. For Mill, this was not simply a concept, but a principle. The ethical rightness or wrongness of an action is based, solely, on the utility (or the pleasure) that action produces. This idea was eventually applied to social contexts. The common expression today is that the best action is the one that produces the "greatest good for the greatest number of people."

While Bentham and Mill understood utility strictly in terms of pain and pleasure, today the concept is understood in a much broader way. We might replace the word *utility* with the word *benefits* to better understand its contemporary usage. Often, the benefit being described is understood in financial terms. In corporate institutional settings, for example, the right activity is the one that will maximize profit. Indeed, nearly every corporate finance textbook will describe this goal on its opening pages: "The purpose of a corporation is to maximize long-term shareholder wealth." With this end in mind, the right course of action that a business should take is the one that best achieves this desired goal.

A classic example of this comes from the construction and manufacturing of the Ford Pinto over half a century ago. As newer, more fuel-efficient cars hit the market, Ford decided to manufacture a vehicle that could compete with them in both performance and price. Considerations in the car's design, however, created an interesting dilemma. Manuel Velasquez summarizes the situation well:

> Because the Pinto was a rush project, styling considerations dictated engineering design to a greater degree than usual. In particular, the Pinto's styling required that the gas tank be placed behind the rear axle, where it was more vulnerable to being punctured in case of a rear-end collision. When an early model of the Pinto was crash-tested, it was found that, when struck from the rear at 20 miles per hour or more, the gas tank would sometimes rupture and gas would spray out and into the passenger compartment. In a real accident, stray sparks might explosively ignite the spraying gasoline and possibly burn any trapped occupants.[9]

With full knowledge of these warnings, Ford proceeded with the production and sale of the Pinto model. What was their reasoning? Simple cost-benefit analysis. Ford concluded that the costs of modifying the Pinto would outweigh the benefits.[10] Ford had produced approximately 12.5 million Pintos, and modifying each Pinto would cost approximately $11 ($11 x 12,500,000 = $137 million). How did Ford determine the benefits to weigh these costs against? Analysts predicted that the modification would prevent 180 deaths, 180 serious burn injuries, and 2,100 burned vehicles. By placing "cost" values onto each of these accidents (death, burns, burnt cars), Ford concluded that the benefits to be accrued from the modification would be less than $50 million (almost a third of the costs). Given this, the "right" activity was to continue production and sales without making the modification, as the costs ($137 million) far outweighed the benefits (less than $50 million).

Many are likely to feel some discomfort with this approach. However, Ford justified their actions by determining that the net costs of the modification would far surpass the net benefits (saved lives, fewer burn victims, and fewer car explosions). That is, they chose the path that produced the best consequence according to their calculations.

Utilitarian reasoning for decision making is not limited to corporations, though. Individuals exercise this very reasoning every day. Consider, for example, a 2010 *Newsweek* article claiming that marriage is no longer beneficial for society. The article, titled "The Case against Marriage," suggests that marital unions are "no longer necessary" because it is more financially advantageous to be single. This "reason over romance" approach is very much a utilitarian argument. In a world of blurred sexual mores, gender equality in the workplace, and favorable tax and benefit policies for singles, the benefits of marriage seem to pale in the comparison to the costs (wedding expenses, risk of divorce, etc.).[11]

Furthermore, if the rightness of an action is based upon the material consequence it produces, then incentives (or disincentives) can be used to cajole us all into better actions and discourage us from undesirable ones. It was this very notion that won University of Chicago economist Gary Becker the Nobel Prize in Economics in 1992. In his work, Becker argued that criminals make choices, just like the rest of us, based upon the costs and benefits associated with potential alternatives. If the benefits outweigh the costs (even if this involves criminal activity), then the crime, so goes the logic, is the optimal course of action for the criminal. With this mentality in mind, Becker has suggested that the key to lowering crime is to make the "costs" (or potential costs) of criminal activity more unattractive (harsher penalties, etc.).

It is not difficult to see how utilitarianism becomes its own ethical system. As a framework for guiding our actions, under the paradigm of efficiency right and wrong are understood in terms of "best" and "worst," often according to purely financial standards. The approach is simple, elegant, and oftentimes unambiguous. However, upon closer inspection, some problems emerge. While much more can be said, I will specifically focus on two problems with this paradigm. First, to judge the "rightness" of an activity solely on the basis of material consequence is a considerable problem for people of faith. Second, many arrangements are efficient, but highly unequal. To the extent that we are concerned with equality and fairness, utilitarianism will at best feel awkward, and at worst, unacceptable.

Problem #1: Efficiency and Consequentialism

While a utilitarian approach might be understood as a helpful means for navigating rights and wrongs, in this ethic the *rightness* of any activity is based upon the material consequence it produces. Unfortunately, this consequentialist approach risks limiting the full range of ethical considerations. This is in contrast to an ethic that is not employed as a means to an end, but is rather an end in itself. Such an ethic asks: "Is it right?" in contrast to "Does it work?"

Recall the basic calculation in consequentialism: an act is considered right or good if it produces a good outcome in material terms. There are three primary problems with this formula. First, there are some acts that we commonly consider to be "right," but that don't produce good outcomes according to the efficiency paradigm. For example, consider a Western retailer whose supply chain involves a garment factory in Bangladesh. In the last few years, a great deal of information has come out about the undignified working conditions that third-world garment workers are forced to labor under. Most would conclude that the "right" thing to do for these workers would be to provide better working conditions (cleaner, safer factories), mobilize worker's rights (work breaks, reasonable working hours, maternity leave), and secure a livable wage that is higher than the pennies per hour that most garment workers are paid. Unfortunately, this would mean a higher-priced garment would be produced, because such input costs must be absorbed into the price. An increase in the product's price would lead to a lower quantity being demanded (particularly given the competitive nature of the garment economy). Should that happen, the company's profits would be forfeited, jobs would be lost, and efficiency would not be achieved. Thus, by the consequentialist formula, just and humane working conditions cease to be "good" because, while morally appropriate, they don't necessarily produce the best financial outcome.

The second problem with the consequentialist formula is that some acts that are commonly considered "bad" produce good, efficient outcomes. I was once made aware of a bank employee who stole a significant amount of money from the national bank he worked for. When confronted by an internal bank investigator, he justified his action by saying, "This money was for my family. It was to ensure that our electricity would not be turned off, that our kids would have food on the table, and that my spouse would have the medicine needed for her disease." As you might imagine, this explanation had little influence on the banking officials, and the employee was terminated on the spot. However, if you were a pure consequentialist, then you might indirectly support stealing bank money. In other words, the gain to the banker's family would be far greater than the loss to the bank. Legal issues aside, under a pure and impartial cost-benefit approach, this employee did the *right* thing. However, we know differently. Lying, cheating, and stealing are morally impermissible—both in our business institutions and in society.[12]

Finally, the consequentialist approach leaves the definition of a "good" outcome open to all. This problem can be better described as the "least common denominator" problem. In other words, in a world of varying conceptions of what is right, good, and true, how can we reasonably expect to achieve consensus as to what a *good* outcome is? The short answer is, we can't. Therefore, we have to distill what is considered "good" down to a basic goal, or outcome, that all can agree upon—the least common denominator.

This line of thinking is pervasive in the world of "business ethics." For example, a great deal of literature encourages business ethics and social responsibility because they "improve the bottom line." Ethical behavior is strongly appealed to in the field of business because it creates the best environment for sustained business growth and development. Or as one business ethics textbook bluntly puts it, "Ethical behavior is *essential* for long-term business success."[13]

Christians have not been immune to this dangerous line of thinking. Phil Clements, the founder of the Center for Christian Business Ethics (CFCBE), describes the motivation for the Center's founding in 2009: "[The center was established] to address the *need* for the application of Christian principles to strengthen business operations."[14]

Clements, like many others, appeals to biblical wisdom as a means to engender market success. Author Larry Ruddell agrees. He writes: "The fact is . . . that companies that set and hold to ethical standards will do better financially and be able to compete more effectively than unethical companies in the long run."[15] Similarly, Christian leadership guru John Maxwell writes: "If you embrace ethical behavior, will it automatically make you rich and successful? Of course not. Can it pave the way for you to become successful? Absolutely. *Ethics + Competence* is a winning equation."[16] This "winning combination" strongly promotes ethical activity as an attractive long-term strategy for any ambitious business. Like competitive prices, quality products, an ambitious marketing strategy, or any other initiative to promote the company's success, moral and ethical behavior is described as a strategic tool to accumulate marketplace profits.

But what if embodying Christian values in business actually harmed profits—would those values cease to be right?

The three issues with consequentialism I have mentioned above should be particularly problematic for those who identify with the Christian faith. Regarding the first problem (some acts are usually considered "right," but they don't produce good outcomes), Christians must realize that many of their actions—by virtue of organizing their lives around faithfulness to God—will fit poorly into the "efficiency" paradigm.

A wonderful example of this was provided by theologian Stanley Hauerwas. In September of 2001, *TIME* magazine declared Hauerwas "American's Best Theologian." Hauerwas responded by saying that "best" is not a theological category; faithfulness is.[17] Here, Hauerwas captured an important distinctive of the Christian faith. "Best" is most often used as an economic expression; the term implies efficiency, maximization, convenience, and effectiveness. However, the Bible is clear that faithfulness cannot cling too closely to such ideas in the lexicon and practice of a disciple. Jesus's idea of faithfulness involves counterintuitive propositions such as "the last shall be first," becoming like "little children," and the idea that the great will be servants and slaves to others. Indeed, he showers blessings on those who are poor, those who mourn, the meek, the merciful, and the peacemakers—characteristics we typically don't celebrate in our modern Western culture. Such directives not only defy our intuition to do what is most economically profitable (i.e., what is *best*), but are often found to be inefficient, inconvenient, sub-optimal, and ineffective.[18] To summarize, the actions and attitudes associated with traditional Christianity are not necessarily prized for their efficacy.

Regarding the second problem (some acts are considered "wrong," but they produce good outcomes), Christians might do well to remember that sin cannot be used to produce a good result. For example, wealth and material sufficiency may very well arise from attitudes of greed, self-regard, and hyper-individuality, but can we support such attributes as people of faith, even though they may bring about seemingly good outcomes? To answer this, we need only remind ourselves of the Apostle Paul's condemnation of undertaking what is morally inappropriate ("continue in sin") for the sake of a good consequence (so that "grace may abound") in Romans 6, to which he responds, "By no means!" Allowing a little bit of sin for a lot of good is not a formula that is traditionally supported in the Christian faith.

Finally, Christians have the DNA to present arguments, not simply in economic terms, but in moral terms. To distill our decisions (especially moral ones!) down to mere considerations of efficiency is to agree to play on the other team's turf. The "least common denominator" approach handicaps the sensibility of our faith, since it reduces our "kingdom logic" to the level of the efficient outcomes that it may or may not produce (more on this in chapter 4).

Problem #2: Unequal Outcomes

One popular critique of utilitarianism and the paradigm of efficiency focuses on the inequality they are said to produce. Award-winning economist and philosopher Amartya Sen, for instance, writes: "The trouble with this approach [utilitarianism] is that maximizing the sum of individual utilities is supremely unconcerned with the interpersonal distribution of that sum."[19] Indeed, notions of efficiency are consistently at odds with our social ideals of equity.

Recall the Greely Expedition story shared earlier. Under the utilitarian paradigm, "killing the fat man" was the right thing to do because—so goes the logic—it sacrificed one life in order to save ten. Interestingly, this story has an important caveat. While Private Henry was guilty of theft and was later killed for his actions, he was not the only person caught stealing. Another expedition member had engaged in theft prior to Henry, but did not meet the same fate. What was the difference? He was the expedition's physician. Indeed, Dr. Octave Pavy was also caught stealing food from the others, but no action was taken against him "on the grounds that the doctor's services were essential to everyone's welfare."[20]

Like the survivors of the expedition, most would contend that executing Private Henry was the action that best ensured the survival of all. In other words, killing "the fat man" produced the best consequence, and this justified their action. However, the situation with the doctor—who was also guilty of stealing—was just the opposite. Allowing him to live was the action that would best ensure the survival of all, and therefore he was not executed.

While this seems efficient, it is likely to strike many as unjust. Are we really to measure life and death based upon a person's perceived utility to others? Imagine if such a philosophy was used to run every facet of our society. Homeless people could be executed on the justification that they offered no value (or offered a negative value) for society. Those with disabilities would also have little worth in public or private settings since the value of their contribution, when measured economically, may be significantly less than average. Further, in many cases, this paradigm would likely guide those in power to wield their influence in a way so that they do not have to bear the consequences of their own actions. To summarize, we would have a world that would be considered unfair, unjust, and inhumane.

For example, consider the infamous 1991 memo written by then World Bank Chief Economist Larry Summers suggesting that an open market in toxic waste between developed and third-world countries was economically efficient and mutually beneficial for both groups. The idea was that developed countries would exchange their toxic waste for cash compensation to the less developed countries who would inherit it. The memo referred to the economic logic of dumping toxic waste in low-wage countries as "impeccable"—but the moral logic will strike many as reprehensible. Such an exchange is certainly efficient, but to sell the rights to dump waste into an already impoverished country hardly seems like a fair and just trade-off—particularly since those countries are in no position to bargain.

Or consider the increasingly popular field of bioethics. In a world where health needs are abundant but health treatment is scarce, how should we distribute health care services? Many contend for efficient solutions, but to what end? For example, a wildly disproportionate amount of money is spent on "end of life" care. One out of every four Medicare dollars is spent on services for the very small proportion of society who find themselves at the end of their lifespan.[21] If such "inefficient" allocations of health services were eliminated, the United States would stand to save over one trillion dollars within a decade. Some see equal health-care treatment as an inefficient waste of tax-payer dollars or medical resources. Others see this as fair and humane. Who is right? What is the right composition between the two? Irrespective of how these questions are answered, most—if not all—would agree that denying a human being health care service is unfair and cruel, regardless of their age.

We are bothered by conflicts like this because they are devoid of a sense of fairness and equality. Indeed, in addition to efficiency, fairness is also a common moral standard that we employ to navigate our lives. We will now turn our attention to this important guidepost for determining morally appropriate action.

Equity: "The Right to be Crude"

Early eighteenth- century Ireland was not a pleasant place to be. Living conditions were harsh, the economy remained stagnant, and food was scarce. Enter Johnathan Swift, who casually suggested "a modest proposal" to correct for such grave material inequality: Eat the children. Swift writes:

> I have been assured by a very knowing American of my acquaintance in London, that a young healthy child well nursed is at a year old a most delicious, nourishing, and wholesome food, whether stewed, roasted, baked, or boiled.[22]

Swift's proposal would solve several problems. First, amidst the rampant starvation in the land, this solution would provide an abundance of food. Furthermore, eating children would bring order to the homes and streets "crowded with beggars of the female sex, followed by three, four, or six children, all in rags and importuning every passenger for an alms." In other words, it would serve as a form of population control and minimize the unpleasant sight of homeless families begging in the street.

Thankfully, Swift was not serious in his proposal. His satirical writing was intended to mock the "can-do" attitude that prevailed at the time. Nevertheless, his essay makes for an interesting thought experiment. One cannot deny the utilitarian logic of his argument. According to the raw calculations, the benefits of eating the plentiful supply of impoverished children seemed to outweigh the costs. And yet we don't take such a proposal seriously. Most would dismiss this depraved suggestion outright on the grounds of human dignity: we cannot steal away another's life. It is, as many would say, a "universal" rule.

Rule is the right term. For while many people today are tempted to live by the utilitarian reasoning found in prioritizing efficiency, others believe that achieving a "good" life requires adherence to principles, guidelines, and rules for living well. One such guideline is the idea of fairness, or equity. In his book *Justice*, Michael Sandel summarizes this principle well: "Persons should not be used merely as means to the welfare of others, because doing so violates the fundamental right of self-ownership."[23] If self-ownership is a fundamental right of every human, then equal treatment of each human being is elevated to the status of a sacred law. Furthermore, equity and fairness seem to be hard-wired ethical sensibilities. Even toddlers can detect an unfair arrangement. The idea of fairness is protected in what I will call the rights-based liberal tradition through the concept of universal, equal rights.[24]

One of the strongest defenses of the paradigm of fairness and rights in the last half century comes from the late Harvard philosopher John Rawls. Rawls's theory of justice, which he offered in the early 1970s, continues to serve either implicitly or explicitly as a guiding principle for how we arrange ourselves in society and seek to live the kind of lives we want to live.[25]

To present his theory, Rawls begins with a simple mental exercise. Imagine that you were in a hypothetical state called the "original position." In this position, you are preparing to enter into the world. However, you don't know anything about yourself. You don't know if you are good-looking, smart, or funny. You don't know where you will live, what color your skin will be, or what your family will be like. You don't know your gender, your health, or any talents you might possess. You are, says Rawls, behind a "veil of ignorance." The only thing you do know is that you want rights, liberties, opportunities, and wealth.

So, if this was all you knew about yourself, what kind of a world would you want to live in? For example, knowing that you might be born as an African American, would you want to live in a world with racial discrimination? What if you were born into an impoverished inner-city neighborhood? How would you feel if you were unattractive or disfigured? Or what if you entered the world with dyslexia or into a family that did not value education? Given these questions, Rawls asks, how would you order the institutions in society so as to assure that whether you were black or white, rich or poor, ugly or attractive, in the west or east, you would be satisfied with the world you were being born into?

Seen through the lens of this hypothetical exercise, Rawls believes we would desire a much more equitable world. He believes that a person behind the "veil of ignorance" would want to improve the position of the worst-off place in society (in case they were to find themselves in that position!). Specifically, he suggests several principles of justice that rational persons in the original position would propose. First, society should strongly promote liberty to let people be free to pursue the kind of lives they want to pursue. Second, society should have equal opportunities for all. Third, and finally, society should be arranged in such a way that inequality is allowed so long as it is in the best interest of the least well off. In other words, Rawls was okay with society having millionaires and minimum-wage households, so long as a society *with* millionaires benefited the minimum-wage households more than a society *without* millionaires. So, to summarize, Rawls argues that we should establish institutions in a way that members behind a hypothetical "veil of ignorance" would agree upon.

Rawls's theory of justice is an exercise in what many call "pure procedural justice." In this theory, all agree upon the procedure as being fair, even though it may potentially produce an unfair outcome. An example may help make this idea more clear. In my neighborhood growing up, the local kids were always getting into disagreements about how we should share food or candy between each other. If, say, a candy bar came into the possession of two people (where neither person merited, or earned, the candy bar) then there was a sense of fairness as to how it should be divided. But how would we determine an equitable distribution? There was no way to be sure that the candy bar would be cut into two equal halves.

To solve this problem, we decided to focus less on the outcome (a potentially unequal candy bar) and more on the rules of how the candy bar would be distributed. What emerged from this was a principle that became common amongst friends: when determining how to share a snack that two people had equal claim to, one person would split the snack in half while the other would get to choose which piece they got. In the candy bar example, the first person had an incentive to split the candy bar as evenly as possible because, if not, the second person would likely choose the larger piece. Notice that this does not prevent an unequal outcome. Rather, both parties agree to the fairness of the procedure to ensure justice. Even though we may or may not like the inevitable outcome, we respect the procedure because it protects our rights, allows us to consent to the transaction, and provides a form of equality between us. The description of justice I have just given would find great support within the rights-based liberal tradition.

When I use the term "liberal," I am not necessarily referring to the political characterizations often used in the United States. Rather, the broader "liberal" tradition emphasizes the importance of human agency as valuable, autonomous, and free. In other words, it begins with the notion that liberty is of great importance in the various expressions of our humanity, and it should therefore be respected and protected.

We can see two primary strands originating from this tradition today. The first is what might be referred to as the liberal-egalitarian approach, while the second is the libertarian approach. Liberal egalitarians believe in respecting the freedom of the individual person, but advocate for a strong welfare state so as to bring everyone up to a position of equality. Thus, notions of equality, opportunity, and fairness are central. The late philosopher Daniel Bell provided a helpful description of the philosophy surrounding the liberal egalitarian position:

> The principle of *equality of opportunity* derives from a fundamental tenet of classic liberalism: that the individual—and not the family, the community, or the state—is the basic unit of society, and that the purpose of societal arrangements is to allow the individual the freedom to fulfill his own purposes—by his labor to gain property, by exchange to satisfy his wants, by upward mobility to achieve a place commensurate with his talents.[26]

Libertarians also value liberty, but according to them, the best way to ensure equality and protect freedom is to minimize intervention in the lives of individuals. Therefore, libertarians are keen to advocate for limited government social intervention so that individuals can voluntarily choose how they want to navigate their lives in a way that is meaningful to them without intervention.

While there are disagreements between these two traditions, both have several features in common. First, they both identity liberty and freedom as supreme values; every human should have the right to live a free and autonomous life. Second, both strands emphasize a rule- or principle-based, rather than consequence-based, way of determining the right action. Finally, and perhaps most importantly, they both emphasize the rights and liberties of individuals to choose and author their own conceptions of what is good. In other words, there is no overarching sense of what is good, except the belief that each person gets to choose the good things they want to pursue in life.

What does this mean for how we should arrange ourselves— socially and politically—in society? Sandel describes what this philosophy looks like in the political realm: "Politics should not try to form the character or cultivate the virtue of its citizens, for to do so would be to 'legislate morality.' "[27] In other words, government should not affirm, through its policies or laws, any particular conception of the good life; instead it should provide a neutral framework of equal rights within which people can choose their own values and ends.

In many ways, this tradition relies upon the notion of consent. To have consent is to have choice; to lack choice is to corrupt liberty. Thus, for liberals, consent is intricately tied to freedom. Rawls, for example, suggests that the proper activity is the one that individuals would consent to in a fair initial situation.[28]

For libertarians, consent is equally important. Philosopher Robert Nozick is famous for presenting a libertarian argument for consent as a matter of justice. In his book *Anarchy, State, and Utopia*, Nozick creatively illustrates his case by referencing NBA basketball legend Wilt Chamberlain. Chamberlain, who was considered one of the best centers in pro basketball, was considerably wealthier than most people. Recognizing the income differential between Chamberlain and the non-wealthy, Nozick made the following argument. Imagine that income in society was completely equal (everyone had the same amount). While in this equilibrium, each person could put 25 cents into a bucket to watch Wilt Chamberlain play a basketball game (each quarter would go directly to Chamberlain). If one million fans put a quarter in the box over the course of the season, Chamberlain would have a quarter-million dollars and income would no longer be equal in society. The question becomes: does Chamberlain deserve the income he received? Is anything unjust about this transaction? Nozick argues (and many agree) that there would be nothing wrong with this new arrangement because it was entered into voluntarily—that is to say, it was *consensual* (formed with no coercion). If people entered into this new, unequal, arrangement on their own volition and as an exercise of their liberty, then there is nothing, morally speaking, to condemn.

Similar to utilitarianism, the liberal tradition and its emphasis on equity appears just and humane on the surface. However, upon closer inspection, it is questionable whether rights, fairness, and consent alone can allow persons in society to fully participate in the good life.

Problem #1: Rights May Undermine Community

It is impossible to read Scripture and not recognize a clear trajectory toward the importance of community. New Testament theologian Richard Hays brings our attention to the importance of corporate worship and community in Paul's writings. He cites Romans 12:1–2, where Paul appeals to his brothers and sisters to present their bodies, or *somata* (plural), as a living sacrifice, or *thysian* (singular). How can a collection of people make a singular sacrifice? The phrase seems awkward, unless one recognizes God's vision of salvation in corporate terms. Hays writes: "God transforms and saves a *people*, not atomized individuals."[29] Yet stressing the rights of individuals may actually serve to undermine this very idea.

A classical argument worth considering suggests that a rights-based society is a conflict society. In other words, when we declare and honor a right, it is often not merely for ourselves, but against someone else. If there is a right to the ownership of property, then this is not a right for me—it is a right against you! This doesn't mean that ownership rights are bad. They are actually quite necessary and very important. However, the point is that the more rights we have, the more conflict we presuppose with someone else. That is, rights may wrongly imply that others are a source of conflict; that humans serve as threats to one another. This is quite different from the conception that our relationships are a source of meaning and fulfillment, or that our connections with others are part and parcel of what it means to live life well.

To illustrate this, suppose that you are about to enter into a contract. However, this contract has, on average, a 50 percent fail rate (sometimes higher). Naturally, this makes you nervous. Who would want to enter an agreement that fails so frequently? Fortunately, you have the right to get insurance on the contract prior to signing up. Furthermore, this insurance has no monthly fees or up-front costs. It is totally free. Would you take out the insurance? Most people would say yes. It would be irrational not to. However, what if I told you that the contract you were entering into was a marriage, and the insurance was a pre-nuptial agreement?

At this point you may likely hesitate. Why? Because while I have the right to secure a pre-nuptial agreement prior to a marriage, and while it would even be rational to do so, capitalizing on this right would undermine the very nature of the institution I was entering into (and, in many ways, might even guarantee that I would need that insurance!). Marriages are about relationship. It is a communal good—something that we share and participate in with another. Marital norms consist of unconditional love, self-giving sacrifice, and trust. To make the most of these norms in a marriage, sometimes it requires that we make less of our rights.

The language of rights and equality may seem to prioritize relationships and communities, but when the curtain is pulled back, its promises are more empty than they first appear. One of the more nerve-racking moments of my doctoral dissertation defense came when John Rawls was discussed. I dedicated a considerable amount of writing to Rawls, and while acknowledging his enormous contribution to contemporary political philosophy, I was rather critical of his individualistic approach to arranging a society. When the conversation turned to this point, one of the examiners cast a concerned look across her face and skeptically stated, "You claim that Rawls is not relational. Unless my reading of Rawls has been incorrect over the last twenty-five years, I disagree." After collecting myself, I simply pointed out that Rawls' original position seems, at first, to emphasize community and relationship because we choose principles of justice that all would agree on without any knowledge of the attributes we possess or what kind of society we may end up in.[30] This, however, is hardly an overture to community. Rather, it is more of an opportunistic community where we create social arrangements that best represent *our* own interests (I want to improve the worst position in society because *I* may be the one inhabiting that position!). This puts us in a strange sort of relationship with others. It is an association held together by tension which requires reciprocity to work—not self-giving love.

To summarize, the liberal tradition's emphasis on rights, which originates from respecting the dignity and self-ownership of each person, may very well protect our own interests and, perhaps, make us more equal. However, basing our lives on rights alone risks undermining the fulfillment of real and meaningful community.

Problem #2: "Doing What Is Right" Different from "Doing What I Want"

Aristotle's classical understanding of justice has been described as "prioritizing the good over the right."[31] In other words, determining what is right to do relies heavily upon a prior understanding of what is good for humanity. We cannot understand whether an action is right or not without first contemplating our human *telos*, purpose, and meaning. With the ascendancy of rights, equality, and fairness—what I have referred to as the liberal tradition—this all changed. Daniel Bell Jr. helpfully describes liberalism's new conception of society, and moreover, a "good" society:

> Liberalism re-imaged society as a teeming mass of individuals, each with their own interests, ends, and conceptions of what constitutes the good life. Consequently, justice was reconfigured; in contemporary parlance, now the right is given priority over the good.[32]

We can easily see the contrast between liberal society and Aristotle's classical vision. In the latter, reflections on justice began with a thick conception of a good life. In modern terms, we no longer seek agreement on what a good life is, but allow each member to make that determination themselves. What condition is necessary to allow people to make such determinations? Neutrality. Neutrality has a lot of advantages. It does not commit to a particular conception of good or bad. Rather, if conditions are neutral, then people can make these determinations for themselves. This allows persons to work around disagreements about the good life and "leave[s] each citizen free to act on the basis of his or her own morality."[33]

In theory, this sounds like a tidy way to minimize moral disputes among citizens living together. However, in reality, respecting rights and maintaining impartiality and neutrality does little to settle deep questions over what it means to live well. If someone trusts that their beliefs, ideas, and actions reflect a moral reality, it is foolish to believe they will be satisfied with simply agreeing to disagree. It is very difficult to follow the "unto each their own" maxim when addressing deeply personal issues such as abortion or a marital affair.

To provide an example, in a conversation with a friend, my wife was once discussing her conviction against buying name-brand, foreign-made clothes without giving any concern to the conditions under which they were made (i.e., sweat shops). After my wife had shared her view, her friend—who was also a person of faith—responded, "Well if God wants you to do something about it, you should." I found this response rather amazing. In other words, the implication was that my wife had a moral responsibility, from God, to take action as it related to supply-chain issues with her clothing—but her friend did not! For my wife, this was an issue of what was "right." It reflected a moral reality about the way we should relate to other human beings who also bear God's image. For her friend, however, it was a matter of individual conviction ("If *you* feel convicted, *you* should do something—but since *I* don't share your conviction, *I* won't").[34]

Principles such as rights and neutrality may create a kind of order, but the order itself implies that all conceptions, beliefs, and

HOW SHALL WE THEN FUNCTION?

pursuits are equally valid. Put bluntly, Debra Satz writes, "In a liberal society, we give people the right to be crude."[35] Beyond crudeness, this framework affords people the right to do nearly whatever they want; to pursue any pursuit. It supports, indeed celebrates, the notion of autonomy. Autonomy, then, becomes a kind of meta-good, or good "from which all others derive."[36] Even Jonathan Haidt, who is not religious, recognizes that autonomy is an affront to the values of faith communities. Where the ethic of autonomy requires that all be treated as individuals with wants, needs, and preferences, the ethic of divinity implies "there is an order to the universe, and things (as well as people) should be treated with the reverence or disgust they deserve."[37] Indeed, people of faith believe that some conceptions of what is good are better than others (and note that to disagree with this statement is to validate its truth). In other words, Christ did not die so I could do what I want; he died so I could do what is *right*.

To summarize, where the paradigm of fairness and equality may correct for some of the more unpleasant features arising from the pursuit of efficiency, it seems to leave some unanswered questions on the table. For many, these ambiguities can be settled not by rational reflection and moral traditions but by simply looking to the laws of the land. For this reason our legal standards often serve as the basis for determining the rightness or wrongness of our actions.

Enforceability: Virtue and Governance

Imagine finding yourself stranded on island with a group of other individuals. The setting is raw. There are no rules, governance, hierarchy, or systems of order. Readers of William Golding's *Lord of the Flies* are invited to imagine such a situation. In his 1954 book, Golding writes about a plane crash that leaves a group of preadolescent boys alone on a remote island. Stranded, and with no adults to guide them, the boys must determine the best way to organize themselves and live among each other. Without an overarching sense of order, how might such a scenario play out? According to Golding, the result would not be good. The book shows how a semblance of order quickly cascades into violence, hierarchy, fear, and control. Forced to survive within the primitive environment of the island, the otherwise civilized boys transform into hostile savages.

Golding's book is no stranger to controversy, and has been banned across various venues over time for portraying man as a barbaric animal.[38] Critics aside, one figure from several centuries earlier who likely would have resonated with the book was Thomas Hobbes. Among other things, Hobbes is famous for his thought exercise about life in a "state of nature," or a setting without any governance. Would a society devoid of structure, regulation, and agreed-upon procedures reflect utopian order, or, in line with Golding's view, would it be chaotic? Hobbes suggests the latter. Life in a state of nature, he famously wrote, would be "solitary, poor, nasty, brutish, and short."[39]

Hobbes believed that legal requirements should ideally reflect what people in a state of nature would accept as governing rules. In other words, if we each give up some of our own rights, we can achieve more order. This idea is referred to as a "social contract." The logic is simple: For any system to work, and work well, there needs to be a baseline of order that prevents people from harming one another and enforces contracts and agreements between individuals. To ensure these key features for a stable society, it is necessary for all to agree upon and erect a legal superstructure. Further, the laws raised up under this structure are binding upon all.

Laws, therefore, have a natural interplay with moral and ethical standards of living. Many laws, for example, reinforce some of our most basic values. These include prohibitions against theft, violence, and various forms of deceit. Oftentimes a law can be traced back to some moral outrage or perceived transgression. Consider, for example, the increase of hotel prices after Hurricane Katrina. It was reported that after the hurricane some hotel rates were increased up to three or four times their original amounts.[40] Charging higher rates to families whose homes were demolished by Katrina floodwaters appears heartless at best and exploitative at worst.[41] As a result, many states have passed legislation to avoid price hikes in the wake of a disaster by placing a price ceiling upon hotels and other important resources for a pre-determined period of time. In addition to the laws created to prevent "price gouging" in the wake of a declared state of emergency, outraged citizens used morally infused language such as *scammer*, *selfish*, or *greedy* to describe those raising prices.

To this last point, Hosmer points out that the life cycle of laws begins with individual values. Individuals partner with like-minded individuals, and soon what is one person's value becomes a shared value. Small groups grow to larger organizations, and eventually evolve into political institutions that formalize their shared values into law.[42] The point is that laws reflect values, and values reflect our deepest-held beliefs about virtue and the good.

Like efficiency and equity before, answering the question of what is "enforceable" can certainly help us to navigate questions of the good, right, and true. However, also like efficiency and equity, reliance upon the guidepost of legality is an impoverished means to apprehend and realize the good life. Here, I want to bring attention to three primary problems with directly equating virtue and the law.

Problem #1: Laws Prohibit; Virtue Empowers

First and foremost, it is important to recognize that laws are, more or less, prohibitive. A law, for example, may say that I cannot throw someone into an icy lake. However, there is no law saying that, should I find someone in an icy lake, I have a legal obligation to try to get them out. In this way, we might say that laws, at best, capture our lowest common denominator when it comes to morality.

To illustrate this, suppose that you are driving and you come upon a stranded car that with a flat tire. We can imagine an array of different responses. Moreover, we can even place these actions on a kind of moral spectrum. On one end of the spectrum, we might not do anything and simply drive by. Or, on the other end, we could assist the motorist in changing their tire, or even give them a ride. Yet what, legally, can we be *required* to do? It would be unreasonable for there to be a law forcing me to help change a tire for a stranger. It would not be unreasonable, however, to require drivers to get over into the far lane opposite the stopped vehicle so as to ensure the stranded motorist's safety and give them space.

This may remind you of another familiar story. In this example, however, the person stopped on the side of the road did not have a flat tire, but rather was severely beaten and stripped by robbers. Further, those passing by were not random cars, but a priest, a Levite, and a Samaritan.

Even today, Jesus's parable of the Good Samaritan has relevance for how we think about laws and virtue. The priest who first "passed by on the other side" would have been considered unclean if he were to tend to a possible corpse.[43] The same action was taken by the lesser official of the temple, the Levite. In contrast, the Samaritan had mercy upon the injured man and tended to him. Samaritans were "despised" by the Jews—a point of irony within the story.[44] Here, the apathy and avoidance of the priest and Levite are associated with distance ("passing by on the other side"). The Samaritan's action, however, is associated with nearness or close proximity with the victim ("came near to him"). Concluding, the audience is charged to "Go and do likewise."

The point is clear: human compassion is a higher law than mere ritual obligations or any other system of rules. Laws may prohibit us from certain actions, including immoral ones. This is quite different, however, from suggesting that laws impel us to virtuous action.

Related to this problem is the assumption that what is legal can be equated with what is moral. It was the Apostle Paul who, in citing the popular Corinthian belief "All things are lawful," responded, "But not all things are beneficial." Or, as Peterson's translation reads, "Just because something is technically legal doesn't mean that it's spiritually appropriate" (1 Cor. 6:12, *The Message*). Similarly, Russian novelist Aleksandr Solzhenitsyn wisely wrote, "I have spent all my life under a Communist regime, and I will tell you that a society without any objective legal scale is a terrible one indeed. But a society with no other scale but the legal one is not quite worthy of man either."[45]

So while laws reflect some semblance of values, and may even aspire to engender a more just, equal, and moral society, doing what is legal is not always closely linked with doing what is right.

We need only imagine early to mid-twentieth-century Jim Crow laws in the pre-Civil War slave-owning society of the United States, German Nazism, or South African apartheid. All were considered to be legitimate legal superstructures but displayed morally impoverished qualities.

Problem #2: Assumption of Rationality

Prohibitive laws, as mentioned, tend to center around what cannot be done. The basis for this system, therefore, is deterrence. Deterrence simply means that we are dis-incentivized through law and punishment from behaving a certain way or acting out of line. The law determines what the boundaries are; the punishment determines what the consequence of transgressing that boundary is. Recall the aforementioned work of economist Gary Becker, who believed that the key to lowering crime was to make the costs of criminal activity more prohibitive. Stronger punishments, so goes the logic, would deter crime because it would reconfigure the criminal's cost-benefit calculations in a way that made the costs exceed the benefits.

This, of course, assumes that people are rational. This term can mean a lot of different things, but here I simply define it as a person who is "goal-seeking." That is, a person who acts purposefully. When a person does anything with purpose, they assume that the costs of the activity will be outweighed by the benefits. So, whether they're cheating on taxes, parking illegally, or even committing murder, rational humans, so goes the belief, will appropriately weigh up the costs and benefits of their actions.

As clean and tightly packaged as this belief is, its claims do not seem to reflect what we know to be true. In reality, many crimes are often done out of passion. As the mathematical genius Pascal once noted, "The heart has its reasons, which reason cannot know." In other words, humans are rational, but we are also passionate, and sometimes irrationally so. Passion may evoke images of romance, heroism, and patriotism but, conversely, it is also passion that explains why people fulminate in rage when they are cut off in traffic.

My father-in-law once visited a man sentenced to life in prison for committing murder. Prior to prison, the inmate had caught his spouse in an adulterous affair, and in a fit of rage he violently shattered her skull with a hammer. When I heard the inmate's story, an odd thought came to mind. I considered Song of Solomon 8:6—a verse that has been read at nearly all of the weddings I have attended (my own included):

> Set me as a seal upon your heart,
>   as a seal upon your arm;
> for love is strong as death,
>   passion fierce as the grave.
> Its flashes are flashes of fire, a raging flame.

Could it be that this verse has less to do with expensive cake, musical bells, color schemes, and other wedding-day accents, and more to do with the imprisoned man who killed his wife with a hammer? In other words, love is so strong (*as strong as death*), that when it goes awry, it is explosive (*a raging flame*). Love is indeed praised and celebrated, and rightly so. But seldom do we describe it with ominous words like *death*, *grave*, and *raging flame*.

Here's the point: laws may assume rational, goal-seeking humans who calculate their actions with respect to costs and benefits. But we know this is not completely accurate. We are creatures of passion, for better or for worse. Further, the law itself is insufficient to keep such passion in check; indeed, a much stronger power is required for that.

Problem #3: Word Games

While in graduate school for business, I took a course in Corporate Tax that was adjunct-taught by a local tax attorney. He unromantically distilled the profession down to a group of attorneys who spent eighty hours a week combing through the Internal Revenue Code. Their aim was to find loopholes for companies that would save millions, if not billions, of dollars. "The goal," he said, "was to find language that could be manipulated in a way to allow for a tax shelter to be built." This seemed to suggest that legal policy had less to do with the spirit of what it was meant to do, and more to do with the semantics of what it could potentially mean.

This "goal" certainly isn't new. Late in his presidency, many recall Bill Clinton suggesting several times that he "did not have sexual relations" with then intern Monica Lewinsky. Yet later, Clinton testified as follows:

> As you know, in a deposition in January, I was asked questions about my relationship with Monica Lewinsky. While my answers were legally accurate, I did not volunteer information. Indeed, I did have a relationship with Miss Lewinsky that was not appropriate. In fact, it was wrong. It constituted a critical lapse in judgment and a personal failure on my part for which I am solely and completely responsible.[46]

This seemingly strategic response puzzled many, prompting the question "When is sex not 'sexual relations?'"[47] In other words, when discussing Clinton's indiscretion, two different strands of conversation seemed to emerge. The first strand was about what could be legally defined as "accurate"—while the second strand related to the truth itself. Interestingly, Clinton himself admitted as much.

Similarly, consider Robert Shapiro's response to Larry King when pressed about the guilt or innocence of his client O. J. Simpson in one of America's most notorious courtroom dramas: "That's a moral judgment. And I can't make moral judgments. I can make professional judgments."[48] The implication is that what is true is different from what is legal, and Shapiro was only obliged to concern himself with the latter.

Whether Clinton, Shapiro, or any other example of parsing out truth and goodness from legality, it is clear that these ideas fit awkwardly at best. Yet it is equally clear that, when convenient, they can be separated to mean completely different things. We see this same line of reasoning from Pilate, who in John's Gospel asks: "Are you the king of the Jews?" only to be answered by Jesus, "Is that your own idea?" (John 18:33–34 NIV). One is left to wonder whether Pilate is truly interested in truth, or simply in the legal process. In other words, does he want to know who the man before him really is, or is he simply trying to sort out, both politically and legally, the death of a man he believes to be innocent?

The parlance of policy, legal language, and prescribed rules and codes is not only a poor substitute for morality, but it risks corrupting and corroding the flavor of virtue, truth, and goodness into something stale and irrelevant.

In summary, as Bruce Weinstein writes, "To be fully human and be a part of civilized society means to go beyond what the law demands of us."[49] A legal superstructure will no doubt reflect values. Moreover, it may incentivize social participants to act and behave in virtuous ways. But such behavior is *shadow* virtue. In other words, it is virtue that is merely mimicked, not embodied. Like efficiency and equity before it, what is enforceable is a poor guidepost for the good life. Laws can make some faint overture toward virtue—but they cannot make me virtuous.

Returning to Unigirl

While certainly not exhaustive, this chapter has given attention to three guideposts for making moral judgments in the absence of a larger vision of design. With these in mind, it is worth returning to the story of Unigirl found at the beginning of the chapter.

Using the guideposts mentioned above, how should we evaluate Unigirl's actions? As it relates to efficiency, we can simply look at the consequence of her action to determine its rightness. She wanted money to pay for college, and auctioning her virginity allowed her to do that. Given the fact that she got what she wanted, her actions may be understood as acceptable. Upon sharing this story, I once had a student tell me that not only were her actions acceptable, they were praiseworthy. "Most girls I know lose their virginity while they're drunk at a party," he reasoned, "at least she got paid and made the most of it." To summarize, the consequence was good, so the action taken to get the consequence must have been good as well.

Under the equity tradition, or what I have called rights-based liberalism, the answer will predictably relate to fairness or consent. Fully informed, she entered freely into a mutually beneficial exchange that was un-coerced. A common response under this line of reasoning might sound like this: "I may not have done it myself, but it is her body, her decision." It is possible, under this tradition, to question whether her actions were justified only by an "ex-ante" argument (Latin for "before the fact"). In other words, while she may be okay with her decision before the fact, she may regret it afterwards. But as true as this may be, it is important to recognize that under this reasoning, the morality of her decision relates not to the decision or action itself, but rather to how it might make her feel. In other words, the action can only be condemned if Unigirl regrets it later.

Finally, one might point to the legal status of the action, which in New Zealand was perfectly legitimate. No law was broken. When news of Unigirl's unusual auction broke, the owner of the website claimed that according to policy, as long as an ad was legal and did not offend the general standards of society, the auction was permissible.[50] Case closed.

So, to summarize, if followed to their natural conclusions, not one of these guideposts gives us grounds to question Unigirl's actions. Yet is this all? Is there nothing left to say? Are we really left to believe that the sale of one's virginity is no different than the sale of coffee, smartphones, or any other everyday commodity? Something seems to be missing. Somewhere, in the background of these guideposts, we hear a faint voice from the classical tradition of virtue. We might imagine Aristotle asking, "What is the *telos* of virginity?" In other words, to determine the right usage, or distribution, of the good in question, it is necessary to determine its meaning. If the meaning of our sexuality, or other human attributes, beliefs, or ideas, is purely relative to the individual (which, in essence, makes it *meaningless*), then the guideposts above serve as nothing more than a convenient set of standards to substantiate a person's preference. Virtue becomes nothing more than a buyer's market.

In contrast to this conception, living the good life and "being the perfect version of ourselves" require us to acknowledge that life was designed to be lived a particular way, and that some forms of living are superior to others. Therefore, the next chapters seek to reconnect how we function with how we were designed to function. The aim of the chapters ahead is to revive and re-invigorate the idea, the language, and the practice of virtue.

DISCUSSION QUESTIONS
FOR GROUP STUDY

1. This chapter mentioned several problems associated with the guideposts of efficiency, equity, and enforceability. Do you see examples of these problems around you in your daily life? What about in yourself?

2. The introductory chapter referenced the legalization of marijuana as a recreational drug. How would the guideposts of efficiency, equity, and enforceability mentioned within this chapter evaluate this legislation? Do you find these answers sufficient? If not, what is missing? Can you think of another example where the E-3 paradigm is, itself, insufficient to capture the moral complexities of a particular issue?

3. Many have made the argument that we should be ethical in business because it is better for business (higher growth and profit). This may very well be true. But why might this argument be problematic for people of faith?

4. What do we lose when we pursue fairness at the expense of other important moral considerations?

5. In his letter to the Corinthians, Paul responds to the common belief that "all things are lawful" by saying, "But not all things are beneficial." What did he mean here? Where might Paul say something similar to us today?

6. The chapter ended by suggesting that if right and wrong are relative, then "the guideposts above serve as nothing more than a convenient set of standards to substantiate a person's preference. Virtue becomes nothing more than a buyer's market." What does this mean? Why might this be problematic for people of faith?

3

THE IDEA OF VIRTUE

"Why do you call me good? No one is good but God alone."

—Mark 10:18

"[O]nce again, what God cares about is not exactly our actions. What He cares about is that we should be creatures of a certain kind of quality—the kind of creatures *He intended us to be*—creatures related to Himself in a certain way."

–C. S. Lewis, *Mere Christianity*

Up to this point, I have tried to argue that without a common moral vision, our tendency is to consult three primary guideposts that are influential in how we navigate our lives and seek to be "good." I have called this the E-3 paradigm (efficiency, equity, and enforceability). Yet upon closer inspection of this paradigm, we see that these standards are corrupted in the absence of design.

Therefore, the chapters that follow will seek to reconnect our activity to God's moral reality, for it is here that we find and participate in "good."

The Marketplace of Ideas

Each year, approximately two million students will walk across a stage, shake the hand of some important administrator, and receive a college diploma. Freed from the burden of lectures, deadlines, term papers, and finals, graduates are released into the open marketplace of commerce. It is here that they will compete for jobs, work late hours, and jockey for promotions. The skills that were introduced, cultivated, and refined in college will presumably help them to successfully foray into the "real world."

College is a rite of passage into today's ever-dynamic and increasingly complex world as preparation for the marketplace is necessary. Historically, nearly two-thirds of eligible adults participate in the labor force. Furthermore, beyond the labor we provide, we participate in the marketplace as consumers—purchasing the goods and services that we value. In a paradoxical way, then, the marketplace is something that we prepare for even though it is something we have always existed in.

At the center of this paradox is commercial activity (exchange, production, distribution, etc.). Indeed, commerce is the engine that drives our economy. It is the invisible force that seems to coordinate our daily affairs. It gets us out of bed, keeps us up at night, dashes our dreams, and drives our future aspirations. In short, we almost unavoidably orbit around the market.

Yet there is another market even more critical than the marketplace of commerce. This is the marketplace of *ideas*. Philosophers have long pointed out that it is difficult to trace "the connection between ideas and practice."[1] But while ideas may be difficult to connect to what we do, that does not mean that they are irrelevant. Rather, it is just the opposite. Ideas (what we think, perceive, and believe) are the cornerstone for activity (what we do; how we behave). Why? Because our view of the world and the beliefs that accompany our perception of reality will ultimately animate our words and motivate our actions. As Ralph Waldo Emerson writes, "that which dominates our imaginations and our thoughts will determine our lives." Historian Glenn Sunshine writes that if you want to understand why, and how, a civilization changes over time, investigate the ideas of that time that make up the dominant worldview.[2] Ideas matter.

Yet not all ideas are created equal. To illustrate this, consider one of the more famous novels, *The Picture of Dorian Gray* by Oscar Wilde (1854–1900). Wilde tells the story of a handsome young intellect and his loathsome journey from innocence to corruption. In the story, artist Basil Hallward captures the strikingly attractive Dorian in a painting. While posing for this portrait, Dorian meets Lord Henry Wotton, a winsome aristocrat who proceeds to entice Dorian with his philosophy of hedonism, or the pursuit of sensual fulfillment as a life-organizing goal. In short, hedonism says that the goodness of an activity is bound up in the pleasure that activity produces.

Dorian readily accepts and embraces Lord Henry's hedonistic philosophy and the lifestyle that accompanies it. However, he is troubled. Henry persuades him into believing that his attractiveness is closely tied to age and that he will lose his youthful splendor with the inevitable passing of time. Dorian then wishes that the portrait would age instead of him, that he would remain just as he was in that moment—even offering up his soul in exchange for perpetual youth.

While it is unclear who Dorian makes this bargain with (though toward the end of the book, someone says, "They say he has sold himself to the devil for a pretty face"), it is transacted nonetheless. His attractiveness secure, he goes on to pursue any and every pleasure available to him. But his lascivious lifestyle and sensual decadence has a cost—not to his outer frame, but to his picture. In a ghoulish twist, it is his portrait, not his actual self, which bears the loss of his beauty and innocence. As he entrenches himself more and more into patterns of corrosive self-gratification and pleasure, the portrait slowly transforms Gray's beautiful features into something horrific, reflecting the ever-increasing ugliness of his decadent, self-indulgent lifestyle. It shows the sin that has ravaged his soul.

The story ends with Dorian tangled in a complicated web of heartache, deception, blackmail, and murder. When he can no longer bear his now grotesque depiction, he wields a knife and proceeds to destroy the portrait. After hearing a bloodcurdling scream, his servants race into the room to find Dorian—now the revolting, disfigured image of the corrupted portrait—dead on the floor with the same knife in his heart.

There is much to reflect upon in Wilde's story. The philosophy of hedonism Lord Henry espoused, and which Dorian embraced, may seem elegant at best or trivial at worst in today's marketplace of ideas. Yet this belies the reality that our ideas, and the actions that so closely follow them, have the unforgiving capacity to corrupt and corrode our very souls. Like young Dorian Gray, we can choose to live however we want, but we invariably discover our innermost self sullied and warped in the process.

In addition to Wilde's novel being a popular story with an eerie conclusion, it is a modern-day tale of morality. It is one that we would do well to consider, as our culture is at risk of a similar Faustian bargain. In exchange for the pursuit of our desires and tastes regardless of their moral significance, we inevitably risk the degradation of the very essence of what it means to be a human proper. To be sure, this is indeed a pursuit of the "perfect version of ourselves"—yet without any notion that there is an overriding reality that we must cohere to in order to realize the completeness, the *shalom*, that we aim toward. Having goodness as an aim doesn't mean that our aim is good.

In contrast, if we were designed, then we have a purpose—some teleological end. This, I suggest, is the *idea* of virtue. It is the belief that how I live is invariably connected to what I was designed for. It is the recognition that the good life is not simply about the exercise of desire as a value in itself; it is about desiring well. The act of choosing does not make a *choice good*. Rather, recognizing such a thing as goodness opens the possibility of a *good choice*.

As I have already mentioned, I want to recapture and revive the idea of virtue. But this very statement suggests that it is missing or even deceased. So what has replaced this idea of virtue? What has dethroned any sense of design and purpose? What is the contemporary *raison d'être* for humanity? What is at the core of how we define goodness?

The answer, I submit, is preference, and in the marketplace of ideas, preference reigns supreme. That is, in the grand competition of beliefs and values, the pursuit of preference wins. Chapter 2 described modern "meta-values" used to guide our actions. While drawn from the well of these values, the "meta-value" of choice almost stands as its own moral and ethical system. Moreover, perhaps more than any other rival tradition, preference and choice contrast sharply with the idea of virtue. Therefore, before we move forward, it will be helpful to first attend to the preference as today's dominant ethic.

The Preeminence of Preference:
Economic and Political Forces

Marx is famous for suggesting that "religion is the opiate of the masses." We live in a rather different age ailed by a variation in Marx's original critique: opium is now the religion of the masses. Not too dissimilar from the hedonism embraced by Dorian Gray, the contemporary pursuit of self-gratification has become a de facto religion. "Happiness," wrote famous philosopher John Stuart Mill, "is intended pleasure."[3] Approximately one hundred and fifty years later, little has changed. How did we get here?

Preference as a meta-value is no mere accident. It is the product of growing economic and political forces.

Economic Forces

In 2013, a Harris Poll was conducted to determine levels of satisfaction and contentment among Americans. Among other findings, the study found that life satisfaction is important to us. The authors of the study write, "Americans are increasingly placing greater priority on living a fulfilling life."[4] This, of course, makes sense. We all seek meaning, significance, and fulfillment in what we do. But how do we do this? What is the best way to increase our satisfaction?

This question has attracted an array of answers, but one popular response comes from the field of economics. Not only do economists have theories about human behavior and well-being, but they can describe and predict humankind's various pursuits using formulas, curves, and models—providing a scientific dimension to the study of human activity. Furthermore, when it comes to increasing, or maximizing, human satisfaction, their prescription is clear: create the conditions under which individuals can have their preferences satisfied.

The general idea of preferences has been around since the earliest periods of recorded history. To have a preference is to possess, or express, a taste, desire, aim, etc. More formally, while many speak of preferences as a taste or a desire, this is only partially true and potentially misleading. Specifically, to have a preference for something is to prefer it to something else. If I have two items before me, I might desire both of them, but I can only prefer one of them. Economists point out that our individual preferences reflect our capacity to confer value upon goods. In other words, something's value is subject to individual appraisal. As one ancient expression put it, *suum cuique pulchrum est*—"to each his own is beautiful." This notion reaches back to early Greek thinkers who suggested that the value of what was preferred was relative to the person doing the valuing. It was Protagoras who "maintained that man was the measure of all things, which, as interpreted by Plato, means that, as things appear to me, so they are to me, or the denial of objective truth."[5] Naturally, what we subjectively value is what we choose to pursue and consume.

In the eighteenth century, a Swiss mathematician named Daniel Bernoulli created a mathematical formulation to describe the expected value one could reasonably achieve for any given action. The value or satisfaction one could derive from an action came to be described as *utility*. So, for example, if I had to choose between eating an apple and an orange, I might say that I would get 50 units of utility from the apple, and 40 units from the orange (naturally leading me to select the apple). This is an example of "cardinal" utility—or placing specific unit values of satisfaction we get from an action.

There is a problem, though. Utility is difficult, if not impossible, to measure across persons—making a cardinal measure both unscientific and unrealizable. Among early critics of cardinal utility was an Italian economist named Vilfred Pareto. Pareto asserted that it was not necessary to quantify a thing's utility. In other words, we don't need to know the exact value of utility one would get from an apple or an orange—we just need to know that a given person would get more enjoyment from the apple over the orange (or vice versa). This came to be referred to as ordinal (rather than cardinal) utility.

The predictive models that were later created based upon this idea suggested that a person can, and will, maximize their utility by choosing the actions, or the bundle of actions, that provide them with the most satisfaction. At this point, one might reasonably ask, "So what?" In other words, there is nothing controversial about this claim. After all, people do the things that they like to do, the things that bring them satisfaction. Not only is this normal, but we claim it is "rational" to act in this way. Conversely, to choose an activity that would not bring satisfaction (or the most satisfaction) is to act "irrationally."

But one important consequence that came with this economic perspective was an enhanced emphasis on preference. As Stanford University's Debra Satz writes, "values and preferences are now shifted outside the province of economics to private individual choice and decision."[6]

In addition to the distinction between cardinal and ordinal utility, Pareto provided a target measure for efficiency, or what has become known as the Pareto criterion. This suggests that the satisfaction of our tastes, or preferences, through markets of exchange will eventually lead to the optimum state where no one person can be made better off without making someone else worse off (what is called Pareto Optimality).

Today, the Pareto criterion has come to be the dominant measure of achieving efficiency in economics. But what is so important about efficiency in this field? First, efficiency is significant because, as mentioned above, interpersonal utility cannot be measured (what brings me satisfaction may differ from what brings you satisfaction). Second, because interpersonal utility cannot be measured, we can assume that people rank the options before them and choose the option that would bring about the most utility given some of their constraints (for example, income). Finally, then, if (1) utility is subjective to each individual, (2) individuals rank their decisions in a way so as to maximize their own personal utility, and (3) we cannot compare utility across persons, then it stands to reason that the best arrangement is the one in which individuals are free to express their preferences through unencumbered market exchange (an "efficient" outcome).

So, if satisfaction is an important goal for human beings, and most would agree that it is, then the fulfillment of our various preferences becomes important as well. This particular philosophy has been referred to as "preference satisfaction"—or the belief that people know what will make them happy, so we should let them consume or act in those ways. Here is the key: the paradigm assumes that my welfare (literally, the "condition of being or doing well") is directly related to giving me what I want. That is, preferences are the key to unlocking human gratification and satisfaction. Furthermore, what we prefer differs from person to person. Some prefer boxers over briefs; movies over concerts; guitars over pianos, etc. While these seem to be matters of taste, it is important to recognize that many of our preferences also have a clear moral dimension. One group of economists states the issue as follows:

> On the preference satisfaction view, one makes Ann better off by satisfying her preferences regardless of how idiosyncratic or obnoxious they are and regardless of how they were formed. If welfare is what matters to social policy, then social policy should be insensitive to the character and origins of preferences.[7]

As mentioned above, the "character and origins" of our preferences in society have been framed as personal value judgments. Indeed, subjective valuations have long been central to post-classical economic theory.

Consider, for example, Austrian economist Murray Rothbard's words over half a century ago: "Individual valuation is the keystone of economic theory. . . . Action is the result of choice among alternatives, and choice reflects values, that is, individual preferences among these alternatives."[8] Authors Edward and Robert Skidelsky state the issue well: "Economists are all for the *satisfaction* of wants, at least within certain limits. But as to the wants themselves, they maintain a fastidious indifference."[9]

Economist Jodi Beggs is rather blunt about the matter. In response to the suggestion that it is important to value goods in an appropriate way, she writes, "Who in the hell are you to tell people what they 'should' be valuing? Some economists may try to account for tastes, but none of us are presumptuous enough to tell anyone what their tastes should be."[10]

I find this to be a rather amazing comment. Aside from someone's preference for sugar over artificial sweetener, etc., when we make moral distinctions between digesting great literature and digesting, say, pornography, is that "presumptuous"? Are we really to be nonjudgmental toward preferences for market goods like extramarital affairs, racially segregated housing, or videos of homeless men pitifully fighting each other for money? When individual valuation is a "keystone" of economics, the answer, unfortunately, is yes.

When we so deeply protect individual value, desire, and choice—even for morally repugnant items for sale—preference can only be understood as a kind of meta-value, or a value from which we derive all other values. By honoring society's many and diverse preferences, we affirm individuals' freedom to choose what they want as a meta-value. Choice leads to the pursuit of preferences, and the pursuit of preferences, at least in theory, leads to satisfaction and fulfillment.

Political Forces

Preference as a preeminent value is not supported by economics alone. Political forces have also served to shape and sustain this cultural standard. To see this, it is helpful to first look at the concept of justice.

Historically, justice has generally been understood to mean "rendering unto each their due." The origin of justice as "to each their due" hails back to ancient Greek philosophers. According to Aristotle, what was "just" related to proportion. For example, if I were to determine who deserves a minivan among a random group of people, the just thing to do would be to give it to the person who has a family. Why? Because minivans were made to cart families around. That is, a family and their transportation needs are best aligned with a minivan. We might say they "deserve" each other.

Notice in this exercise that a just distribution requires us to understand the nature of the thing being distributed. Aristotle believed that questions about what someone deserves require us to first define the aim and character of what is being distributed. An example that Aristotle himself used was a flute. That is, who deserves a flute? Before answering this question, we must first define the purpose (the *telos*) of the flute. Among other things, flutes exist to make beautiful music. So, according to this logic, the person who deserves the flute is the person who can play it well (because that is what a flute is made for!). Imagine if I were to use one of the most expensive flutes in the world, a Verne Q. Powell Flute, to stir my coffee in the morning or smash hard-to-reach cockroaches on the floor—all while living next door to award-winning Irish flutist James Galway! Not only would this arrangement be unfortunate, it would be patently unjust. Expertly crafted flutes are made for expertly trained flutists. They are *proportionate*; they deserve one another.

So, whether it is a family and a minivan or a flute and a flutist, the proportionate link between the item and the recipient represents the historical understanding of justice. However, something changed when we entered into the modern era. Justice was no longer about achieving proportion, but about achieving equality—more specifically, equality among individuals and their rights.

This is a major assertion of Alasdair MacIntyre's popular work *Whose Justice? Which Rationality?* In this book, MacIntyre traces Western conceptions of justice from Aristotle to Thomas Aquinas (thirteenth century) and on to David Hume (eighteenth century), making the case that they each appeal to a particular tradition engaging moral theory. However, after Hume and the Scottish Enlightenment, a new kind of thinking—what we can call "liberal" thinking—emerged.

But what was this new liberal thinking? What were its features? Similar to what I've mentioned in the discussion of the E-3 paradigm, Michael Sandel defines liberalism as the idea that "society is best arranged when it is governed by principles that do not presuppose any particular conception of the good."[11] Similarly, MacIntyre describes this as a commitment "to there being no overriding good."[12]

Think of it this way: society once began by starting with a conception of the good life, and then organizing itself in such a way as to best achieve this life. By first determining the best way to live, the proper end of humanity, such a society could then be arranged to pursue this desired outcome. The traditional expression of this perspective was that "the good was prior to the right"—or determining the good life came before the determination of individual rights. To provide just one example, early American founders such as Thomas

Jefferson judged economic and political arrangements by their capacity to promote character among citizens, because character, by their conviction, was fundamental to human flourishing. In other words, the pursuit and development of human character was a standard by which to arrange society's members socially, economically, and politically.

Liberalism, however, flipped this ancient maxim around: "the right is prior to the good"—or individual rights, desires, tastes, and pursuits come first. In the ancient expression, people were encouraged to conform to goodness. Under the liberal expression, people are encouraged to define their own idea of goodness (recall this discussion from the rights-based liberal tradition in chapter 2).

John Rawls, whom I mentioned earlier in chapter 2 and described as one of the leading "liberal" philosophers of the twentieth century, justifies this shift away from Aristotelian justice: "Human good is heterogeneous because the aims of the self are heterogeneous."[13] In other words, people have different perceptions of what is good, right, and true. Why force them to conform to one overarching definition of goodness? Why not create the conditions by which people can define and pursue what they want, so long as it does not prevent other people from pursuing what they want?

What was the result of this emerging philosophy? Society came to be understood as a collection of rational subjects defined by their choices and preferences. Indeed, preference was considered a "central" value of liberal modernity.[14] "The just society," writes Sandel, "seeks to provide a framework within which its citizens can pursue their own value and ends."[15]

So, to summarize our modern view of justice, society should not begin with a thick moral conception of what is good, and arrange itself in such a way as to best achieve this end. Rather, there is no overriding good, no moral vision that all can agree upon and aspire toward. In its place is the proposal to let people determine what is good for themselves. Furthermore, the role of governing bodies is to create the conditions by which citizens can pursue their conception of what is right and good (so long as their pursuit does not infringe upon or prohibit someone else's pursuit)—a liberal arrangement.

Liberalism can means lots of things to lots of people—but here I simply define it as the philosophy that an *individual's* rights supersede any notion of what it means to live a good life. Furthermore, one of the primary conditions necessary to make this arrangement possible is the presence of neutrality.

To be neutral is to allow people to satisfy their desires without placing any kind of moral significance on the things they might value. For example, philosopher Michael Philips suggests that while it is impossible to describe a good that everyone would agree on, we can confidently assert that "Everyone wants their preferences satisfied."[16] Respecting individuals, so goes the belief, means respecting their preferences. Maintaining neutrality of this sort requires that we value individuals and their preferences without any reflection on the very things they actually prefer. MacIntyre describes such neutrality as giving each individual "freedom to express and to implement preferences and a share in the means required to make that implementation effective."[17]

What does this mean? It means that what I want to pursue, my preferences, becomes sacrosanct. Moreover, value is determined by the individual doing the valuing. Daniel Bell's blunt description, mentioned in chapter 2, is worth repeating: "Liberalism re-imaged society as a teeming mass of individuals, each with their own interests, ends, and conceptions of what constitutes the good life."[18]

If the individual is the reference point for modern liberal society, and society is thus arranged around the individual, then it is little wonder that choice and preference have become central values for a "just society." The just society is no longer about determining and participating in what is good; it is about letting each individual define it on their own. In this way, justice is closely correlated with preference. The new "good" was the declaration that there was no absolute good worthy of everyone's pursuit. If there was to be a shared value, it was the agreement to let individuals—and their various beliefs, values, and aims—determine what they wanted to pursue. Indirectly, then, choice becomes our absolute good.

Whether through economic, political, or other sociocultural forces, preference has acquired a significance that could be described as nearly religious. It is a characteristic to be evangelistically proclaimed, zealously defended, and sacredly upheld. Naturally, this implies an overly optimistic view of humanity and, specifically, the capacity and potential of the individual.

"Be True to Yourself"

In 2005, after he was diagnosed with the pancreatic cancer that would eventually take his life, Apple founder and technology genius Steve Jobs regaled Stanford's graduating class with the following advice:

> Your time is limited, so don't waste it living someone else's life. Don't be trapped by dogma, which is living with the results of other people's thinking. Don't let the noise of others' opinions drown out your own inner voice. And most important, have the courage to follow your heart and intuition.[19]

In essence, Jobs was sharing advice that is as old as time itself: *Be true to yourself.* Unlocking your potential, overcoming your fears, and achieving your dreams is all a matter of authenticity, we are told.

In the early twentieth century, Alfred Lord Tennyson wrote, "Ah, for a new man to arise in me—that the man I am may cease to be."[20] A century later, our cry is not for our authentic self to "cease to be," but to come into being. Today, Oprah Winfrey's advice to "love yourself first" is the solution, not the problem, to whatever may ail us. Indeed, the mantra to "be true to yourself" is so ubiquitous and oft-repeated that it has the status of a metaphysical principle for regulating our lives.

Interestingly, this was the very logic used by the serpent in Genesis: "Did God say, 'You shall not eat from any tree in the garden?' . . . You will not die; for God knows that when you eat of it your eyes will be opened, and you will be like God, knowing good and evil" (Gen. 3:2–5).

You will be like God. You will know good and evil. You will determine right and wrong as you see fit.

The lie that deceived Adam and Eve remains our illusion today. The good, the right, and the true aren't out there to be sought, discovered, and apprehended; they are inside of me. I am the arbiter of right and wrong. It is me, not others, who can best evaluate the choices that will maximize my satisfaction.

If all of life's answers are to be found within me, then the expression of preference—in itself—is its own goal. In other words, the thing I choose no longer communicates its goodness—the very act of choosing does! In this sense, choice is not just a tool to maximize utility (as suggested by economic forces) or establish a just society (as suggested by political forces). We are led to believe that goodness comes in exercising choice, not in choosing things that are good. Ethicist Thomas Jensen calls this "values clarification"—where something becomes good because I first of all want it. It begins inside of us, and then moves outside.[21]

We might say that the very exercise of choice is a modern virtue. To illustrate this, consider an article posted by *The Economist* in 2013. Seeking to tackle the nuances of gay marriage, the article cites author Alexander Borinsky's reflections on his own sexual promiscuity:

> My promiscuity served a purpose. Abandoning myself to alcohol and flirtation felt like a salvific, if reckless, kind of machismo. Uncommitted sexual encounters meant self-reliance. I vividly remember leaving the house of a waifish, doe-eyed dancer from Devon who grinned and giggled and wore a ripped army jacket. It was around four thirty in the morning. The sex had been terrible, but outside was a lovely, warmish night. As I waited for the night bus I felt disappointed, embarrassed, and a little frightened. I also felt brave, dangerous, and grown. . . .
>
> The urge to prove that I could stand on my own two manly legs came, in part, from the language of helplessness that pervades most messages of gay acceptance: "It's okay that you're gay, because you were just born that way. It's no one's fault." Binging and [having sex] made my gayness into, yes, a "lifestyle" choice—not just a hormonal tic I couldn't help. I was a person making choices, not a sexuality unfolding itself.[22]

The point to be made does not necessarily relate to sexuality—rather, Borinsky captures the spirit of the age in matters of preference. Borinsky may have had feelings of disappointment, embarrassment, or fear. But once he determined that he was not an organism passively subject to the ebb and flow of some mysterious sexual psyche, but an active choice-making man electing his lifestyle, all apprehension was replaced with bravery. The expression of his preference was not simply an expression of autonomy—it was an act of courage; an overture toward self-reliant maturity. According to him, choice is heroic. Choice defines what is right. Choice fashions the chooser.

Indeed, although preference reigns supreme across many aspects of our lives, it is particularly evident in discussions of sex. Consider the language surrounding the growing acceptance of polyamorous relationships. "Polyamorous" literally means "many loves," but in reality the term seems to double as a euphemism for uncommitted sexual exploration. While some may describe having multiple sexual relationships as a "constant, evolving, open, and transparent conversation," attachments inevitably take on an entirely different meaning.[23] The problem isn't simply that one is having sex with multiple partners (potentially breeding jealousy, etc.). Rather, the larger concern relates to the polyamorist's user-friendly, consumerist approach to relationships in general. No longer is a relationship constituted by norms of trust, sacrifice, and self-giving love; it is about satisfying one's various desires without being burdened with any one partner's relational baggage or other potentially hurtful outcomes.

This attitude is also supported by new platforms that have emerged to facilitate casual, serial relationships. With innovative technology, we have entered into the realm of "Big Dating" (a play on the phenomenon of "Big Data"). One defender of polyamory describes it well:

> Today's most interesting apps are designed to support Big Dating, offering discreet, asynchronous, anonymish, non-exclusive communications. Multiplied against algorithms that optimize the pool of potential partners for connection (requiring no more than swipe left, swipe left, swipe right to operate), romantic partners are now more fungible than ever. Scary! Exciting![24]

In his fascinating book *The End of Absence*, author Michael Harris explores how technology (e.g., smartphones and the Internet) is forming and reforming today's social landscape. In his chapter on "hooking up," Harris highlights the now-numerous sex apps sweeping the marketplace that serve to gratify our desires, whatever they may be. In Harris' words, we are "emboldened . . . with the possibility of getting what we want whenever we want it."[25]

Whether it is a dating site trying to match couples or an app disclosing the proximity of like-minded folks desiring a casual hook-up, algorithmic technology plays an increasingly significant role in plugging the hot-wire of human desire into the appropriate outlet. Just as the online music establishment Pandora can better match your musical preference as you provide them with more information about yourself and your musical tastes, dating apps can "do their job properly" when provided with more and more detail about their users.[26]

For example, Neil Biderman, founder of AshleyMadison.com (a website that facilitates adulterous relationships), describes the future of relationships in terms of data: "If we can use science, use algorithms, to make our relationships more successful, then that's a positive. We need to get over this idea that infringing on privacy is such a problem. Does it matter if a computer knows what you watch on television?"[27]

Advanced match-making algorithms may perhaps be one of the most telling expressions of preference as an ultimate value. To illustrate why, we might imagine a dating site with a highly-advanced algorithm. Furthermore, imagine that the site has access to your entire neural network (desires, beliefs, experiences). In the world of technology, more data equals enhanced predictive capacity. If such an arrangement were a possibility, then who would the algorithm choose as my partner? The model, in its perfect form, would choose another individual who feels what I feel, thinks what I think, likes what I like, and believes what I believe. This person would meet each and every desire I had in a relationship. She would perfectly match the sum of my preferences.

But if an individual is indeed nothing other than the sum of their preferences, then in a very odd way, I would be dating . . . *me*. That is, if the process worked to its maximum capacity, I would be connected with a person who, in every way imaginable, reflected my full laundry list of desired attributes.

Technology, of course, does not say anything normative about what I choose or the kind of desires I should have. It would be unreasonable to expect it to do so. Moreover, technology most certainly has the capacity to connect couples in meaningful, fulfilling ways. However, it also has the capacity to reinforce the expression of choice as its own value. In the example above describing dating algorithms, advanced technological approaches to relationships do not necessarily improve my life or my relationships (though that is the promise)—rather, they offer an innovative, twenty-first-century way of expressing my own love of self. It is the autonomous self, not the distinct other, that we are encouraged to pursue in order to achieve meaningful and significant fulfillment in our lives.

New York Times writer and prolific author David Brooks has given considerable attention to the "autonomy ethos" that seems to dominate our current culture. In his book *The Road to Character*, Brooks traces the twentieth-century shift from self-skepticism to self-praise. Regarding the former, many thinkers, both ancient and modern, possessed a "limited view" of our individual power and reason. According to these thinkers, humans have the capacity for unaided reason and right action, but ultimately we are fallen creatures who tend toward self-destruction, not self-actualization, when we are left alone. In contrast, after World War II, Brooks writes, a new wave of optimism about human potential gripped the culture. Humans were equipped, not limited; rational, not incoherent; good, not corrupted. Human perfectibility resided within everyone—it only needed to be tapped correctly. Under this belief, it is often external circumstances, not interior wiring, that are understood to prohibit human flourishing.

Under the autonomy ethos, attributes such as self-esteem and authenticity have come to define the systematic philosophy that ultimately animates our actions in today's world. This may not seem bad on the surface, but these positive attributes risk becoming mere euphemisms for other, more insidious, characteristics. Self-esteem becomes self-centeredness. Similarly, authenticity becomes self-worship. Regarding the latter, Brooks writes:

This mindset is based on the romantic idea that each of us has a Golden Figure in the core of our self. There is an innately good True Self, which can be trusted, consulted, and gotten in touch with. Your personal feelings are the best guide for what is right and wrong.[28]

Notice that under this philosophy, which is often called "emotivism," our sentiments serve as the arbiter of truth and morality. In a 1948 debate, Frederick Copleston pointed out that Bertrand Russell, his atheistic counterpart, distinguished between blue and yellow by sight—but how, Copleston asked, did he distinguish between right and wrong? "By my feelings," Russell bluntly responded.[29] Over half a century later, when superstar cyclist Lance Armstrong came clean about his doping activity, he justified his actions to Oprah Winfrey by sharing that "cheating didn't *feel* wrong."[30] In other words, Armstrong was appealing to Oprah and her army of viewers, not on the basis of predefined cycling standards, personal integrity, or appropriate social convention, but on the basis of his feelings.

Personal feelings, and the desires, preferences, and choices they are so closely associated with, have come to serve as the de facto gold standard for individual and social pursuits. But, as we've seen, it was not always so.

"Educating the Sentiments"

Ancient philosophers such as Aristotle and Plato did not simply discuss good, but *the* good. The word "the" here is what linguists refer to as the definite article. One of the primary reasons we use the definite article ("the") is to denote that there is a specific thing we are speaking about. That is, we are drawing the reader's attention to a particular object (in this case the noun *good*).

Adding "the" seems subtle. But there is an important philosophical point to make here. Goodness is not something we generate or define on our own; it is something we apprehend. We participate in goodness. It is not unique to each individual. It is not manufactured. It is not relative. Goodness is outside of us, a thing to be perceived, grasped, and embodied. Goodness is not created, it is joined. *The* good.

C. S. Lewis recognized this. In his short essay *Men without Chests*, Lewis provides a brief but unforgettable philosophical reflection based upon a textbook that had come into his possession. The book itself analyzed a writing piece by poet Samuel Coleridge. Accompanied by two other tourists, Coleridge writes about his experience standing before a majestic waterfall. One of his fellow tourists describes the waterfall as "sublime." The other simply acknowledges it as being "pretty."

The first description receives praise from Coleridge—the waterfall was indeed sublime, and not merely pretty. Yet the authors of the textbook believed that Coleridge had made a mistake: "When the man said *This is sublime*, he appeared to be making a remark about the waterfall. . . . Actually . . . he was not making a remark about the waterfall, but a remark about his own feelings."[31]

According to the authors of the textbook, there is no such thing as sublimity (outside of ourselves), and certainly no such thing as a sublime waterfall. When the tourists commented on it, rather than saying something about the waterfall itself, its beauty and essence, they were saying something about themselves—more specifically, their emotions.

The authors of the textbook are basically asserting that the world has no essence to it. Rather, according to them we react to the environment around us in various ways and simply project those reactions onto it. This is the very definition of "existentialism"—our existence and our experiences create the essence of the world around us, and not the other way around. To navigate the world, then, we must simply navigate our feelings. In this sense, goodness (or any other quality) is something that is contrived or manufactured within us. A waterfall is not sublime in itself. Rather, I *feel* sublime and project this onto the waterfall.

In contrast, if the world has an essence or a design—what has traditionally been referred to as the *created order*—then living well and virtuously requires us to order our thoughts, language, and ultimately our lives to the essence of the world around us. Yet without a sense of this order, and mixed with the all-too-popular belief that we are the best judges of what is good for us, our aims become arbitrary at best, as if we were "firing arrows into a barn door and drawing targets around them."[32]

So what does it mean to participate in goodness? If there is a good to be sought, discovered, and apprehended—what are its characteristics? A key to the answer can be found in Lewis's response to the authors of the textbook: "The good life is not simply one of satisfied desire; it indicates the proper *goal* of desire. Desire is to be cultivated, directed to the truly desirable. Moral education is an education of the sentiments."[33]

Moral education is an education of the sentiments. What does this mean? While much can be said, I want to highlight three important areas related to educating the sentiments, and ultimately to the idea of virtue.

Denying Self

In his book *Your God Is Too Safe*, author Mark Buchanan shares the story of a couple undertaking pre-marital counseling. In place of traditional vows, the couple chose to write their own. Upon Buchanan's inspection, the vows looked fine—until he came to the phrase, "I promise to be true to myself." Concerned, he confronted the couple:

> "Um," I said, "I'm pretty sure you don't want that in the vow." "I'm pretty sure we do," the man said. "Maybe you're very different from me," I said. "There's part of me, I'm glad to say, that is joy-filled, generous, trusting, trustworthy. But there's another part of me—maybe the larger part—that's slothful, lustful, greedy, miserly, apathetic. I could go on. Which part should I be true to?"[34]

Buchanan shares his revelation,

> It occurred to me then that to take traditional marriage vows is to pledge, in essence, that I won't be true to myself. I will be true to another. I will be true to God. But in order to do that, I will often have to deny myself—deny my impulse to run, to retaliate, to sulk, to self-indulge, to self-destruct.[35]

Buchanan's insight stands in contrast to the popular belief that people are, at their core, good. Many hold the view that we are made up of impulses that incite us to perform good actions and bad actions over the course of our lives, with, ideally, the good outweighing the bad. Some believe religion is a key to tipping the scales toward traditional virtues and good living. Some believe the opposite. More recently, the so-called "new atheists" such as Richard Dawkins, Sam Harris, and Christopher Hitchens have argued that humans are inherently good, and religion makes us bad. Get rid of religion and its tyranny, they claim, and the world will be a much better place.

Religion, however, and especially Christianity, has a much different narrative. Martin Luther's definition of sin is particularly helpful here. We tend to think of sin as a bad, or evil, action. For Luther, though, it was a disposition: *cor incurvatas ad se*—or "the heart curved in on itself."[36] Historical Christianity has long recognized the self as the problem, not the solution, to achieving human excellence. The British journalist Malcolm Muggeridge has described man's depravity as being the most empirically verifiable reality while also being the most intellectually resisted fact.

"Empirical" is a good description of sin. Inside or outside the faith, many people witness or experience an inclination—or an incapacity—for right living. As a teenager, I recall listening to a popular alternative band whose lyrics caught my attention: "It's hard to rely on my good intentions, when my head is full of things I can't mention. It seems I usually get things right but I can't understand what I did last night."[37] I wasn't exactly a reflective thinker when I was younger, but I can remember pausing upon hearing these words. "That is exactly how I feel," I thought. There seemed to be a gap between my own good intentions and my actual performance, between the goodness I desired to embody and the badness that took its place.

As I would come to learn, I was experiencing what people across ages and cultures have long recognized and lamented in the human experience. *I am not good.*

As the late pastor A. W. Tozer bluntly states, in matters of character and moral development, the wind blows toward hell. That is, we have an inclination to serve ourselves. This may not sound too bad on the surface, but it is literally the bane of our desire to do, and be, good. A heart curved in upon itself is a heart that desires *autonomy*—total freedom, not for the sake of others, but from others. It is prideful, lustful, conniving, and caustic. In an insidiously ironic twist, the very liberty we are promised in ourselves is not very liberating at all. It is bondage. "Nearly all men die of their medicines," writes French playwright Molière, "and not their maladies." What a prophetic, and instructive, insight for those who are led to believe that "being true to themselves" is a necessary medicine.

John Wesley understood this. He called the problem *independency*, or the desire for autonomy masked as liberty. Independency is not freedom *for* another (God or neighbor); it is freedom *from* all constraint. However, to shun constraints is to invite self-rule. And self-rule, as mentioned, is self-enslavement. Understood in these terms, staying "true to myself" is most certainly a recipe for destruction. Moreover, this insight can be acquired without a theology degree. " 'Be yourself,' " Mark Twain warned, "is about the worst advice you can give to people."

Luther had it right.

From Disconnected to Connected Desire

If the Christian narrative has it right, and being "true to myself" promises destruction, what is the solution? What good can we aspire to when our very selves are so corrupted? Here, Paul's letter to the Philippian church offers guidance.

> [For] many live as enemies of the cross of Christ. Their destiny is destruction, their god is their stomach, and their glory is in their shame. Their mind is set on earthly things. But our citizenship is in heaven. And we eagerly await a Savior from there, the Lord Jesus Christ. (Phil. 3:18–20)

There is much to reflect on here, but Paul makes two important points in this passage that are worthy of immediate consideration. First, those who seek a life constructed around fulfilling their own worldly desires ("their god is their stomach") are enemies to the sacrifice Christ made on the cross. Second, we will never find salvation in "earthly things." Therefore, our minds should be occupied in altogether different territory—the true region of our citizenship (heaven). We see two commands, one in the negative sense and one in the positive. *Don't* look to yourself or earthly things and *do* look toward heaven, toward your Savior. If we forsake the latter (heavenly), and seek the former (self), we risk losing our reference point for organizing our lives in the way they were meant to be organized. In short, we lose the notion of design. As we saw in chapter 1, when how we function is disconnected from how we were designed to function, questions about our identity and our action become simply a matter of taste. We might say that our desire becomes disconnected from what is truly desirable.

One of the more powerful testimonies to these truths comes from St. Augustine. While many recognize Augustine as a saint, and rightly so, a significant part of his life was far from "saintly."

The issue was disconnection. Like those before and after him, Augustine's problem was not desire itself. In other words, our goal as humans should not be to eradicate our desire. This, of course, is in contrast to Buddhist philosophy, which claims that perfect peace ("Nirvana") is achieved through the complete suppression of individual desire. According to Augustine, God blessed us with desires, so the goal should not be to suppress them. Rather, the goal is to desire *well*.

Recall C. S. Lewis's story about Samuel Coleridge and the "sublime" waterfall. Coleridge recognized that the waterfall had an objective, powerful beauty. It was as though he could perceive its essence and not merely his own experience of it; or perhaps we might say that his experience was true to its object. The waterfall had beauty regardless of whether or not Coleridge had the eyes to see it. He recognized that goodness was something outside of himself that is comprehended and captured, not created from within.

Lewis points out that upon hearing the waterfall being described as "sublime" and "pretty," Coleridge endorsed the first judgment but was disgusted with the second. In other words, the beauty of the waterfall deserved a better description than merely being "pretty"—it was *sublime*. The description fit. It was rightly ordered.

Similarly, I recall being asked to describe a renowned renaissance painting in a high school humanities class. After fumbling around for what to say, my mind completely blank, I awkwardly blurted out that it was "neat." My teacher stared at me in silence, offended by such a pathetic answer. I will never forget his sarcastic response: "*Neat?*" Embarrassing as it was for me, his reaction was appropriate. The painting was not merely neat. It was profound. Inspiring. *Sublime.*

Lewis writes, "The reason why Coleridge agreed with the tourist who called the cataract sublime and disagreed with the one who called it pretty was of course that he believed inanimate nature to be such that certain responses could be more 'just' or 'ordinate' or 'appropriate' to it than others."[38] The preeminent philosopher Peter Kreeft has wisely noted that beauty is not in the eye of the beholder, but it is in the power of the beholder's eye to see beauty.[39]

What does this have to do with desire? In the same way that some judgments are more appropriate than others (for example, it's better to call a painting by Michelangelo "sublime," not "neat"), some desires are also more appropriate than others. But what is worthy of our desire? How can we determine the appropriate objects of our desire? Notice that this question cannot be answered from myself alone. An outside measure must be present: a fixed reference point, or a standard for human excellence. One author, writing on Augustine's famous work *Confessions*, puts it quite well:

Augustine's favorite argument is based on the hierarchy of being that we discover in the world. We judge that some things are more perfect than others. We judge that things which are alive are more perfect than inanimate things. We judge that things that are alive and can sense (animals) are more perfect things that are alive but cannot sense (plants). And we judge that we who think, sense, and live are more perfect still. However, the existing human being is not the ultimate key to understanding reality; for when we judge, we judge by some criterion of truth, goodness, or beauty. And if our judgment is correct, then the criterion we use must be certain and unchanging. We judge by the truth; we do not judge the truth. Thus, the truth is something above us.[40]

The Christian call to deny one's self is not simply arbitrary rule-making or ascetic fundamentalism. Rather, it is the recognition that nothing good lies within me. I am not, and cannot be, my own reference point for navigating through life. My judgments, desires, and preferences are not good in themselves. Disconnected from their design and their proper objects, at best we can say that they simply are. At worst, though, we risk incoherence, confusion, frustration, and hopelessness. Seen through this lens, are we surprised that we suffer from broken relationships, social distrust, and rampant anxiety? Could this play a role in creating the lives of "quiet desperation" that Henry David Thoreau famously recognized?

Of course this doesn't mean that we don't desire to be good. We do. Few people make it a life aim to live in a morally impoverished way. Yet when we live under the illusion that goodness can be unlocked within ourselves (i.e., by "being true to ourselves") without looking beyond ourselves, even our best intentions for virtuous action and meaningful significance are thwarted.

As David Brooks writes, "The result is that people can understand themselves only by looking at the forces that transcend themselves. Human life points beyond itself."[41] Augustine himself came to realize that it would be better to be a slave to another human being (especially if the person was virtuous and wise) than to "fall under the tyranny of one's own corrupted and confused desire."[42] Similarly, in Romans 6:22, Paul writes that after being set free from sin (or the heart curved in on itself) the benefit of "slavery to God" is holiness, and the result is eternal life. Disconnected from sin and the rule of self, we become connected to a Savior, Creator, Designer: God.

Ordo Amoris—*Desiring Well*

Today, however, the educational trends that C. S. Lewis observed more than half a century ago are more prevalent than ever. For example, in their 2010 book *The Heart of Higher Education*, Parker Palmer and Arthur Zajonc reflect on the difference between possessing what Zajonc calls the "Socialized Mind" and achieving the more mature "Self-Authoring Mind."

If an adult has a Socialized Mind, they argue, then he or she is well-adjusted enough to make sense of the world and its meaning. However, Zajonc warns, this is not enough. A more mature learner will move on to develop the Self-Authorizing Mind, which is characterized by an individual harboring various beliefs and viewpoints but ultimately being able to "author his or her own independent one."[43] Self-Authorship, it is claimed, "should be heralded as a central purpose of higher education."[44]

The thought is interesting, but can we really distill education, whether formal or informal, down to successfully authoring one's own viewpoint? Does not the viewpoint itself make a difference? It is not difficult to imagine tyrannical monarchs, KKK officers, Nazis, or antebellum slave owners who managed to achieve a Self-Authored Mind. It is foolish to praise someone's authorship and ownership of a particular viewpoint without scrutinizing the nature of the viewpoint itself. In contrast, C. S. Lewis provides an alternative vision of what education should aspire to be:

Aristotle says that the aim of education is to make the pupil like and dislike what he ought. When the age for reflective thought comes, the pupil who has been thus trained in *ordinate affections* or 'just sentiments' will easily find the first principles in [Aristotle's] Ethics; but to the corrupt man they will never be visible at all and he can make no progress in that science. Plato before him had said the same. The little human animal will not at first have the right responses. It must be trained to feel pleasure, liking, disgust, and hatred at those things which really are pleasant, likeable, disgusting and hateful.[45]

Unfortunately, properly educating our desires cannot be achieved by merely sitting in a classroom and taking good notes. This is because education is not simply a matter of mental maturation—understanding and authoring one's own desires and values. Rather, it is about aligning those very desires and values with what is truly desirable and the truly valuable. By this very definition, it is impossible to find the answers within myself. To declare the aim to orient my life around truth, beauty, and goodness is to concede that those very qualities must be discovered, apprehended, and embodied. In a paradoxical way, then, the center of our lives is not *in* us, but rather *outside* of us. Desire cannot be justified by the person doing the desiring alone; it must align with the created order. Attempts to arrive upon the good, the right, and the true are inseparable from the notion that how we function must match our design. Anything else is *disconnected*.

Despite some of our contemporary expressions of faith that (wrongly) emphasize individuality, preference, and choice, the Christian faith tradition has long been suspicious of disconnected desire. As Rodney Clapp writes, "For Christian spirituality, desire can never be considered apart from its object. A desire is known as 'good' or 'evil' only when we take account of what is desired— the object of desire."[46] Our desires should be ordered to cohere and conform to the person, place, or thing being desired. Not the mere expression of preference, but aligning what we prefer to what should be preferred—desiring well.

Augustine referred to this as *ordo amoris,* or "ordered love." For him, ordered love is the center of virtue itself. In his most popular book, *The City of God*, Augustine writes, "We do well to love that which, when we love it, makes us live well and virtuously. So that it seems to me that it is a brief but true definition of virtue to say, it is the order of love."[47] Virtue and goodness are not first about rules but about loving what is good. We go astray when we desire what is not good. Thus, virtue is about "educating the sentiments"— recognizing, appreciating, seeking, embracing, and sustaining what is worthy of our affections and pursuits. The truly good person acts virtuously not out of fear of breaking the rules, but out of sincere desire to do what is right.

Why is this important? What is at stake? I submit that it is our very humanity. It is fulfillment, significance, and meaning; it is being who we were created to be. Properly ordered love is not simply about our lives becoming better; it is about being able to become whole. You may recall from the opening chapter of the book that to have a virtuous life is to have a "perfect" life, or the best life we can lead. Aligning ourselves to God's created order does not dismiss our humanity (i.e., being "true to ourselves")—it is an overture toward discovering our best self. It is, as Stuart McAllister writes, "restoration and re-creation, a physician's meditation; it is about human flourishing and discovering life."[48] Goodness is not bound up in our choices. Rather, a choice can be considered good insofar as it is bound up with goodness.

Conclusion—"Something Lives in Every Hue"

My pastor once shared with me that he commits a day out of the week to spending time alone in the woods. "That must be relaxing," I said. His response startled me, "It's not relaxing at all. I spend most of my time stomping around out there thinking about the thousand things I could be doing." Recognizing my curiosity as to why he committed himself to this routine if it was so unpleasant, he offered this: "I believe that there is a human tendency to try to control our reality. I am one of the worst offenders. But when I go out into the woods, *I sober up*."

I love this expression. For one, I like that idea that we are drunk with excessive work, deadlines, activities, etc., and that removing ourselves into a realm of stillness and reflection allows us to sober up from our productivity-driven stupor. But, more to the point, I think this statement says something important about the reality around us and how we might participate within it.

In his hymn "Loved with Everlasting Love," George Wade Robinson writes:

Heaven above is softer blue,
Earth below is sweeter green,
Something lives in every hue,
Christless eyes have never seen.

This is not simply a songwriter expressing that his faith-life makes him feel warm and fuzzy. Rather, I believe this is a man who recognizes connections, interrelatedness, and order around us. When we fully grasp the nature of the created order, it is impossible not to conceptualize the world in unique and beautiful ways. It is not that the world creates arbitrary feelings within us; rather, our sensibilities conform and adhere to the order around us. We *participate* in beauty and thus experience the beautiful.

This direction comes not by orienting the world to yourself—the tastes and preferences within you. Instead, it comes by orienting yourself to the essence outside of you. Pastor Steve Deneff of College Wesleyan Church says that if life is a story, then this is the plot: "It's not just about you 'discovering yourself'—it's about you losing yourself to something bigger than yourself because it was here before you got here and it will be here long after you are gone. That's the plot."

If we had the eyes to see it, not only would we recognize beauty, but we would see and partake in essence, design, and order. In this discovery, we are invited to participate, to lean into, this design. For in syncing up with this order, we discover the best version of ourselves. This is the *idea* of virtue.

DISCUSSION QUESTIONS
FOR GROUP STUDY

1. Wilde's character Dorian Gray lived under the belief that hedonism and the maximization of pleasure was the best way to
   organize one's life. Where do we witness this philosophy in our
   culture? What are some of the consequences?

2. The chapter discusses the economic and political forces that have
   served to create, or perhaps reinforce, preference as a preeminent cultural value. What, specifically, would you say is wrong
   with "preference" as a cultural value? What should take its place?

3. David Brooks has praised the self-skepticism or "self-effacement"
   found in earlier generations. What risk does this conception of
   self pose? Contrastingly, what can be gained by having this conception? Which conception better aligns with the Christian faith
   tradition?

4. What is wrong with a world in which our moral duties, determinations, and obligations are all predicated upon our feelings?

5. Can you provide a personal example of "disordered desire" that
   you would be willing to share?

6. In an appeal to recapture our "moral imagination," Michael Miller
   of the Acton Institute has argued that we need to recover silence
   in contemplation so "that we allow the world to present itself to
   us." Do you agree? If so, why might this be a difficult mandate?
   What conditions are necessary for us to recover silence so as to best
   comprehend the world and its essence?

7. Read Philippians 2:5–11. If someone asked you how "emptying
   yourself," like Christ, could lead to wholeness (seemingly a contradiction), how would you respond?

4

THE LANGUAGE OF VIRTUE

Be ready to speak up and tell anyone who
asks why you're living the way you are, and
always with the utmost courtesy.

—1 Peter 3:15 (*The Message*)

Introduction: *Exchanging* Language

In 1776, the year America declared independence from the British, Adam Smith published one of the most famous pieces of literature in Western history: *The Wealth of Nations*. Frequently referenced today, his masterpiece would become a blueprint for modern democratic capitalism. Today, we still reflect on Smith's economic genius—which is ironic given that he would have referred to himself as a moral philosopher.

As a philosopher, he sought to account for what it meant to be human. Specifically, what made humans unique? Smith had much to say here, but one of his more interesting observations was the human capacity for exchange. This does not simply refer to exchanging goods and services in a modern economic sense, though that is something people certainly do, but our exchange of language. The capacity to vocalize enables humans to exchange "sentiments."[1] Our words allow us to convey a range of information and emotions, from the basic to the complex, the technical to the abstract, the profound and meaningful to the lighthearted and meaningless. Part of being a human being, Smith observed, is communicating with each other.

If human exchange includes goods, services, and *sentiments*, then we are right to suppose that our language, like everything else, is also subject to market forces—particularly the marketplace of ideas. Moreover, markets facilitate competition. This is not necessarily a bad thing when we think of goods and services, but it is reason for concern when we consider our sentiments and, more specifically, the language we use to articulate answers to life's big questions or, in the words of Eugene Peterson, to adequately "tell anyone who asks why you're living the way you are" (1 Pet. 3:15, *The Message*).

In light of this, this chapter aims to look at three dimensions—three pressing questions—that churn their way through today's marketplace of ideas. First, what is valuable? That is, what is worthy of our pursuit? Second, what is morality? How do I best speak to what guides my behavior? Third, who is God? Who or what constitutes the church—God's people?

These questions have a religious undertone, but they are familiar to all. Directly or indirectly, we inevitably answer them in the way we live. Even not answering is a form of an answer. We "exchange" language to help make sense of these dimensions, which, in a competitive environment, means some of the vocabulary evolves, or adapts, and some does not. In other words, some expressions better satisfy the collective preferences of those buying and selling in today's market of ideas. The result? We risk losing our words. For people of faith, this is a significant risk, for in the absence of appropriate discourse, these important areas suffer the likelihood of being re-described and thus redefined altogether.

Chapter 3 argued that we do not necessarily determine the good through our preferences, but rather, our goal is to discover, embrace, and embody the good through the education of our sentiments, or learning to desire well. However, it is not simply enough to comprehend the "idea" of virtue; it must also be articulated. Therefore, this chapter will concern itself with these aforementioned areas—the big questions. In doing so, we can best set forth a path to revive and cultivate a richer moral vocabulary: the language of virtue.

What Is Valuable? From Instrumentalist to Essential

The Price of "Dignity"

It was Aristotle who long ago made a distinction between "use value" and "exchange value." For most of us, use value is a familiar idea. There are certain goods that we desire for their own sake: friendship, education, a peaceful and comfortable family life, and above all, the virtues. To attain these, there are certain external goods that are necessary to have in our possession. For example, having hot water and heat in our homes, or chairs to sit on, or a car to drive, provides a measure of practicality that is central to so much of what we do. This is use value.

Exchange value is different. More often than not, exchanging something requires us to standardize various goods into a common currency. So, for example, if we were to ask how many chairs one car would be worth, we would first have to designate a way to parse out the worth of each good in order to answer. Exchange involves comparison, but this can be complicated when we are comparing many different goods. The solution? Find a common denominator. In other words, we can simplify the complexity of diverse goods by incorporating some external unit of measurement. This is our modern day notion of money. It may be unclear how many chairs a car would be worth, but we can more accurately compare the two if we first determine how much *money* a chair and a car are each worth. In other words, money serves to reconcile the difference in value between chairs, cars, and a variety of other goods and services.

But for Aristotle, the shift from use value to exchange value was a problem. Why? Can the full value of all goods be captured in a standardized unit of currency? If we are talking about chairs and cars, the answer may be yes. But if we are talking about more complex goods, like reading a book to a child, there is reason for skepticism. In other words, not all goods are *instrumental*. By "instrumental," I mean a place or thing that serves as some kind of a means to an end. For example, gasoline is instrumental for a car to function correctly. Moreover, if something is purely instrumental, then its value is bound up in its degree of usefulness. The more useful something is, the more valuable it is. My VCR used to be instrumental for playing VHS movies, but now it is not (since VHS movies are obsolete). Thus the value of the VCR is effectively zero.

But can value be relegated to a good's usefulness alone? If there is an essence to our reality, the answer is no. If some things are intrinsically valuable, then merely instrumental language is awkward at best, and corrosive and degrading at worst. Such language might be appropriate for goods we use to achieve specific ends, but not for what philosopher Elizabeth Anderson calls "higher goods."[2] Higher goods are persons, places, and things that are not—and cannot be—valued for their usefulness alone. Their value comes from their inner substance; it is an "intrinsic" value. Consider the words of philosopher Immanuel Kant, who famously wrote on this issue:

> Everything has either a *price* or a *dignity*. Whatever has a price can be replaced by something else as its equivalent; on the other hand, whatever is above all price, and therefore admits of no equivalent, has a dignity. But that which constitutes the condition under which alone something can be an end in itself does not have mere relative worth, i.e., price, but an intrinsic worth, i.e., a dignity.[3]

Here's the problem: "dignity" doesn't price very well in the marketplace. Our dominant Western form of measuring value is reflected in the market, where "finding out what something is worth to people is easiest when they engage in observable transactions involving it."[4] In other words, the most prevalent language used to capture instrumental value is economic. It's as though we're relying on the market to tell us what everything is truly worth.

Market economies use the forces of supply and demand to create a price signal. The benefit of a natural price is that it minimizes excess demand and excess supply. This is because the natural price will ideally reflect the market's value for a particular good or service. While this seems logical for basic commodities, more thought must be given to the value of what we might refer to as "social goods" and "complex social goods."

A social good is something that serves a beneficial purpose for society. Take, for instance, the field of higher education. Many people value education for the benefits it can produce (landing a job, promotion, etc.). That is, there are clear economic advantages associated with possessing a degree. For example, one way to determine the value of education is to take the present value of future earnings that one might command by virtue of being educated, and measure this against the cost of the education itself.[5] In contrast, though, some people view education as beneficial—a "good"—for reasons outside of what it produces in the job market. An educated life, we often hear, is a more enriching, fulfilling life. As John Dewey famously stated, "Education is not [just] preparation for life, education is life itself." According to this perspective, placing a dollar value on education fails to fully capture all the dimensions of its value.

To go a step further, as the complexity of social goods or services begins to increase, simple calculations of dollars gained not only fail to comprehensively capture our ideas of ultimate value, but even risk corrupting the very nature of the things we are attempting to value. Let me provide an example of what I mean.

Several years ago, my wife and I had dinner with a couple who are close friends of ours. The husband, who is an engineer with a major multinational firm, began discussing the unique nature of his pay structure. He had no formal working hours—that is, no time when he was scheduled to clock in and clock out. "I can technically work twenty-four hours a day from anywhere," he said. Knowing that he was compensated handsomely for each hour on the job, I realized that his lack of formal working hours created an interesting dilemma: how did he decide how to separate his time between paid work activities and unpaid non-work activities? Put differently, how did he know he was done with work? After presenting this question to him, he acknowledged the nature of the problem and said, "I put a dollar value on every activity."

One example he gave related to mowing his yard. Even after paying someone to cut his grass, he could still earn more money working for that hour (as opposed to using that time mowing the lawn). In economic parlance, working (instead of mowing) was the activity that minimized his *opportunity cost*. Assigning a price tag to each activity allowed him to calculate the best way to spend his time. After all, if every activity has a sticker price on it, then simple cost-benefit analysis is all that is necessary to determine how one should allocate time in one's schedule.

This is good economic logic. However, what if instead of mowing his lawn, the activity was doing a puzzle with his daughter? Or helping a neighbor? What is the right price for reading scripture, attending a funeral, or committing time to secluded, contemplative stillness? How much do those activities cost? The questions do not stop here. If monetary values can be placed on such goods, can they be invested? Divested? Diversified? Optimized?[6]

The point is not that it is difficult to place dollar values on such activities (trust me, economists find a way to do it). Rather, by putting price tags onto everything that we do, we inevitably shift and radically revise the nature of the conversation altogether. The very set of values we rely on changes. Their meaning is altered. Language that fails to reflect reality is one thing; language that changes that reality altogether is another, more critical, matter.

Examples are not difficult to come by. Chapter 2 referenced a *Newsweek* article by Jessica Bennett and Jesse Ellison titled "The Case against Marriage."[7] They argue that at one point in history, marriage made sense for women as it "ensured their financial security, got the fathers of their children to stick around, and [helped them gain] access to a host of legal rights." However, with changes in the workforce in today's labor market, marriage no longer seems to be practically reasonable, leading the authors to conclude that reason has triumphed over romance.

What do they mean? What reason do they give for ditching our long-held marital covenants? *Money*. The "icing on the cake," they write, is that it is financially optimal to avoid marital commitments: "Federal law favors unmarried taxpayers in almost every case—only those whose incomes are wildly unequal get a real tax break—and under President Obama's new health plan, low-earning single people get better subsidies to buy insurance."

Now, one must admit, this is a pretty good argument against marriage—if you think that the benefit of marriage boils down to

long-term wealth accumulation.[8] More realistically, the authors
have provided a rigid and utterly impoverished view of marriage.
To define marriage strictly in financial cost-benefit terms is to
minimize the institution and dismiss a host of other "higher" purposes or ideals for marital unions—purposes that cannot necessarily be standardized to financial, legal, or practical units of
measurement. What if marriage was not necessarily constituted
by its financial benefits, but by norms consisting of trust, sacrifice,
and self-giving love?[9] How much weight would their argument
hold then?

Or consider a much more difficult topic: self-selective abor-
tions that frequently occur in India. Often times, daughters are
seen as less "useful" to a family unit than sons. Specifically, they
tend to have less economic value in the marketplace, and parents
are expected to pay their dowry upon marriage. On a balance sheet,
female children are more of an economic liability than an asset to
some Indian families. Consider this passage from the 2010 book
Poor Economics:

> Self-selective abortions, which are now widely available and ex-
> tremely cheap, allow parents to choose whether they would rather
> abort a female fetus. As the stickers pasted on the dividers in Delhi's
> main road advertising (illegal) sex-determination services put it:
> "Spend 500 rupees now and save 50,000 rupees later" (on dowries).[10]

I shared this quote once with a student who had ties to Indian
culture, and she quickly pointed out that the funerals for selectively
aborted females are carried out in a reverent and respectful manner.
True as this may be, I said, the very fact that young female babies
would be conceptualized in economic terms (monetary costs/ben-
efits) was highly offensive and extraordinarily irreverent. It is nothing short of profane to expunge a child under a financial pretense
and subsequently mourn their loss as a human being.

As these stories make clear, when we describe "higher goods"
purely in terms of their instrumental value—their usefulness for
something else—we inevitably corrupt or degrade their very meaning. Marriage is minimized to a money-making institution, not
a lifelong commitment of self-giving love and sacrifice. Innocent

female children are reduced to being understood as economic liabilities. Under this paradigm, their right to exist is contingent upon their ability to produce financial benefits that exceed their costs. Marriage, human life itself, and an array of other "higher goods" are bound up in larger systems of meaning, moral significance, and sacredness. When you put a price tag on virtue, it ceases to be understood as virtue.

It is worth pointing out that there is another cost to describing morality and virtue in economic terms. That is, you get an economic response, not a moral one. The very language establishes the nature of the discussion. It was Marshall McLuhan who famously suggested that "the medium is the message." In other words, the way we communicate the message will play a significant role in determining how that very message is understood.

To provide an example, consider this story from Harvard's Michael Sandel. He writes:

> In the 1970s, when I was a graduate student at Oxford, there were separate colleges for men and women. The women's colleges had parietal rules against male guests staying overnight in women's rooms. These rules were rarely enforced and easily violated, or so I was told. Most college officials no longer saw it as their role to enforce traditional notions of sexual morality. Pressure grew to relax these rules, which became a subject of debate at St. Anne's College, one of the all-women colleges.
>
> Some older women on the faculty were traditionalists. They opposed allowing male guests, on conventional moral grounds; it was immoral, they thought, for unmarried young women to spend the night with men. But times had changed, and the traditionalists were embarrassed to give the real grounds for their objection. So they translated their arguments into utilitarian terms. "If men stay overnight," they argued, "the costs to the college will increase." How, you might wonder? "Well, they'll want to take baths, and that will use more hot water." Furthermore, they argued, "we will have to replace the mattresses more often."
>
> The reformers met the traditionalists' arguments by adopting the following compromise: Each woman could have a maximum of three overnight guests each week, provided each guest paid fifty-pence per night to defray the costs to the college.[11]

Sandel's point is that the norms of the argument were given, not on moral terms, but on economic terms. And yet, the discussion had both moral and economic implications. The traditionalists communicated their moral problem (men and women cohabitating) in terms of utility (costs will go up). The answer was presented under the same utilitarian terms (men will pay money to defray the costs).

As we might predict, the existing rules of separating men and women were waived altogether, leading Sandel to conclude: "The language of virtue had not translated very well into the language of utility."[12] Herein lies the problem: arguments for virtue are often lost when decisions are distilled to their bare economic features. Usefulness equates poorly with essence. If we have a moral issue we want to raise, it must be communicated in similar moral language—especially if we expect to get a moral response. That is the lesson from the St. Anne's College story: when you communicate a moral argument on economic grounds, you will get an economic answer.

Speaking about Essence

So what does this have to do with our ability to speak the language of virtue? We have to learn to present our arguments, not simply in terms of what is useful or instrumental, but also in terms of what is essential. An essence is the nature, or substance, of something. It is its irreducible quality, its center. Recall the story of Samuel Coleridge describing the waterfall as "sublime." Sublimity was not something he felt inside himself, it was something he apprehended outside of himself. That is, the waterfall had an essence of beauty.

Let's go a step further: What is the essence of a human? Human beings are more than a mere collection of biological mass. On the orthodox Christian account, men and women are image-bearers of a creative, loving, relational God. While we have a physical makeup, we are also constituted by an "innermost self" that is immaterial (more on this later in the chapter). Glenn Sunshine writes that being made in God's image "is the *most essential element* of what it means to be human."[13] That is, at the core of our humanity is our

God-like resemblance. Among other things, this elevates the notion of human dignity. We were not created for our instrumental value. It is impossible to set an exchange value for a human being.

It is important to note that our understanding of the value of human life is not relegated to the religious realm alone. Politics, science, technology, and economics all possess creative mechanisms by which to say that a life is valuable in some way. However, not one of these realms can say that life is *sacred*. The scientific method cannot verify that I have a soul. The marketplace does not aim to edify one's "innermost being."[14] Political structures may protect my rights, but they do not inherently recognize the Creator's thumbprint on my life, nor do they aim to cultivate my interior self.[15] Such territory is sacred, hallowed. It is beyond modes of valuation. It cannot "do" anything in an instrumentalist sense.

To summarize, what is valuable is not always the same as what is useful, and this has implications for how we talk about virtue—particularly as it relates to discussing human beings and virtuous action. Christian virtues and values translate poorly when expressed in economic parlance. Indeed, to borrow a phrase from Kathleen Norris, as people of faith, we "traffic in intangibles . . . that are not easily manipulated by corporate concerns, not easily identified, packaged, and sold.[16]

What Is Morality? From Incoherent to Consistent

Several years ago I participated in a one-day seminar held at a secular university. The topic of the event—described as an "interactive dialogue"—was religion and violence. To start the day, one of the school's religious professors read a position paper to the audience. After finishing, with the help of a moderator, he answered topically related questions to start the discussion.

The paper was based upon the professor's PhD work, and suggested that religious institutions were a natural recipe for conflict (Christianity included). Religion, so went the argument, has animated and motivated aggression, violence, and war over the centuries in the name of God. Dogmatism and irrational religious zeal unavoidably pits one group against another. Using fancy theological rhetoric and vivid, gruesome expressions to describe the violence carried out in God's name, he lamented the bloody past of history's religious traditions. When he finished, there was little doubt as to his point: religiosity was clearly and undoubtedly a threat to humane and peaceful social arrangements.

After the speaker fielded a few questions, a retired biology professor with a skeptical look on his face raised his hand. His question would alter the course of the event entirely. Appearing offended, and with a note of scorn in his tone, he asked, "Are you suggesting that violence is . . . bad?"

There was a moment of silence as the speaker wisely waited to let the questioner elaborate. "You see," he went on, "I am an evolutionist. Violence is a part of the development of our species. Without it, we would not be here today." Another pause. Finally, after some uncomfortable fidgeting, the speaker, staring at the ground, managed an awkward response, "I, uh, wouldn't necessarily say that violence is, um, *bad*." I could not help but grin. The speaker had spent the previous hour excoriating the "badness" of the violence he believed was so closely correlated with religion. His answer effectively de-legitimated everything he had said up to that point.

The exchange was eye-opening. The speaker had to decide which grouping of values he wanted to maintain fidelity to. If he opted for open-minded tolerance, particularly tolerance toward other worldviews like evolution, then he could no longer be consistent with his conviction that violence was bad. If he opted for the "violence is bad" position, he would have to challenge the evolutionary premise of the retired biologist's question. What was unreasonable, though, was the belief that both realities could be equally valid—a belief the retired biologist himself would also deny.

The problem can be easily summarized: not all ideas are created equal. Moreover, this is not simply a religious mantra. For example, atheist philosopher Simon Blackburn argues that much of what moral relativists try to do is actually unhelpful for solving disagreements. If we were to have a dispute over who is the best all-time MLB player or which actress deserves an Oscar award, then we would only be saying something about our tastes. In matters of taste, it is easy to "agree to disagree." However, as the issues become more complex, such conclusions are not so simple. For example, if one party believes that abortion is murder and the other believes that it is the legitimate expression of one's political rights, it is difficult, if not downright silly, to suppose that we are only making statements about taste. Both sides cannot be "right" about this, nor would they ever "agree to disagree." If anything, each side aims to impose their beliefs onto the other. To summarize, the suggestion that both parties' beliefs are accurate is not only untenable, but it is patently unsatisfactory. Writes Blackburn, "The idea that we are not in conflict just starts to look farcical. And the conflict has not been resolved by [the relativist]—it hasn't even been helped."[17]

So, some ideas are better than others. Moreover, this has implications for how we express ourselves. If our language reflects the belief that all value systems are equally valid, then, at best, we will sound incoherent. In a postmodern age, one might ask, "What is wrong with incoherence?" First, and ironically, we can rightfully assume that the hypothetical questioner would desire a coherent answer to the question. Second, incoherence comes with its own costs. C. S. Lewis concludes his essay *Men without Chests* with the warning that to divorce truth and morality from education is to remove the heart—creating men without chests. He writes, "In a sort of ghastly simplicity we remove the organ and demand the function. We make men without chests and expect of them virtue and enterprise. We laugh at honor, and are shocked to find traitors in our midst."[18]

His words are prescient. We live in a society where Americans are horrified at the thought that their elected leaders may be dishonest or misuse funds, and yet, each year an estimated 1.6 million Americans cheat on their taxes.[19] (One 2012 study found that if Americans were honest in reporting, we would have increased tax revenue to the tune of 450 billion dollars!)[20] We speak out against sex-trafficking, but pornography usage has never been higher. We consume the Hollywood glorification of violence, but throw up our arms in confusion and anger when mass school shootings occur. We treat our children as if they are the center of the universe, but criticize them as being narcissistic and vain when they act like it. Ironically, inconsistence may be our society's most consistent feature.

These are just a few examples demonstrating our lack of coherence. That is, our beliefs—and the language used to articulate our beliefs—seem disconnected from a larger comprehensive framework or value system—or a "coherent moral ecology."[21] To be clear, there are always going to be tensions that occur between the City of God and the City of Man, to use Augustine's famous expression. Similarly, New Testament theologian Richard Hays has talked about the "interval in which the 'already' and the 'not yet' of redemption exists in dialectical tension."[22]

Tensions aside, there are some values that simply cannot exist together coherently without altering or corrupting their essence. I am reminded of an adage that was tossed around back in my banking days: "When you mix clean water with dirty water, you get . . . dirty water." Our allegiance to multiple values means fidelity to none.

Foundations of Consistency

In a world with so many values, how are we to navigate the marketplace of ideas in a coherent way? What does it mean to live, and speak, consistently? In a fundamental sense, it is important to first take stock of the very foundations that our beliefs and values are built upon. All coherent structures have an architecture, which invites us to explore the very scaffolding we erect our moral edifice upon.

For help, consider a famous illustration given by C. S. Lewis. If a fleet of ships were to go out to sea, there are certain considerations necessary for the voyage to be successful. First, the ship must avoid getting in the way of other ships or, worse, colliding with them. Second, the ship's instruments must be operating correctly (engines, sails, etc.) But, Lewis writes, this is not enough. There is an important question preceding both of these considerations: Why is the ship out there in the first place? What is its destination?

What is the point of determinations in social ethics (how to avoid hitting other ships) or individual ethics (how to "tidy up" or keep my instruments working), if we have not first determined our purpose? Or, put another way, what is existence for?

Lewis offers this wonderful summary:

> Morality, then, seems to be concerned with three things. Firstly, with
> fair play and harmony between individuals. Secondly, with what
> might be called tidying up or harmonizing the things inside each
> individual. Thirdly, with the general purpose of human life as a whole:
> what man was made for: what course the whole fleet ought to be on.[23]

As argued in chapter 2, morality—bereft of the foundations of
design—is left to be determined by the guideposts of efficiency, equity, or enforceability. Chapter 3 described a more modern "meta-
value": preference and choice. To be clear, these traditions employ
moral language. One cannot participate in the world and not en-
counter morally-infused prescriptions related to fair play, harmony,
or individual improvement (to speak in terms of Lewis's metaphor).
However, such prescriptions are seldom connected back to "the general purpose of human life as a whole" or "what man was made for."

This is a critical element. It joins morality with purpose. It was
Aristotle who rightly linked "goodness" to a thing's apparent aim
or nature. For example, as mentioned earlier, a *good* chair does
what a chair is designed to do—allow me to sit well. Goodness, for
humanity, also requires us to inquire as to the meaning or purpose
of a human. This does not mean that questions surrounding human
purpose are relative to the inquirer. Morality cannot be, in Lewis's
words, a private *taste*. By its very definition, morality implies our
conformity to goodness or proper behavior—standards attained
outside of a person, not defined by a person according to his or her
whims. Thus, in the faith tradition, to understand our design, we
are impelled to look to the Designer.

The orthodox faith tradition begins with the perspective that
because of God's incarnational act in Jesus, we have the capacity to
fully love God, love neighbor, and to "take hold of the life that really
is life" (1 Tim. 6:19)—which is the "abundant" life (John 10:10). The
more we are like Christ, the more we fulfill our original design—the
"perfect version of ourselves." For this reason, Jill Carattini writes
that the Christian's most significant task is not to defend the faith,
but to embody it, "participating in the vision of God with a love for
both Word and neighbor."[24]

Much more can be said (or explained), but this is a conception of reality that properly speaks to why we exist—why "our boat" is out to sea in the first place. Moreover, when we have a strong sense of our own human purpose, we can best apprehend what is good. Not only does this allow us to better articulate morality, but it best ensures a truly consistent message.

Who Is God? From Individualistic to Communal

"I Could Believe in God If . . ."

Christian music has been described as the only genre that is defined by lyrical content instead of musical style.[25] In other words, if you want to know what makes a song "Christian," look at the words. This is not necessarily bad. There is much to appreciate in the rich theological language found in hymns by Spafford, Watts, Wesley, and a host of others.

But what about the words found in music today? Although contemporary praise and worship music is often pitted against traditional hymns in modern ecclesial circles, some have suggested that—in a theological sense—the two styles share more resemblances than differences.[26] After all, there is no single way to praise God. Moreover, while God-honoring language may change over time, the intended purpose of worship remains the same. However, when we look specifically at the pronouns used in hymns and contemporary worship music, a potentially different story emerges.

A recognizable difference between classical hymns and contemporary Christian music popular on the radio becomes apparent when both are analyzed using twenty-first-century linguistic software. This difference is particularly evident when one looks at the proportion of self-referencing words within a given song (i.e., "I," "me," "mine"). Upon comparison, classical hymns have a lower proportion of self-referencing language than contemporary worship songs. Moreover, this difference is considered to be "statistically significant"—which simply means that the effect is real (not simply an effect accidentally found in the sample). Interestingly, though, if one were to compare the proportion of self-referencing language in contemporary Christian radio to that of self-referencing language found in today's secular pop radio hits, one would find no statistically significant difference. That is, the two are nearly identical.[27]

So, in summary, self-referencing words like "I," "thine," "mine," or "me" are used more in our contemporary worship music than in our classical hymns. However, when compared to other pop culture music, there is no difference.[28] Contemporary Christian songs that are popular on the radio use "I" language just as much as their secular counterparts.

This is what the data tells us. What this means, though, is another issue. Some are likely to blame our narcissistic culture. Alternatively, others might suggest that our "I" language reflects a more insecure culture.[29] While I am less concerned with trying to get underneath what the data reveal, it might not be a stretch to suggest that this is evidence of our cultural tendency to speak in relation to ourselves. That is, in our language, we have become the ultimate point of reference.

Such self-reflection can be a good thing. The ancient adage to "know thyself" is just as relevant today as it was thousands of years ago. Yet if we are not careful, our "I" language can quickly cascade from the healthy to the hollow—missing a much wider dimension of what it means to be human.

In their oft-cited 2008 book *Soul Searching: The Religious and Spiritual Lives of American Teenagers*, Melinda Denton and Christian Smith describe the dominant religious spirit among American teenagers as "Moralistic Therapeutic Deism" or MTD.[30] The name is derived from three distinguishing features of American teens in their attempts to voice their religious beliefs and describe God.

First, they believe in a moral approach to life. For some, this was rather opaque: "My whole religion is where you try to be good and, uh, if you're not good then you just try to get better." For others, morality was about the absence of certain features. "Just don't be an asshole, that's all," replied one respondent. Regardless, the primary idea held by many teens is that being moral has some degree of importance.

But to say that the teens prize "morality" can be misleading. In other words, their appeal to moral excellence is weak at best. According to this theology, God is not demanding, allowing morality to rise to the level of what makes people feel good. In other words, the pursuit of virtue and character is only attractive insofar as it is convenient. Second, MTD has less to do with organizing my life around the good, the right, and the true, and more to do with improving myself. One's feeling of well-being—one's happiness, state of mind, etc.—is at the center of religious experience. "When I pray, it makes me feel good afterward," offered one fifteen year old. Reflecting on the therapeutic element of MTD theology, Ross Douthat writes, "Niceness is the highest ethical standard, popularity the most important goal, and high self-esteem the surest sign of sanctity."[31]

Third, and finally, MTD affirms belief in God, but not necessarily a supreme being that concerns themselves with the affairs of men and women throughout the world. Rather, to use an expression coined by the popular naturalist philosopher Daniel Dennett, the MTD god is at best a "benign overseer." But this is not necessarily the god of Deism, who gets the creation process started and then tucks himself away into a corner of the universe. Unlike the Deists' distant god, the god of MTD is available upon request to consult with and counsel the religiously-minded in their times of need. Once their needs are addressed, the two parties are free to ignore each other once more. God, in this sense, functions more or less like a twenty-four-hour urgent care clinic: available for an emergency ailment, but considered unnecessary otherwise.

In addition to their seemingly heterodox views of faith, Smith describes those whose beliefs fall into the category of MTD as being "religiously inarticulate." Denton and Smith tracked the language use of US teens and found a considerable lack of reference to historically popular religious, spiritual, or theological ideas. Smith writes:

> When teenagers talked in their interviews about "grace," they were usually talking about the television show *Will and Grace*, not about God's grace. When teenagers discussed "honor," they were almost always talking about taking honors courses or making the honor roll at school, very rarely about honoring God with their lives. When teens mentioned being "justified," they almost always meant having a reason for doing something behaviorally questionable, not having their relationship with God made right.[32]

We might conclude that such a phenomenon is unique to teen-agers, but this would be a mistake. In his follow-up book *Lost in Transition*, Smith finds that emerging adults in the United States reveal a similar impoverishment when it comes to conceptualizing and articulating moral issues relative to their faith: "The center of gravity among emerging adults is definitely MTD."[33] Smith writes:

> The majority of those interviewed stated . . . that nobody has any natural or general responsibility or obligation to help other people. . . . Most of those interviewed said that it is nice if people help others, but that nobody has to. Taking care of other people in need is an in-dividual's choice. If you want to do it, good. If not, that's up to you. . . . Even when pressed—what about victims of natural disaster or politi-cal oppression? What about helpless people who are not responsible for their poverty or disabilities? What about famines and floods and tsunamis? No, they replied. If someone wants to help, then good for that person. But nobody has to.[34]

What about full-fledged adults? Contrary to the belief that teens depart from the values held by their parents, Smith and Den-ton found that teens are not reacting against the teaching of their parents, but rather they are reflecting them. Conversations with teens suggested that "in most cases teenage religion and spiritu-ality in the United States are much better understood as largely reflecting the world of adult religion, especially parental religion, and are in strong continuity with it."[35] They are being "socialized" into adult religion. In other words, the *moralistic, therapeutic deism* embraced by teens and emerging adults is simply downstream from what adults, in general, believe in religious circles today.

What are we to make of this? In the realm of experience, beliefs, and values, it would appear that religion, and God, is largely under-stood to be relative to the individual. Naturally, this translates into our language. Smith writes,

> The language—and therefore experience—of Trinity, holiness, sin, grace, justification, sanctification, church, Eucharist, and heaven and hell appear . . . to be supplanted by the language of happiness, nice-ness, and an earned heavenly reward.[36]

A great deal is at stake here. It was German philosopher Ludwig Feuerbach who suggested that the religious tradition had it all wrong. God had not made man in his image, but rather, man had made god in his image. That is, man had collected his supreme attributes together with his best hopes and projected them onto a fictitious god-figure. Similarly, in his *Lettres persanes*, French philosopher Charles de Montesquieu suggests that "if triangles invented a god, they would make him three-sided." Under this line of thinking, our conception of God is not determined by our theology, tradition, etc., but by our preference. This, writes A. W. Tozer, is the very definition of idolatry: "[Imagining] things about God and [acting] as if they are true."[37]

Take, for example, a satirical article that appeared in *The Chronicle of Higher Education* in 2011 titled "I could believe in God." I could believe in God, the author writes, but God would have to meet several criteria. He would have to be Protestant, specifically, Northeastern Protestant (living in Connecticut). God would have to be mildly secular, dress like an Ivy-league graduate, and speak with a mid-Atlantic accent. He would need to smoke, and his smoking should only be surpassed by his drinking. In an old leather armchair, God would read novels in a book-lined den overlooking a slightly overgrown garden. In addition to owning a dog, he would play golf and watch college football. He would give charitably, but would consider tithing to be "tacky." And to top it off, the author concludes, "All my God would demand of me as a worshipper would be that I give Him a friendly smile every time I encountered Him on His walk. He'd be fine with that."[38]

In other words, she could (or would want to) believe in a god that would satisfy all of her preferences. Yet before we are tempted to criticize her consumerist approach to religion, it would do us good to recognize that many of us have a similar idea that we "could believe in God if..." In his book *With*, Skye Jethani discusses a short exam that religious professor Scot McKnight gives to seminary students on the opening day of class. The test begins with questions asking students to reflect on the personality of Jesus. Students are then asked a series of questions related to their own personalities.

Most interestingly, the personality attributes that students associate with Jesus are the same ones they claim to possess themselves! Jethani writes: "McKnight is not the only one who has administered this exam; it has been field tested by other professionals as well. But the results are remarkably consistent—everyone thinks Jesus is like them."[39] The point to be made is this: we are all at risk of imagining, and worshipping, a god who perfectly coheres with our idiosyncratic tastes and cultural sensibilities. That is, sometimes we are the triangles, and our god is conveniently three-sided.

Beginning with the End: Communal Clarity

This has clear implications for the way we collect ourselves in the church. In other words, can a church be organized around conceptions of God unique to each individual? Is the "bride of Christ" simply an amalgamation of our own quirky preferences? Is our only commonality the very fact that we do not require anything in common? If so, this is a very odd description of God's Kingdom manifest in the church. A primary part of being able to articulate answers to big questions about God and the church is to point to the good outside of us and show that it is worth striving toward. When we process our faith through the filter of our own self-focused language, we inevitably get a distorted outcome.

In contrast, consider a comment by Christopher Wright that describes the difference between our current notions of community and the biblical concept of community. He writes,

> We tend to begin at the personal level and work outwards. Our emphasis is to persuade people to live a certain kind of life according to this and that moral standard. If enough individuals live up to such-and-such morality, then, almost as a by-product, society itself will be improved or at least maintained as a healthy, happy, safe environment for individuals to pursue their personal goodness. *This* is the kind of person you should be; *that* kind of society is a bonus in the background. The Old Testament tends to place the emphasis the other way round; here is the kind of society God wants. His desire is for a holy people for his own possession, a redeemed community, a model society through whom he can display a prototype of the new humanity

of his ultimate redemptive purpose. Now if that is the kind of society God wants, what kind of person must you be once you belong to it?[40]

The difference is subtle, but significant. Religious affiliation and church participation are not about each of us making individual determinations about God, morality, and so forth; rather, we should start with the attributes of "the new humanity" and conform to the standards of this community. The language of virtue does not start with me; it starts with God's community. When the church capitulates to individualism, writes David Atkinson, it loses the "distinctive approach both to community and to justice as inclusion within the community."[41]

Individuality, which stands as a cultural value, also poses an impediment to the articulation of authentic Christian language. In concert with the multitude of scriptural references that advance an other-centered attitude, Paul tells the Philippian church to "be of the same mind, having the same love, being of full accord and of one mind" (Phil. 2:2). And what "same mind" should they all aim to share? The mind of Christ,

> who, though he was in the form of God, did not regard equality with God as something to be exploited, but emptied himself, taking the form of a slave, being born into human likeness. And being found in human form, he humbled himself and became obedient to the point of death—even death on a cross." (Phil. 2:5–8)

Emptied. Slave. Humility. Obedience. Death. These are the words Paul uses to describe "the mind of Christ." This is the humility we are called to collectively imitate.

To be clear, a great deal of self-referencing language is helpful, since it is necessary; or perhaps it is innocuous, since it is innocent. However, great care must be given to how we express our faith. We would be mistaken if we believed that a more robust vocabulary will solve the shortcomings of the "religiously inarticulate" young adults interviewed by Denton and Smith. The problem does not occur simply in the words; rather, it originates in the conception. Beginning with a right conception of our relationship to God, the pursuit of virtue, and our role in the wider church will provide the right intellectual basis by which to more coherently articulate our faith life.

Who is God? What is the church? What is religion? These questions cannot be answered in reference to me. That is, they are insufficiently addressed independent of the faith tradition. It is in our communal experience—our collective attempt to embody the "prototype of the new humanity"—that our understanding of God, church, and religion best reflect reality.

Conclusion

Given my age, I may appropriately be referred to as a "digital immigrant."[42] I grew up in a world absent of online connectedness and I now inhabit a world utterly dependent upon it. So I have seen a lot change over time. Interestingly, one thing that has not changed is the perception of an ever-diminishing moral climate. When it comes to morality, many believe that the current generation is always worse than the one preceding it.

This may or may not be true. Perceptions aside, a less disputed claim relates not to the decline in our moral atmosphere, but in our moral language. "I doubt people behave worse than before," writes David Brooks, "but we are less articulate about the inner life."[43] Brooks criticizes the lack of moral conversation in the public square, which leads to a world where people who have a hunger for meaning "don't know the right questions to ask, the right vocabulary to use, the right place to look or even if there are ultimate answers at all."[44]

As stated in the opening of this chapter, language is something we exchange. In this sense, it can be a beautiful gift. Our language eulogizes, praises, inspires, encourages, and edifies. Yet the very tongue that can bless has an equal capacity to spoil. Language can mislead, degrade, deflect, discourage, and corrupt. How do we reconcile such a contradiction in the power of our words? As James warns, "With the tongue we praise our Lord and Father, and with it we curse human beings, who have been made in God's likeness. Out of the same mouth come praise and cursing . . . this should not be" (James 3:9–10).

If we are not careful to redeem our words—particularly as they concern life's big questions—we let the forces of a competitive marketplace of ideas provide their own articulation. Essence is reduced to what is instrumental; our deepest held values are left to be understood in financial and economic lingo. Questions of morality bypass purpose and design, settling for incoherent discourse over a more consistent moral expression. Our understanding of God, church, and religion risks being distilled to considerations in individual taste and interpretation. When asked who God is, we talk about ourselves.

This chapter looked at three dimensions, three big questions, where we exchange language or "sentiments" in the marketplace of ideas. When we survey these dimensions, common themes emerge. I have argued that in today's culture our ideas about value, morality, and God are filtered through expressions that are instrumental, incoherent, and individualistic. This simply expresses the fact that our marketplace of ideas reflects some of the more dominant cultural values today. For example, our culture tends to eschew what is sacred, so how can we discuss what is essential? Further, we place an extraordinary premium on relative, individual preferences, so how can we ever expect our guiding principles to reference a transcendent logical structure? Finally, if we were to name a secular principle that has been baptized in religious language, it is certainly individuality and "being true to yourself." So how can we ever properly define, let alone follow, a Creator God or his people, the church?

In contrast to these trends, this chapter sought to present a morally richer and traditionally orthodox articulation. First, there is an essence and an inherent value to our existence. That is, God called his creation "good" well before man ever used the term. Goodness is not an arbitrary concept we create to make societies work; it exists outside of us to be understood, apprehended, embraced, and embodied. Second, men and women were created with a purpose. To understand what goodness means for humans, we have to understand the human aim, that is, what we were designed for. Naturally, then, to understand our design, we have to understand our Creator—the One who deliberately conferred meaning and purpose onto our existence. This relates to the third theme: we are incomplete, insufficient, in ourselves. To properly conceive of God and his people, the church, we are called to not only look beyond ourselves, but to empty ourselves.

Now, some may find this account wanting or perhaps dissatisfying. However, I would like to suggest that at the very least it is a helpful overture toward cultivating our language about "the inner life." Moreover, while these ideas are inherently religious, the language I've used in this chapter is not exclusive. Goodness, purpose, and human fulfillment set the stage for a drama we all participate in. All of us, in some way, invariably give an answer to "why we are living the way we are" (1 Pet. 3:15) with the way we live and the language we use. The only question is: Are we answering well? Does our language capture the full spectrum of God's created reality? If so, we are speaking the *language* of virtue.

DISCUSSION QUESTIONS
FOR GROUP STUDY

1. The beginning of the chapter suggests that we exchange language to help us answer life's big questions. Furthermore, in the marketplace of ideas, our language risks being replaced with other sentiments. Can you provide an example of where you have seen this happen? That is, can you think of traditionally Christian language that has been co-opted or hijacked?

2. In Michael Sandel's "St. Anne's College" example, the argument by the traditionalist women was presented in economic terms and thus received an economic answer. Can you think of an example, today, where a moral issue has been expressed in non-moral terms (e.g., in economic language)? What was the result?

3. If someone asked, how would you describe the "essence" of a human?

4. The Moralistic Therapeutic Deism highlighted in Denton and Smith's work with teenagers was said to also reflect similar language in adults. Where have you been guilty of using this language? Can you provide an example?

5. We are told to take on the "mind of Christ," to "empty" ourselves. What does this look like for us in everyday life?

6. The chapter ended with the suggestion that speaking the language of virtue does not necessarily commit us to overtly religious language. That is, "Goodness, purpose, and human fulfillment set the stage for a drama we all participate in." Can you provide an example where a robust vocabulary of virtue could be used that would transcend religious boundaries?

5

The Practice of Virtue: "He Has Shown You What Is Good"

Not in the flight of ideas but only in action is freedom.
Make up your mind and come out into the tempest of living.

—Dietrich Bonhoeffer

"Let me ask you something. If someone prays for patience,
you think God gives them patience? Or does he give them
the opportunity to be patient? If he prayed for courage, does
God give him courage, or does he give him opportunities
to be courageous? If someone prayed for the family to be
closer, do you think God zaps them with warm fuzzy feelings,
or does he give them opportunities to love each other?"

—"God" (Morgan Freeman) in *Evan Almighty*

He has shown you, O mortal, what is good.
And what does the Lord require of you?
To act justly and to love mercy
and to walk humbly with your God.

—Micah 6:8 (NIV)

Introduction: You Are What You Do

Between 1989 and 2003, the Liberian civil war was responsible
for nearly a quarter million lives lost. At the center of it all was
Joshua Milton Blahyi, better known as "General Butt Naked." A

Liberian terrorist leader, Blahyi has claimed responsibility for upwards of twenty thousand deaths. Often fighting unclothed (hence the name), he has been described as one of the most wicked men in the world. In addition to his notorious cannibalistic practices, the general was ruthless toward enemies and even went so far as to sacrifice children to appease what he understood to be evil spirits. When he wasn't carving up the bodies of his victims, he was recruiting child soldiers to assist him against his foes. The man was pure evil.

Yet after a "road to Damascus" experience not unlike that of Saul in Acts 9, the once-notorious warlord was miraculously converted to a pastor, husband, and father. Today, when he is not preaching, he is trying to reconcile with the families of his victims. In one account, Blahyi found himself at the hands of a former enemy who was wielding a machete and threatening his life. He dropped to his knees before him, offering to let the man kill him if he thought it would help.[1] The transformation from warlord to pastor explains the radical shift in Blahyi's behavior (reconciliation, peace building, and preaching).

General Butt Naked's testimony, and the thousands of others like it from throughout history, remind us that our actions (what we do) are preceded by our identity (who we are). When it comes to being and doing, many presume that the causal direction is a one-way street. In other words, we believe that our sense of self comes first, and then our behaviors follow. Determining who we are naturally precedes deliberation about what we should do. This notion is certainly not foreign to those within the faith tradition. The logic is simple: change a person, and you change their actions. Not only is the logic simple, it is also proven. History is replete with stories of men and women like General Butt Naked, whose radical conversion was followed by a fundamental transformation in lifestyle.

Yet perhaps there is more to the story. Yes, our personhood—who we are in our innermost self—plays a significant role in motivating our behaviors. But what if our behaviors—our *habits*—also play a role in cultivating our innermost self? That is, what if doing actually has an influential effect on being? This reverse logic is an example of what social scientists call *mutual causality.* The term describes two variables that are causing, or reinforcing, one another. Could it be that who we are and what we do are understood best not in a cause-and-effect paradigm, but as being mutually causal? Could it be true that our sense of self influences our habits *but* our habits also influence our sense of self?

A helpful picture of this can be found in Steven Spielberg's 1998 film *Saving Private Ryan.* Though disturbingly violent, the film offers a redemptive scene not easily forgotten. The revered Captain John Miller (played by Tom Hanks) is leading his troops on a mission to find a missing solider, Private Ryan, and bring him home. Miller has all the ingredients of a battle-tested captain: he is deeply respected, experienced, resolute, and cool under pressure. Little is known about him outside of the army, leading the soldiers to speculate about his personal life before the military—a "big mystery."

At one point during their mission, Miller and his troops stumble onto enemy gunfire, and one of his soldiers is killed. While the loss is tragic, they manage to capture the culprit, presenting Miller with an opportunity to avenge the death of his officer. This is where things get interesting. Against all convention, Miller decides to free the captive. Incredulous with this decision, the soldiers revolt. In their eyes, the prisoner deserved death. Not only were they within their rights to kill him—it was their duty. As the scene plays out, the order and structure so closely associated with a military operation quickly gives way to chaos.

Amidst the disarray, Miller inexplicably blurts out his identity prior to his military service: "I'm a schoolteacher." His men grow silent, as if introduced—all over again—to humanity. He wistfully opens up about his quaint hometown, his wife, coaching baseball, and so forth. But then he reflects upon his identity in the military— the death, darkness, despair, and suffering he is forced to participate in each day. Justifying his decision to set the enemy soldier free, he makes this appeal to the men: "Just know that [for] every man I kill, the farther away from home I feel."

Miller addresses the men not as the fearless captain with black and white answers at his disposal, but as a broken, confused, and scared man who wants to return home to his wife. His appeal is to something deeper: "So I guess I've changed some. Sometimes I wonder if my wife is even going to recognize me when I get back to her." He confesses that his real "mission" is not simply to follow military orders, but to go back home as the same person who left. What good does it do to win a war when you have lost your soul, your essence, in the process?

This scene is not only memorable, but relatable. It arouses a kind of sympathy, a rationality not easily described. But what is it? Here we find guidance from ancient wisdom. As odd as it sounds, Aristotle would likely resonate with Miller's decision to let the soldier go free. Why? Because, he believed, *we become what we repeatedly do*. Miller intuited that with each death he was responsible for—even when following military protocol—he became less the small-town English Composition teacher, and more of an inhumane version of himself. His exterior actions as a captain occurred at the expense of his interior self. The habits of war were transforming his sense of identity.

Who we are plays a role in what we do, but as this powerful scene makes clear, what we do can also impact who we are. More to the point, this has implications for virtue. In his highly influential book *Nicomachean Ethics*, Aristotle claims that we do not become virtuous by nature, but rather, "this capacity is brought to maturity by habit."[2] Yes, we can expect a virtuous person to do virtuous things, but no one can attain this state of character without first practicing and inculcating habits that cultivate virtue. In other words, virtue requires experience and effort. Furthermore, suggests Aristotle, it is in the exercise of virtue that we realize a happy, significant, meaningful, fulfilling, and satisfying life. The *good* life.

Chapter 3 articulated the idea of virtue—that is, that goodness is not defined within us, but exists outside us to be sought and embraced. In chapter 4, we explored what it means to articulate this idea in a manner that is essential, consistent, and communal. Now we turn our attention to the practice of virtue.

This chapter explores the virtues famously laid out by God in Micah chapter 6: justice, mercy, and humility. In line with Aristotle's dictum that our habits serve to form our inner selves, we will explore the meaning of these virtues and their necessity for living well.

He Has Shown You What Is Good

"Micah 6:8," writes Tim Keller, "is a summary of how God wants us to live."[3]

Regardless of their level of biblical literacy, many are familiar with the prophet's dictum to "act justly and love mercy and walk humbly with your God." The text is simple, yet powerful. Whether in the form of a T-shirt slogan, a ministry ethos, or a global poverty reduction campaign, this often quoted expression has made the rounds throughout evangelical culture. But to understand why the verse is a summary of how God wants us to live, we must first take a look at the text that precedes it.

The opening of Micah 6 plays out like a courtroom scene. The people of Israel feel burdened by all of the seemingly unreasonable expectations God is placing on them. So God, you might say, brings them to court. Moreover, he is not passive in his approach. He wants Israel to lay all of their complaints on the table: "My people, what have I done to you? How have I burdened you? Answer me" (Mic. 6:3 NIV). God has only been good to them—what do they have to complain about?

We do not hear a response from Israel (almost implying a silence), so God continues. He reminds his people that he brought them out of Egypt—out of slavery. He provided them with leaders (Moses, Aaron, and Miriam), and delivered them from the clutches of a hostile Moabite King and into the promised land. In short, God has given them the freedom, structure, and resources to prosper and flourish as a people. Furthermore, God's goodness has occurred not because of Israel's faithfulness, but in spite of its absence! They have transgressed his law, and yet he has remained charitable and kind toward them.

Recognizing that they have fallen short of God's standards, Israel responds by asking what God expects in return for his goodness. Does God expect burnt offerings, the sacrifice of a thousand rams, or even ten thousand rivers of olive oil? Would that please God? Or, even more radical, should the people of Israel offer their firstborn—their very offspring? Would that suffice? In other words, we can almost imagine the people of Israel throwing up their arms and saying: "What do you want from us?"

Perhaps these are genuine questions. Alternatively, they may be cynical ("What in the world does it take to please you?"). Either way, an assumption rises to the surface: God has been good, Israel has been bad, and now Israel needs to give God something to restore the relationship—calves, rams, oil, or even a firstborn. Israel assumes that they must part company with treasured possessions or make elaborate sacrifices in order to be "right" in God's eyes.

It is here that Micah speaks up. We might think that sacrificing one's child or collecting "rivers of olive oil" is radical piety on the part of Israel, but that would be incorrect. In reality, they have completely overlooked what God desires of them. While basic and simple, God's requirements are fundamental to the Christian way of life. "He has [already] shown you what is good," the prophet says, "And what does the LORD require of you? To act justly and to love mercy and to walk humbly with your God" (6:8).

Justice. Mercy. Humility.

The point is not to give their possessions away (rams, oil, children); it is to give themselves away. God doesn't want their belongings; he is asking that they consecrate their lives. *They* are the offering God desires.

Note, too, that these aren't simply ideas—they are actions, and are expressed as such. *Act* justly. *Love* mercy. *Walk* humbly. As one commentary puts it, Micah 6:8 "is like a summary of much that is presented throughout the Bible."[4] To understand this summary, the balance of this chapter will attend to the virtues of justice, mercy, and humility as expressed in Micah 6:8. For in understanding we can be led to practice, and from practice we can be led to embodying, and in embodying these virtues we can better cultivate a virtuous self.

Act Justly and Love Mercy

Justice is nothing new. From ancient philosophers to emerging twenty-first-century adults, justice inevitably seems to surface within social, political, economic, and cultural discussions. If anything, the popularity of the concept is on the rise. For example, the millennial generation has been referred to as the "social justice" generation. One author even describes them as being the most justice-minded generation in United States history. Millennials, and many others, are concerned with issues of inequality and environmental injustice, and overwhelmingly support efforts that address social problems.[5] So justice is not necessarily new, and may be as popular as ever—but what exactly is it?

The term *justice* implies fairness in matters of distribution (and retribution in a criminal justice context). Perhaps the clearest description of what is meant by *justice* in both a classical and contemporary context is this: justice is "giving each their due," or giving people what they deserve. As mentioned in chapter 3, the origin of justice as "each their due" hails back to ancient Greek philosophers and finds its greatest development in Aristotle.[6] It was Plato who credited Simonides as defining justice in this way: "it is to give each what is owed."[7]

In a formal sense, few dispute that justice is giving someone what they deserve. Unfortunately, in reality, determining what someone deserves is much more difficult than it sounds. For many, this is realized by achieving "fairness" or a fair arrangement (fair opportunities; fair outcomes, etc.). For others, justice is less about procedural fairness and more about free exchange without the presence of coercion. Some hold that determining what each person is due is based upon the individual's contribution to society, which can be measured by effort or by productivity. Others define justice based upon the Marxist maxim: "From each according to his ability, to each according to his needs."[8] Here, what is deserved is based upon need and not effort. These various articulations of justice aside, in modern terms, justice is most often equated with "ensuring equal opportunity, giving equal pay for equal work, guaranteeing equal protection under the law, or avoiding favoritism and scapegoating among one's children or students."[9]

To be clear, evaluating these various expressions of justice is very important. However, these descriptions miss a larger, more comprehensive biblical conception of the term. The Hebrew word for justice in Micah 6:8 is *mishpat* (an expression that occurs over two hundred times in the Old Testament). At face value, *mishpat* implies judgment in an equitable, or fair, manner. However, like so many ideas in Scripture, the word itself is far more rich and packed with nuance than a surface-level view would suggest. To best understand this, we must first take a broader view of justice. In the Bible, to enact justice is to bring about an order, that is, the way things are supposed to be. For this reason, Scripture seldom describes justice apart from the notion of righteousness, or "right relations." Micah 6:8 is no different. Tim Keller writes, "The text says to 'do justice and love mercy,' which seem at first glance to be two different things, but they are not."[10] Mercy, or *chesedh* in Hebrew, is a covenantal word implying loving-kindness, generosity, or goodness toward another. As Keller describes it, *mishpat* describes the action of justice, while *chesedh* describes the attitude behind it.[11] Justice, then, is not simply about our practice, but also about our posture—our attitude.[12]

Why is it important to place justice (*mishpat*) side by side with the notion of mercy or loving-kindness (*chesedh*)? Precisely because, understood by themselves, these ideas are radically different. Theologian Emil Brunner contrasts the classical understanding of justice as giving each person what they deserve with the general idea of self-giving love.

Who or whatever renders to every man his due, that person or thing is just; an attitude, an institution, a law, a relationship, in which every man is given his due is just. Thereby justice is clearly distinguished from love. Love does not ask what is mine and what is thine: it does not render to the other what is his due, what belongs to him "by right," but gives of its own, gives precisely that to which the other has no right.[13]

Justice, as a stand-alone concept, is quite different from loving-kindness. For example, many are familiar with the Roman goddess Lady Justice, or *Justitia*, whose statue still decorates courthouses and judicial buildings. Blindfolded, she holds scales in one hand and a sword in another. This is the personification of justice: impartial, calculated, and swiftly executed.

Yet God does not simply want justice—he wants justice and mercy. Mercy, or *chesedh*, moderates the otherwise icy expression of justice. When the two combine, we get a virtue that makes sense of justice and mercy in tandem: *charity*. This is giving people what they deserve, but with a sense of self-giving love. Gordon Graham describes this notion of justice as "an active concern to help others in their poverty or weakness."[14] This is not simply help in the form of almsgiving, but includes an expression of sympathetic understanding as well. In other words, sympathy is granted to someone who has encountered hardship irrespective of whether they deserve such hardship or not.

This perspective helps us to understand justice as "righteousness." Justice is not simply about doling out rights in a fair and impartial way. It is about making our relationships right; it is an other-centered overture motivated by an attitude of self-giving love and mercy.

Moreover, a charitable expression of justice mirrors the very character of God himself. Consider again the backdrop of Micah 6. The people of Israel have not only fallen short of God's design, but have further complicated the relationship by complaining about their situation. This seems particularly brash given that God rescued them from slavery and delivered them into the promised land. No Israelite would be so bold as to stand before God and say, "I demand justice!" That is, we do not really want God to give us "what we deserve." Thankfully, God is not a god of scales and swords in matters of justice. This is the very definition of mercy: saving us from something we deserve—a punishment that is merited. Unlike *Justitia*, God does not blindfold himself, distributing justice in a cold, impartial manner. Just the opposite. As Daniel Bell Jr. writes, in God's judicial math, "true justice is formed by charity and its rule is mercy."[15]

The Practice of Justice and Mercy

There is an elegant quality to the biblical notion of justice as righteousness, but it is not a concept to be admired; it is to be practiced. More specifically, it is to be woven into the fabric of human character.

When God says, "I have shown you what is good," one way of understanding this text is that God has redirected Israel's attention to what he is concerned with. As mentioned earlier, he does not require, nor desire, the sacrifice of rams, oil, or even children. God wants his people to offer themselves. In other words, God is saying: "You have it wrong. This is what I want you to focus on."

However, we may just as easily understand God's words in a more literal sense: "I have *shown* you what is good." That is, "I have demonstrated the kind of sacrifice I want;" "I have exhibited self-giving love right in front of your eyes;" "I have embodied, myself, the very humility that I require of my people." Israel need not listen so much as look at what God has already done for them. God is not simply a theoretical God; he is also practical. God has *shown* them.

Regardless of how we might understand Micah 6:8 (God has redirected us; God has demonstrated for us; God has done both), this raises the question: What does it look like to do justice and love mercy? Much can be said here—but my goal is not to spell out an all-encompassing list. Rather, I want to identify several practices that are specifically oriented around the cultivation and refinement of justice and mercy (*mishpat* and *chesedh*). In *doing* these practices, we inevitably influence our *being*.

Generosity

We will begin with the practice of generosity. More often than not, the practice of giving is associated with charity drives, love offerings, or ministry donations. Parting company with our money for such efforts is certainly an act of generosity, but the term itself has a much broader application. In addition to our money, we can be generous with our time, our care, and our effort. We can even be generous in disposition, such as giving someone the benefit of the doubt.

Giving is not a confusing idea. We all know how to give (writing a check; creating time in our schedule). Oftentimes, we even know what to give (money, time, possessions, or compassion). Further, it is also often clear whom we should give to (friends, family, spouse, stranger, etc.). These do not tend to be the prohibitive issues when practicing generosity. The real crux of the problem relates to *why* we should give.

While generosity is indeed something we do, it first starts with a conception of what has been done for us. A helpful example of this comes from Paul in his letter to the Corinthians. Specifically, in 2 Corinthians 8, Paul directs attention toward the Macedonian churches in Thessalonica. He praises their rich generosity, as they "gave as much as they were able, and even beyond their ability" (v. 3). The text reads as if Paul is about to strongly exhort the people of Corinth to be more like the Macedonians (the way parents nag their problem child to be more like their older, more responsible sibling).

But Paul takes a different tack. Instead, he says this: "I am not commanding you . . . [but] you know the grace of our Lord Jesus Christ, that though he was rich, yet for your sake he became poor, so that you through his poverty might become rich" (vv. 8–9 NIV). In other words, Paul does not directly command the church to be like the Macedonians and emulate their abundant giving practices. Rather, he is simply reminding them of what Jesus gave to them.

You see, Paul understands a very simple but profound truth: giving begets giving. When Jesus taught his disciples to pray saying, "And forgive us our debts, as we also have forgiven our debtors" (Matt. 6:12 NIV), the implication is that being forgiven and the act of forgiving are not two independent ideas. That is, our generosity toward others should be a natural overflow of the generosity God has extended toward us (forgiveness has been described as "giving excessively").[16] Richard Longenecker, for example, writes that when moral questions arise about how we should treat others who are powerless, without status, or in need, we should begin by asking, "How did God treat me when he sent his Son to deliver me?"[17] Our generosity is prompted by the recognition that we have received generously.

As mentioned earlier, in stark contrast to the norms of justice based upon a defined sense of merit, God's grace and mercy toward us are unjust, partial, and unequal. They are unjust insofar as they celebrate relational norms that are not based upon scales and swords; they are partial insofar as they recognize distinct human dignity and protect the plight of the helpless, the stranger, and the outcast; and they are other-oriented as they recognize that our completeness is to be found in others, not ourselves. We are prompted toward generous action, not because we are receiving a tangible return (exchange) or because it is a divine rule, but because we have already been the recipients of the "gift of Christ."

Charitable Judgment

Related to generosity is the practice of charitable judgment. To judge charitably means to see things as God sees them. It is the practice of changing how you view, and therefore how you evaluate, a given situation.

Being a person of faith in this world poses an interesting dilemma. Though our "citizenship is in heaven" (Phil. 3:20), we find ourselves situated in a particular time, place, and culture. Speaking about this dual citizenship, Miroslav Volf writes:

> Christians inescapably inhabit two worlds—they are "in God" and "in the world"—the world of the biblical traditions and the world of their own culture. Consequently, Christian "tradition" is *never pure*; it always represents a merging of streams coming from the Scriptures and from given cultures that a particular church inhabits.[18]

Fortunately, this "merging of streams" creates space for what Volf calls "double vision." On the surface, this may appear to be an outlook, but it is also a practice: specifically, the practice of "seeing with the eyes of the others, accepting their perspective, and discovering the new significance of one's own basic commitments."[19]

The practice of "double vision" is, according to Volf, "indispensable" in matters of justice. In other words, to arrive at agreement upon justice, one must be willing to embrace the conception of the other. As Volf writes, "When we are looking at each other through the sights of our guns we see only the rightness of our own cause."[20] In contrast, Volf submits that the will to embrace the other must precede any agreement on justice.

A wonderful example of this is found in the famous story of the prodigal son. The youngest son in a well-off family asks for his inheritance early, only to squander it in "dissolute living." Impoverished and broken, he returns home to work as a hired hand for his father. When he returns, his father races out to meet him. Far from accepting him as a hired servant, his father says:

> Quickly, bring out a robe—the best one—and put it on him; put a
> ring on his finger and sandals on his feet. And get the fatted calf and
> kill it, and let us eat and celebrate; for this son of mine was dead and
> is alive again; he was lost and is found! (Luke 15:22–24)

This is *not* justice in our conventional sense of the term. Quite the opposite. The elder son in the story is deeply angered. For him, this arrangement is patently unjust. Recognizing this, his father responds: "But we had to celebrate and rejoice, because this brother of yours was dead and has come to life; he was lost and has been found" (Luke 15:32). Regarding this story, Volf writes:

> It was "unjust" of the father to receive back the prodigal as a son and,
> on top of that, to throw a party for him after the son had just squan-
> dered half of his inheritance. But the father was not interested in
> "justice." He acted in accordance with a "must" that was higher than
> the "must" of "justice" (v. 32). It was the "must" of belonging together
> as a family. *Put differently, the relationship defined justice; an abstract
> principle of justice did not define the relationship.*[21]

Similarly, in another passage, Jesus describes, in parable format, the kingdom of heaven as being "like a landowner who went out early in the morning to hire laborers for his vineyard" (v. 1).[22] The land-owner agreed upon a daily wage (understood as the "usual" wage) with potential laborers as the workday began. However, afterward, he proceeded to go into the marketplace to appeal to more workers to come, work, and be paid "whatever is right" (v. 4). Men were hired throughout the day to work until evening. Finally, the story ends:

> When evening came, the owner of the vineyard said to his manager,
> "Call the laborers and give them their pay, beginning with the last and
> then going to the first." When those hired about five o'clock came, each
> of them received the usual daily wage. Now when the first came, they
> thought they would receive more; but each of them also received the
> usual daily wage. And when they received it, they grumbled against
> the landowner, saying, "These last worked only one hour, and you
> have made them equal to us who have borne the burden of the day

and the scorching heat." But he replied to one of them, "Friend, I am doing you no wrong; did you not agree with me for the usual daily wage? Take what belongs to you and go; I choose to give to this last the same as I give to you. Am I not allowed to do what I choose with what belongs to me? Or are you envious because I am generous?" So the last will be first, and the first will be last. (Matt. 20:8–16)

According to Joachim Jeremias, Jesus is telling a familiar story, as this was a common narrative in the Jewish rabbinical oral tradition.[23] However, the rabbinical version had a far different ending:

When the labourers came to receive their wages, each of them received the same amount as all the others. Then they murmured and said: "We have worked the whole day, and this man only two hours, yet you have paid him the full day's wages." The king replied: "I have not wronged you; this labourer has done more in two hours than you have done during the whole day."[24]

If justice is about proportion or impartial calculation, then Jesus' departure from the rabbinical version of the story is confusing at best. Yet "kingdom" justice has less to do with proportion, and more to do with God's partiality: "Take what belongs to you and go; I choose to give to this last the same as I give to you. Am I not allowed to do what I choose with what belongs to me?"

But how do we practice this kind of charity? How do we achieve the double vision Volf speaks of? There is no simple answer to this, but part of the answer can be found in the practice of proximity. In other words, to see "with the eyes of others, accepting their perspective, and discovering the new significance of one's own basic commitments," we must place ourselves within the realm of the other in a very literal sense.[25] Theologian Timothy Gorringe notes that it is within close proximity, within the most fundamental forms of face-to-face relationship, that the moral sense is most acute. He writes:

In the experiences we have of the varieties of love, partial, flawed, and often corrupted as they are, the *depth* and *mystery* of what it is to be human is revealed to us, and it is from this revelation that awareness of the sanctity of life springs. Love of *life*, or awareness of its sanctity, then becomes the basis for all ethical systems.[26]

Such love, Gorringe continues, is not natural, that is, it is not like loving a child or a spouse, etc. Rather, it is *agape* love: the Greek term used to express the biblical idea of unconditional love. Gorringe writes: "What is implied by agape, on the other hand, is love for the totally unlike, love for the enemy, turning the other cheek, forgiveness."[27] For Gorringe, this occurs in face-to-face interaction—in closeness to one another.[28] Thus, while proximity is not the supreme solution to all matters of justice, without it, we are left to construct our preferences, morals, and rights bereft of a distinct "other."

Steadfast Love

The final practice related to cultivating justice and mercy is steadfast love. In his article on "Extreme Virtues," David Fillingim writes that "Steadfast love means continuing to practice devotion through the changeableness of religious feelings."[29] To love mercy as described in Micah 6:8, writes Fillingim, requires us to practice steadfast love in all of our relationships. In a culture where choice, preference, and feeling are dominant, Fillingim is right to label this virtue as being "extreme."

Love that is steadfast does not ebb and flow with the changeability of human emotion and feeling. It is quite literally devotion: an unchanging commitment of love toward God and others. Yet how does one develop the practice of steadfast love? How does one cultivate the habit of commitment? Quite simply, you commit. I am reminded of a conversation I once had with an athletic trainer for a national sports program. "The best way to improve your ability to jump," he said, "is to jump." The logic is simple. The more we do something, the better we become at it. This is illustrated in Malcom Gladwell's popular book *Outliers*, in which he suggests that those who have achieved extraordinary mastery in a field have committed at least ten thousand hours to their skill.

Why is this important? Because steadfast love will not magically happen on its own. Unfortunately, how we choose to use our time often betrays this simple truth. I once had a sports teammate who seldom exercised, ate poorly, and spent copious amounts of time in front of his television. He was consistently the last person to arrive when practice started and the first to leave when it ended. Given this, it was bewildering that he complained about his playing time and lack of respect amongst our teammates. Similarly, I have had dozens of students through the years express frustration that they did not understand a concept when they skipped class regularly, failed to read the text, rarely studied, or all of the above. Given this, would it not be more surprising if they actually did understand class concepts?

This naturally has implications for our relationships. How can we expect to have a vibrant relationship with a friend, partner, son, daughter, spouse, or supervisor when there is little to no investment? Similarly, who are we to complain about not "feeling" God's presence in our lives when we neglect devotional time alone or communal worship in church? How can we expect God's word to be "a lamp unto our feet and a light unto our path" when the average person in the United States spends approximately 444 minutes (or nearly seven and a half hours) looking at a screen per day and disproportionately less time studying scripture?[30] In short, we can't.

We might be tempted to believe that the aforementioned examples represent people who simply lack discipline. But if discipline is a regimen of practices that trains or inculcates us to think, act, and speak a certain way, then we cannot accurately say that they lack discipline; rather, they are exercising the wrong discipline.

I once heard a journalist recalling an interview with a woman who was guilty of a fatal hit-and-run. Several years later, in prison, the perpetrator was asked about her thought process in the instant of the crash that fatefully led her to flee the scene. "There was no thought process," she answered. "Prior to that night, I had made thousands of little decisions in my life where I had abdicated responsibility for my actions. When the wreck occurred, I instinctively fled. Fleeing was second nature—I didn't even think about it."

It would be easy to declare that this woman was unethical or lacked discipline—at least at the time of the hit-and-run. But this is not necessarily true. More accurately, her actions were a product of disciplined thoughtlessness and recklessness. Her character had been warped, sullied, and corroded over a long span of time and an even longer series of iniquitous patterns. She had *habituated* moral irresponsibility.

Though we are often unaware of it, we are constantly training ourselves into certain patterns. Our thousands of atomistic and seemingly harmless actions aggregate to mold our nature. We inevitably become someone—but who? Each of us will answer this with our actions. Steadfast love is not simply a disposition—it is a deliberate movement toward others: God and neighbor. Moreover, the perfection of this love requires our commitment to classical spiritual disciplines. Reading scripture (individually and communally), prayer, worship, fasting, and deliberate stillness—these are the fertilizers necessary to grow our relationships into healthy, vibrant, and sustainable commitments with God and others.

There is nothing innovative about spiritual disciplines. They have been around for thousands of years. Nor are they sexy. We can superimpose all the glitz and glamor we want onto these practices, but at the end of the day, they are what they are: reflective scriptural reading, communal liturgy, heartfelt petitioning through prayer, willful fasting, deliberate listening, and meditative stillness. As the old saying goes, "Everyone wants to have read the classics, but no one wants to read the classics." That is, everyone wants the benefits of discipline, but no one wants to undertake the disciplines themselves (especially when they come at the cost of our time and attention).

However, there is a counterpoint to be made here. Spiritual disciplines do not simply exist for the sake of achieving a result. Rather, as suggested at the beginning of the chapter, they have the capacity to change the very nature of our being. To provide an example, my father had to undertake a significant and radical transformation in his diet nearly two decades ago. Had he continued to consume high cholesterol food, the health ramifications would have been severe. Thankfully, he committed himself to a disciplined diet of fruits, vegetables, and other seemingly bland, but healthy, food. Years after this, I once asked him if he was ever tempted by hamburgers, fries, pizza, or other unhealthy but seductive dishes. "Not at all," he responded. "I strongly desire the foods I eat now, and further, I have no desire whatsoever for what I used to eat." Similarly, recall the findings mentioned earlier from Gladwell's *Outliers*. In addition to noting the ten-thousand-hour threshold for mastery, Gladwell found that those who achieved mastery not only practiced, but grew to love—to *desire*—practicing their skill. Their desire bred discipline, but their discipline also bred desire.

Let us turn our attention back to steadfast love. As Dallas Willard has pointed out, spiritual disciplines are not primarily for solving behavioral problems (though it would not be unreasonable to expect that as a by-product). Rather, the disciplines exist to renew us from inside out.[31] Our commitment to classical spiritual disciplines such as scripture reading, prayer, or fasting does not come out of a self-imposed piety, but rather, out of an overture of love toward God and others. To act justly and love mercy is to have steadfast love as an impulse, a default reaction. There may be no better description of committing ourselves to "right relationships" with others.

Walk Humbly

Years ago, after having established my own pattern of devotional time in the morning, I copied a well-known poem and placed it in a conspicuous spot in my study space. In addition to committing the words to memory, the strategic placement of the poem would force me to consider its words and their meaning during my most reflective time of the day.

The poem was "Invictus" (Latin for *unconquered*) by William Ernest Henley. It reads:

Out of the night that covers me,
  Black as the pit from pole to pole,
I thank whatever gods may be
  For my unconquerable soul.
In the fell clutch of circumstance
  I have not winced nor cried aloud.
Under the bludgeonings of chance
  My head is bloody, but unbowed.
Beyond this place of wrath and tears
  Looms but the Horror of the shade,

And yet the menace of the years
      Finds and shall find me unafraid.
It matters not how strait the gate,
      How charged with punishments the scroll,
I am the master of my fate,
      I am the captain of my soul.

Henley's 1888 work has all of the elements of great writing. It is inspirational, invigorating, and incorporates rich imagery for the reader. The rhythmic and melodic language smolders with heroic undertones, inviting the reader to raise their chin and straighten their back with each stanza. Henley's words are also relatable. The seemingly random, bleak forces of life create a sense of being an underdog. Subject to "bludgeonings of chance," it is natural to cheer on the resilient, gritty personality whose "head is bloody, but unbowed."

So there is much to praise in this popular literary work. Yet I did not deliberately commit this poem to memory for these reasons. Rather, I wanted "Invictus" before me each and every day to remind myself of its *foolishness*.

In spite of its praiseworthy attributes, Henley's gallant speech and cavalier spirit risk leading the reader into an implicit celebration of self-referential autonomy. This is no innocent shift. Autonomy and virtue do not play well together. Autonomy values freedom and liberty from others, but virtue extols freedom for the sake of others. Autonomy prizes choice for its own sake, but virtue aims to link our desire to the truly desirable. Autonomy sees others as a constraint, but virtue recognizes our relational commitments as a source of fulfillment. Autonomy says that I raise myself, make myself, and save myself—but virtue realizes that how I function is aimless, worthless, and harmful when disconnected from human teleology (our design).

I am not the master of my fate. I am not the captain of my soul. It is one thing to state this, but quite another to live it out. This is what it means to "walk humbly with your God"—the other necessary ingredient in God's recipe for virtuous living in Micah 6:8. Humility, in this sense, has been described as wisdom.[32] More specifically, having wisdom means recognizing God and your place within his created order. "The fear of God is the beginning of wisdom" writes the psalmist, or as *The Message* puts it, "The good life begins in the fear of God" (Ps. 111:10, *The Message*). This is not the same fear we feel during a scary movie or, say, holding a tarantula. Fearing God means holding him in awe. It is reverence and respect. To fear God is to rightly admit who God is and who you are in relation to him.

What would keep us from such wisdom? What would prohibit our ability to "walk humbly" with God? Our inability to fear God is often less about how we see God and more about how we see ourselves. We might say that wisdom means knowing who we are, as well as knowing who we are not.

In contrast to the puffed up, autonomous spirit evident in Henley's words, Paul tells us to "have the same mindset as Christ Jesus"—a mindset constituted by taking on the form of a slave, emptying ourselves, and acting with humility and obedience (Phil. 2:5–8). Yet, this picture of humble wisdom is a not so subtle contrast to the thousands of invitations we receive daily to make ourselves the point of reference. In the 1970s, it was estimated that Americans saw, on average, approximately five hundred advertisements a day. Thirty years later, the new estimate was five thousand—a 900 percent increase.[33] Advertisements aren't benign. They do not exist to simply inform you—they exist to seduce you. A successful advertisement does not just enlighten you; it *persuades* you—and persuasion isn't cheap. Companies mobilize an army of resources to either subtly or explicitly shape your perception of reality. They tell you what to think, what to believe, and what you deserve.

Consumerism's invitation to construct our own edifice is not the only wind that blows in the opposite direction of humility. Indeed, the increasingly innovative tools of technology not only fail to reinforce, but in many ways discourage, the good life that "begins with the fear of God." Author Tim Urban, for example, has suggested that today's social media fixation has led to the phenomenon of "image-crafting," or the embellished maintenance of one's online personality. Urban writes:

Social media creates a world for [participants] where A) what everyone else is doing is very out in the open, B) most people present an
inflated version of their own existence, and C) the people who chime
in the most about their careers are usually those whose careers (or
relationships) are going the best, while struggling people tend not to
broadcast their situation.[34]

In essence, image-crafting involves a flattering depiction—an exag-
gerated version of ourselves—that people can admire, with little to
no relevance to reality.

Whether through rampant advertising and consumerism, or
image-crafting with the help of our technology, we all risk failing
to walk humbly with God. Thankfully, humility is not just an ideal
to be dismissed in action but admired in theory. It is a practice—a
habit that can be sewn into the fabric of our everyday lives. I want
to draw your attention to two distinct practices that can help to
establish and develop a humble walk.

The Practice of Humility: "Agreement"

This is strange. I have no interest in running and am not a partisan
in the British class system. Then why should I have been so deeply
moved by . . . a British film that has running and class as its subjects? I
believe the answer is rather simple: Like many great films, [the movie]
takes its nominal subjects as occasions for much larger statements
about human nature.[35]

So said Roger Ebert in 1981. Ebert was describing the classic film
Chariots of Fire, which won four Academy Awards and is considered
one of the best British films ever produced. (While I was studying
at St. Andrews in Scotland, I attempted to run on the same beach
filmed at the opening of the movie. Unfortunately, awkwardly slog-
ging through sand was, for me, a stark contrast to the effortless
trotting exhibited by the youthful runners in the film.)

A true story, the movie focuses on running legend Eric Liddell.
At the beginning of the movie, Liddell, who would go on to be a
famous missionary in China, is preparing for the 1924 Olympics in
Paris. At one point in the movie, he famously tells his sister: "Jenny,

I believe God made me for a purpose [China], but he also made me fast. And when I run, *I feel his pleasure*" (a sermon illustration I have heard at least a dozen times). Liddell amassed widespread attention for his refusal to compete in his best race, the 100-meter sprint, which was scheduled to occur on the Sabbath. Because of this, Liddell was forced to participate in another event entirely, the 400-meter sprint. Despite never having run this race before, he secured his spot in the annals of Olympic history by inexplicably winning a gold medal.

Liddell's Olympic performance, coupled with his uncompromising principles, make him the perfect candidate for timeless storytelling. Indeed, the "flying Scotsman," as he would come to be called, is central to the *Chariots of Fire* plotline, and responsible for endearing millions of viewers to this story of faith. To many, Liddell was, and is, a Christian hero.

Naturally, viewers are attracted to Liddell as the movie's protagonist. But as the film progressed, my attention drifted away from Liddell and was redirected to another character: Harold Abrahams. Abrahams is himself a very talented runner, and also secured a spot in the 1924 Olympics. In contrast to Liddell, Abrahams is committed to a singular life aim: winning an Olympic gold medal. At one point in the movie, he admits that running is an addiction, a compulsion. Upon being asked how he feels about the prospect of losing, Abrahams answers: "I don't know. . . . I've never lost."

One of the most important scenes of the movie occurs, I believe, just before Abrahams's Olympic race. This was the moment he had been working toward his entire life. Yet something is not right. Previously motivated by the fear of losing, he is now confronted with a new, unfamiliar, concern: the fear of *winning*. Prior to the race, he shares a moment of vulnerability with a teammate ("Aubrey"):

> You, Aubrey, are my most complete man. You're brave, compassionate, kind. A content man. That is your secret: contentment. I am 24 and I've never known it. I'm forever in pursuit and I don't even know what I'm chasing. Aubrey, old chap, I'm scared. . . .
>
> And now in one hour's time I will be out there again. I will raise my eyes and look down that corridor, four feet wide, with ten lonely seconds to justify my whole existence. But will I? Aubrey, I've known the fear of losing but now I am almost too frightened to win.

It is a profound reflection. Abrahams suffered a void in his life that he presumed would be filled with the glory that accompanies Olympic success. Yet when the moment arrived, a new angst arose. What if this moment did not deliver the satisfaction he so desperately lacked, and so fiercely sought? *"With ten lonely seconds to justify my whole existence."*

He wins the race, but there is no celebration. Rather, Abrahams drops his head and slouches into the locker room, seemingly oblivious to the spirited fans around him. His realization becomes clear to the viewer: winning a race, and even an Olympic gold medal, was still insufficient to deliver the fulfillment absent in his life. The satisfaction he had hoped would accompany his accomplishment was only a mirage.

The movie seems to invite us to celebrate with Liddell and mourn with Abrahams. In contrast to Liddell, Abrahams's abundant talent for running belies his hollow interior life. Yet there is something redemptive, even beautiful, in this scene. We might be tempted to look at Abrahams as inept, or worse, pathetic, because his dogged pursuit of worldly success proves insufficient to satisfy the desires of his heart. We criticize his shortsightedness. We revile his blindness. We secretly assure ourselves that we are above such shallow exploits.

I see it differently. I see a person who has explored the contours of his innermost self: the ugliness, the duplicity, the emptiness—and has marshalled an expression that accurately describes his findings. Abrahams seems to lack the meaningfulness to his existence so evident in the movie's hero, Liddell. But he recognizes something we would do well to reflect upon. He perceives that his contentment is tied to something deeper than accomplishment. He discerns that he is comprised of two selves—an interior self and an exterior self. Moreover, he acknowledges—rather eloquently—that the two do not seem to match: *"I'm forever in pursuit and I don't even know what I'm chasing."* So while we might be tempted to dismiss Abrahams as shallow or pathetic, we are also invited to identify with him, acknowledging the hollowness and misalignment within ourselves.

The faith tradition has a term for this practice: it is called confession. Confession is not exactly a fashionable idea. The term conjures up images of the guilty shamefully standing before the judgment of others. Yet the idea itself is often misunderstood. Confession, in a biblical sense, means not simply to convey information to God—but to *agree* with him. The Greek word that gets translated as "to confess," *homologeō*, means "to agree with or assent to." This puts an interesting spin on an otherwise unpopular term.

When we share our failures, our disappointments, or our struggles with God, we are agreeing with him. God is not taken by surprise. Rather, we are saying, "I recognize what I have done. I recognize who I am." Further, confession is acknowledgement that we, alone, are insufficient to settle these shortcomings. Something more, or rather someone more, is necessary. Consider one of the more profound confessions in the Bible, which came from King David in Psalm 51. Broken, he cries out to God, "You desire truth in the inward being; therefore teach me wisdom in my secret heart" (v. 6).

According to our faith, we are all in need of a "true" life. Christianity begins with the conception that we are not complete. Left to ourselves, we are inept, inadequate, and found wanting. In Romans 7, Paul, when reflecting on trying to live above reproach by strict adherence to the law, puts words to the condition that has shackled humanity for ages: "Nothing good dwells within me" (v. 18). Further, if nothing good dwells in me, then why would I want to be autonomous? The notion of autonomy would suggest not freedom, but bondage. In addition to Paul's words, the whole trajectory of Scripture invites us to constantly revisit this important truth in our human nature: our autonomy is inadequate and found wanting.

To recognize this is the essence of humility and wisdom. To walk humbly means to recognize that we are not the point of reference. Rather, our Creator is. It is to agree that we are insufficient in ourselves. Recall the "Christian irony" discussed in chapter 3: having a whole self requires us to empty ourselves wholly.

There is an important caveat in God's third entreaty in Micah 6:8—not simply to act with humility, but to "walk humbly." The expression implies activity that is continual and sustainable. In other words, humility is less like a weapon we unsheathe and brandish at the right moment, and more like a character trait deeply ingrained into our very essence. Think walking, talking, eating, sleeping, and breathing. God's wants humility to be our reflex, our default activity and attitude.

This means we need to think carefully about the habit of confession—that is, training ourselves to constantly be "in agreement" with God about who we are and who he is. When Christ taught his disciples how to pray, he emphasized that they should ask God for "daily bread" (Matt. 6:11). This was a calculated statement. That is, we are to depend upon God, daily, for sustenance and survival. To ask for daily bread is to implicitly recognize that we are dependent beings. Moreover, we are asking God to "give" to us. This is not a market transaction where God is the seller and we are the buyer. Nor is this conventional reciprocity. We have done nothing for God that would merit an expected gift from him in return. Rather, we ask for God's gift so as to be reminded of our faithful dependence upon him, as well as his loving generosity to us. To ask God to provide us with daily bread is to *agree* that it is not something we can manufacture in and of ourselves.

But can confession be a habit? Absolutely. Every Sunday our church participates in a corporate expression of confession. For some, this practice might seem strange. For example, many believe that confession should only occur where sin has occurred. Similarly, some say that regular confession is an implicit statement that we cannot help but sin every day in thought, word, and deed.

However, quibbling over this common practice risks missing a larger point: corporate confession is an opportunity to bring ourselves before God and agree about who we are and who he is. It is to bring ourselves into unity with God and with one another. As Enuma Okora writes, "For many of us, that weekly point of confession might be the only time we acknowledge to ourselves, to God, and to one another that we cannot be left to our own devices without making grave mistakes."[36]

The practice of confession is not limited to our public spaces of worship. It can be cultivated in our private life as well. Like Abrahams's experience before the race, confession begins with quiet, contemplative reflection. As one commentary puts it, it is in our quiet practices (prayer, scripture reading, reflective meditation, etc.) that we assume our most "advantageous posture" for hearing and responding to God.[37] It is within God's presence that we actually know where, and who, we are.

An example may help to make this clear. Not far from where I live, a forty-minute hike can take you to the top of a natural rock structure. Towering above the forest and trees, the hiker is rewarded with a panoramic view of pure nature. The sight is breathtaking. However, when standing at the summit, you are also very aware that a wrong step here or a careless slip there can send you careening down a precipitous drop to your death. I think the fear of God is something like this. *It's wildly beautiful, but watch your step.*

Coming into the presence of God is like hiking up the rocky slope I just described. We are captivated by beauty, wonder, and grandeur. However, we become instantly aware that we are not in control. We quickly ascertain a healthy respect for our surroundings, aware of our own shortcomings and limitations. We assume humility. Humility is indeed a practice, but its most natural expression can be found when we come before our Creator.

Understood in these terms, humility becomes interchangeable with the idea of reverence. Indeed, reverence has been described as "a deep understanding of human limitations." Further, "from this grows the capacity to be in awe of whatever we believe lies *outside* of our control."[38] Agreement with God is not simply an expression of humility. Nor is it just an agreement about who we are. Ultimately, it is to agree with the Creator about who we are and who he is.

The Practice of Humility: "Works of Mercy"

Humility may be naturally invoked before our Creator, but it can also be kindled before our fellow human beings. Strategically placing ourselves in front of the needs of others, referred to as "works of mercy" in the Catholic and Methodist traditions, can serve to fashion us into a posture of humility. Actions such as visiting the sick, feeding the hungry, clothing the naked, and ministering to prisoners can have a positive effect on the "least of these."

However, works of mercy are not simply about ministering to others; they are also in many ways about ministering to ourselves. Ask anyone who has set out to serve another, and more often than not they will describe the change they themselves have experienced. Why? Because contact "reminds." We are reminded that where we have thrived, others have suffered. Where we have been fortunate, others have faltered. Where our health has been sustained, for others it has failed. Where our relationships have held, for others they have not. Most importantly, though, we are reminded of our common link with humanity: we all share this journey called life, and navigating through it requires the presence, love, help, and support of each other. Thus, among other things, contact with those unlike us will inevitably change our understanding of others, ourselves, and of the very way we organize our lives.

A wonderful example of this comes from the work of Michael Emerson and Christian Smith. In their book *Divided by Faith* the authors provide an in-depth analysis of evangelicalism and racial bias in America.[39] They conclude that modern Christianity is unable to effect change when it comes to our overtly segregated society.[40]

Their study itself was rather straightforward. When meeting with a Caucasian respondent, the authors would begin by sharing statistics that spoke to the enormous gap between white and black Americans (e.g., white households have higher income, are more educated, less prone to crime, etc.). Next, they asked respondents to choose the explanation that they thought best made sense of this phenomenon. Respondents were given four choices: (1) Black individuals are biologically inferior to white individuals; (2) Black individuals are lazy; (3) Black individuals often receive an inferior education to that of white individuals for social, economic, and political reasons; and (4) Black individuals have been the victims of systematic discrimination and racism, creating an array of disadvantages.

The first two options describe individual-level problems, and the latter two options describe structural-level problems. The authors found that an overwhelming majority of self-described white evangelicals chose one of the first two explanations. In other words, according to their study, most white evangelicals frame the problem of racial inequality as an individual-level problem, and have therefore failed to recognize the structural attributes of racism that have perniciously maintained its existence.[41]

But there was an interesting wrinkle to this study. Emerson and Smith discovered that white individuals who had more contact with African Americans on a daily basis held views that were more sympathetic to, and reflective of, the structural influences on contemporary racial differences. That is, greater exposure to African Americans changed the perceptions of white evangelicals, leading them to describe race and segregation in much different terms (less individualistic, more structural).[42]

So what was going on? The authors called it "contact theory," which asserts that having contact with people from other groups can reduce prejudice and other fears that might be otherwise understood as mere "preference."[43] The authors summarize their theory:

> The higher the contact with black Americans, the less likely our respondents attribute primacy to individual-level explanations of the racial gap, and the more likely they are to attribute primacy to structural-level explanations. This appears to result from increased contact.[44]

Contact theory is a promising sociological view, but if its underlying assertion is that contact with others (particularly those who are different than us) can refashion us, then we cannot say that the theory is new. Indeed, this is what theologians in the "works of mercy" tradition have long understood: *relationships change us.* In particular, closeness with people whose background is different from ours facilitates the process of humility in each of us. John Wesley understood this as a "means of grace"—an opportunity for God to channel his grace to us through our direct interaction with those in need.

As a final note, works of mercy remind us that our lives are but a few events away from being altered dramatically. Once while hiking with some friends near a steep cliff, my friends' toddler broke from the ranks and inexplicably darted for the edge. Thanks to quick action by his father, he was stopped short a few precarious feet away from what would have been a fatal plummet. We all collectively gasped, knowing the traumatic turn our otherwise pleasant trip could have taken. At the end of the day, when asked whether he enjoyed the hike, the toddler responded, "Not really—I got my shoes wet." I recall thinking, "Trust me, your day could have been a lot worse than wet shoes!" We all hiked off the mountain with a renewed sense of gratitude, knowing that mere inches would not only have altered the day, but our lives.

Here is the point: works of mercy remind us that we are human like so many others. We become acutely aware that we are "inches" from swapping places with those we minister to. As my father used to remind me, "We are all an event away from tragedy." Thus, works of mercy and contact with the least and the last are helpful reminders of our precarious earthly walk and our necessary link with all of humanity. Understood in this context, gratitude and humility become unavoidable.

Conclusion

Before ending this chapter, two important points need to be made.

First, as mentioned earlier in our discussion of Micah 6, God does not desire the sacrifice of calves, rams, oil, or even our firstborn—he desires that humans offer themselves in service and in love to both God and others. Furthermore, virtues of justice, charity, and humility reflect the very character attributes of God himself. That is, God has first put forward a picture of the very love he commands ("I have shown you what is good").

But don't miss this: the call to justice, mercy, and humility is not simply a sacrifice to God; in fact, it is not a sacrifice at all. These virtues are not for God's benefit alone—they are for Israel's benefit. They for are our benefit today. Micah 6:8 is indeed a summary of how God wants us to live, but not as a down payment for his goodness or a penance for our badness. Ultimately, these virtues are for our own sake (and for his glory). Micah did not say, "He has shown you what he wants"; he said, "He shown you what *is good*." In this passage, God is turning our attention back to the essence of what it means to be a Christian and, at the same time, what it means to be a human.

Second, these aforementioned practices are rightly referred to as "disciplines" because they are within our realm of control. If the Christian practices of justice, mercy, and humility were not possible, then we would not refer to them as disciplines. The very word implies our capacity to carry them out. As this chapter suggested in its introduction, who we are will have an impact upon what we do. However, what we do can also influence who we are. That is, change can also come from the outside in.

And yet, true as this may be, there is another important caveat that demands our consideration. Being who God desires us to be is not entirely a matter of discipline and practice. Our innermost self cannot be restored by our actions alone. As James Loder writes, "It is the personal author of the universe whose Spirit alone can set the human spirit free from its proclivity to self-inflation, self-doubt, self-absorption, and self-destruction."[45] Spiritual disciplines are fundamentally necessary in the life of faith. However, if they were all that was necessary for robust Christian virtue and transformation, then we would risk creating a Christian version of "Invictus," where we raise ourselves up by our own moral bootstraps. That, of course, is not possible. Our "being" is more than the sum of our actions.

The virtuous life—the life where we best apprehend the good, the right, and the true—is certainly cultivated through disciplined Christian practices. However, these practices cannot be understood outside of a rich and robust relationship with our Creator. To know the best way to organize and arrange my life, I must know what my life purpose is, what I was designed for. Therefore, I must know the Designer. So, answering "What should I do?" requires the answer to an antecedent question: "Who is Jesus?" It is in relationship with him that we discover our freedom to participate in the highest form of human potential—the good life.

Therefore, we will explore this idea more carefully in chapter 6.

DISCUSSION QUESTIONS
FOR GROUP STUDY

1. The chapter began by suggesting that human transformation tends to come from the inside-out: change the person, change the behavior. This is particularly true in modern evangelical thinking. However, it was suggested that behavior can also influence the person. Can you provide your own example of this, where repeatedly doing something influenced who you were?

2. Recall Tim Keller's suggestion that "Micah 6:8 is a summary of how God wants us to live." Would you agree with this? Why or why not?

3. It was suggested that "giving begets giving." Provide an example where you have seen this occur in your own life.

4. The chapter described practices associated with "justice and mercy" as generosity, charitable judgment, and steadfast love through a regular regiment of spiritual disciplines. What might these practices look like in your own life today? How can they evolve from practices to habits?

5. The chapter also described practices associated with humble wisdom such as confession (or "agreement") and works of mercy. What might these practices look like in your own life today? How can they evolve from practices to habits?

6. What is keeping you from a more disciplined life of faith? If you are not being disciplined into a life of faith, what are you disciplining yourself into? That is, who are you becoming based upon your actions today?

7. What does it mean that "God has first put forward a picture of the very love he commands"?

6

Virtue beyond Habits

The incarnation took all that properly belongs to our
humanity and delivered it back to us, redeemed. All of our
inclinations and appetites and capacities and yearnings are
purified and gathered up and glorified by Christ. He did
not come to thin out human life; He came to set it free.

—Thomas Howard, *Evangelical Is Not Enough*

The idea of reaching a "good life" without Christ is based on a
double error. Firstly, we cannot do it; and secondly, in setting
up "a good life" as our final goal, we have missed the very point
of our existence. Morality is a mountain which we cannot climb
by our own efforts; and if we could we should only perish in
the ice and unbreakable air of the summit, lacking those wings
with which the rest of the journey has to be accomplished.
For it is from there that the real ascent begins. The ropes
and axes are "done away" and the rest is a matter of flying.

—C. S. Lewis, "Man or Rabbit?," *God in the Dock*

Introduction

In chapter 5, we explored how disciplines (things within our
control) can help to cultivate our inner self. According to Aristotle,
our repetitive habits play a significant role in shaping our character and identity. That is, we become what we do. The apostle Paul
would certainly agree that habits play a role in shaping character.
After all, Paul compares spiritual training to athletic training: disciplining oneself in such a way as to "get the prize" (1 Cor. 9:24 NIV).
Elsewhere he encourages people of faith to practice godly training:

"Exercise daily in God—no spiritual flabbiness, please! Workouts in the gymnasium are useful, but a disciplined life in God is far more so, making you fit both today and forever" (1 Tim. 4:7, *The Message*).

Yet we would be making a considerable mistake if we believed that Paul was simply superimposing Aristotelian ethics over his own spiritual and theological grid. Aristotle and Paul may share some similarity when it comes to the language of training for character, but they part company dramatically when it comes to the degree of change we can command in and of ourselves.

For Aristotle, characteristics of a moral life reflect virtue, and such virtues are cultivated through training and practice.[1] He describes goodness as exercising the capacities that make us distinctively human. Namely, this is our ability to reason and to exercise our will. Here, reason and will are benign: blank slates to be developed for better or for worse. Further, this places the responsibility for moral excellence upon us. If character is realized through our efforts alone, then each individual is accountable for their virtue or lack thereof. That is, they are *self*-sufficient for *self*-actualization.

In contrast, for Paul, virtue has less to do with self-development and cultivation. Rather, human excellence is necessarily bound up in a person's life of faith. Scholar Kelvin Knight writes:

> Whereas Aristotle praises self-cultivation and condemns what is servile, Paul commends the service of others. Self-sufficiency is something of which human beings are utterly incapable, and for self-sufficiency to be an ethical ideal is the sin of philosophical pride. The temporal perfection that marks out some is due to their faith, not to any habitual excellence gained through personal practice.[2]

In the Christian community, someone's worth or goodness is not achieved through self-development. Rather, goodness is an attribute of God that is conferred upon men and women through God's own love. Such love is offered in a charitable sense, and righteous behavior toward one another reflects a similar charity. Knight writes: "This idea of charity—of the goodness of God, or of any agent, being manifest in his generating or producing something for its own good, or for the good of others—is something utterly alien to Aristotle."[3]

So while Aristotle and Paul share similar conceptions of actions, disciplines, and development, they differ in matters of self-sufficiency and the breadth of human potential. Put differently, in Paul's theology, there are some things that God must do in us that we cannot do in ourselves. Before exploring this in more detail, it is first necessary to understand why we lack sufficiency in and of ourselves.

Creation, Communion, and "Flat Tires"

The Christian metanarrative can be summarized in five simple phases: God, Creation, Fall, Redemption, and Restoration. While seemingly basic, a close inspection of this outline reveals a complex and significant storyline. Specifically, there are two areas worth concentrating on for our purposes.

Although this will be counterintuitive to how we think of storytelling, it is helpful to start by exploring the middle of this metanarrative: we are *fallen*. That is, the presence of sin has distorted God's original design for humankind. In Matthew 19, Jesus has a thought-provoking interaction with the Pharisees relating to marriage and divorce. After they question him about the permissibility of divorce, Jesus responds by pointing them to God's purpose for marriage: "'For this reason a man will leave his father and mother and be united to his wife, and the two will become one flesh.' . . . Therefore what God has joined together, let no one separate" (Matt. 19:5–6). Not satisfied, the Pharisees quickly point out that Moses allowed for divorce, to which Jesus responds: "Moses permitted you to divorce your wives because your hearts were hard. *But it was not this way from the beginning*" (Matt. 19:8 NIV; italics mine).

According to Christopher West, this reply ("it was not this way from the beginning") provides a key to understanding the gospel message in its entirety.[4] In other words, Jesus is telling the Pharisees that if a relationship is so dysfunctional and acrimonious that it requires divorce, something has gone terribly wrong. Jesus is pointing them to what humans were designed for—*relationship*—not simply what is right, wrong, or permissible.

For clarity, West gives a helpful modern day reading of this text:

> It is as if we are all driving around town in cars with flat tires. The
> rubber is shredding off the rims; the rims are getting all dented up;
> and we just think this is normal. After all, everyone's tires look this
> way. According to the analogy, Jesus is saying to the Pharisees (and
> to all of us), "In the beginning, they had air in the tires."[5]

In a play on John 3:16, West continues, "But do not despair! Christ
came into the world not to condemn those with flat tires. He came
into the world to re-inflate our flat tires."[6] This leads to the next area
of the Christian metanarrative worth considering: the beginning.
Prior to the fall, or what orthodox faith calls "original sin," there
was God and creation.

But why did God create? This was a question posed by the German philosopher Friedrich Hegel. After considering the Genesis
narrative, he asks, "If God is all-sufficient and lacks nothing, how
does he come to release himself into something so utterly unequal
to him?"[7] In other words, if God is sufficient in and of himself,
why did he need to create a world, and moreover, people to inhabit
that world?

Hegel attempts to answer his own question by suggesting that
God is insufficient without a creation to confer his *god-ness* upon
him: "Without the world," he writes, "God is not God."[8] This picture,
at best, makes God seem insecure: a cosmic creator in need of a
creation to reinforce his lordship. The implication is that creation
does not exist because God *is* sufficient, but rather so that he can
be sufficient.

A more theologically sound answer can be found by rearrang-
ing the question. Not "why" did God create, but rather, what does
creation tell us about God? Among other things, it tells us that God
is loving and relational. West writes, "And here is why we exist: Love,
by its nature, desires to expand its own communion."[9] Creation is
not a function of God's insecurity; it is an *overflow* of his love. It is
in God's nature to relate and commune.

This allows us to draw back the curtain and discover the Designer's grand storyline for our lives. In his book *With*, Skye Jethani
writes, "If the Bible were the script for a play, both the opening

scene and the final act of this drama would focus on God's desire to live and rule with his people."[10] Not only do we know the beginning of this story, but we know the ending too. The narrative begins—and ends—with communion. That is, the fall ruptured our communion with God, but our teleological purpose is to be brought back into communion with him so that humanity can properly reflect his image ("Restoration").

So what is preventing us from communion with God? We could distill the problem down to *confusion* and *capacity*. Continuing his analogy, Jethani writes, "It is as if we entered the theater late and left before the final curtain. As a result, we have a skewed understanding of the story."[11] In other words, as characters in this metanarrative, we are confused about our purpose. This is not meant to suggest that people are purposeless or that their lives lack meaning. On the contrary, observe anyone's life and you will see a series of overtures toward what that person considers to be meaningful. Ideas of purpose, meaning, and significance almost always animate our actions and behaviors.

And yet, according to the Christian metanarrative, virtue cannot be defined based upon our own idiosyncratic preferences, but only in relation to our teleological end as humans. In other words, questions of purpose, meaning, and significance cannot be separated from questions of design. Function must always flow from form. As mentioned, if we understood God's metanarrative from start to finish (rather than, as Jethani describes, wandering in during the middle of the act), we would recognize that a core component of human excellence relates to our communion with God.

God is love. As image-bearers of a loving God, we have been endowed with the capacity to love ("We love because he first loved us," 1 John 4:19). Love, by definition, spills over into the life of others, and this was God's grand design for humanity. It is for this reason that Jesus declares that no greater commandments exist than loving God and loving others (Mark 12:30–31). Love overflows; love communes with others.

But confusion is not the only factor prohibiting our communion with God. We must consider our capacity—or, in West's terms, our "flat tires." This is a significant problem, because unlike confusion, which can be sorted out intellectually, our capacity is not something we can so easily remedy, particularly on our own. To understand why, we have to consider the nature of sin. Our common definitions of sin include "missing the mark" or "transgressing the known will of God." While not untrue, these descriptions risk suggesting that sin is about an ethic (what we do), and not an ethos (our disposition). We make a mistake if we understand the former independently of the latter.

Why? Because we may master an ethic, but if we lack the ethos, we are no better off. Even worse, in some ways we may be more dangerous, since "a good doctor is also a good poisoner."[12] In a more comprehensive sense, sin, as an idea, implies "forfeiture"— that is, we are forfeiting God's power and instead turning to our own self-sufficiency, or what is referred to in the New Testament as "the flesh." Here, our *flesh* is the dimension of our humanity that is alienated from the one we were meant to be in harmonious communion with: God.[13] Not only are we alienated from God, our self-referencing posture inevitably alienates us from others as well. So while love spills over into the life of others as mentioned above, our inward-curving nature (our ethos) prohibits us from realizing fulfillment and wholeness in our relationships with both God and neighbor. What, then, are we to do?

In short, we cannot do much of anything. That is, there are some things that only God can do for us that we are unable to do for ourselves. To summarize the problems associated with being fallen: there is a fracture between ourselves, others, and our Creator, God. Moreover, our habits, practices, and piety alone cannot reconcile this fracture. Not because it is difficult. More accurately, it is unattainable. It is impossible to enter God's kingdom on our own merits (Mark 10:27); it is impossible to eradicate the problem of sin through man-made sacrifice (Heb. 10:4); it is impossible to please God without trusting and saving faith (Heb. 11:6). Thankfully, while the faith life is impossible in and of ourselves, "all things are possible" with God (Matt. 19:26).

Therefore, if we are sticking to the script—that is, to the overarching metanarrative of the orthodox faith tradition that begins and ends with communion—then there are at least three relevant forms of empowerment that must come through God alone: harmony with ourselves, harmony with others, and harmony with God. Before concluding, the balance of this chapter will look at each in turn.

What God Does for Us—Identity and Self-Harmony

To understand what it means to be in harmony with ourselves, we must understand our true identity. To understand our true identity, we must look at the concept of narrative.

Among other things, narratives are useful because they provide a lens for us to make sense of reality. As Alasdair MacIntyre has argued in his influential book *After Virtue*, life's random data (actions, ideas, events, phenomena, etc.) become intelligible when understood within a larger narrative. This claim is true for nearly everything, including our existence. To paraphrase Ross Douthat, we find ourselves born into a mysterious and mysteriously ordered universe.[14] What are we to make of this? Where did this order come from? Who am I in relation to the order I see around me? Part of being human is attempting to make sense of the world we occupy and its origins. To do this, we start with a story.

But the stories differ. One narrative, for example, speaks to a deliberate Creator. This is the narrative associated with traditional orthodox faith. Another narrative, what we might call the humanist narrative, describes the universe as mechanical, with our world and its inhabitants coming into existence as a random by-product.[15] They each have their own explanation of humans, the world, and humans within the world.

More specifically, the latter story goes something like this. First, our population is just a collection of individuals. That is, people are "the basic unit of society." From Margaret Thatcher's famous proclamation that "There is no such thing as society"[16] to Ayn Rand's assertion that "a man must be free from his brothers" to attain true freedom, the individual is often emphasized at the expense of the larger idea of society.[17] What is a society, so goes the narrative, if not a collection of individuals?

Second, in this story, the rights conferred upon individuals within a fair and equitable democracy are meant to offer persons in society the opportunity to conceive of, and cultivate, their conception of what is best for their life. We might call this a *pragmatic* conception of society, since members of society have competing visions of what a good life is. Therefore, "A consensus on these principles thus insulates the political process from fundamental moral conflict."[18] In other words, if we cannot agree upon a common vision of humanity worth organizing ourselves around, it is best to simply create the conditions that let people pursue their own vision.[19] At the very least, this perspective is fair, impartial, and neutral (recall the description of a "liberal" society in chapter 2). As Michael Sandel has pointed out, whether one identifies as a Republican or Democrat, this conception "assume[s] that freedom consists in the capacity of people to choose their own ends."[20] As emphasized in chapter 3, these conditions promote choice as the dominant cultural value.

There is a third characteristic to this story worth mentioning. With the state serving as guarantor of our individual rights, the marketplace is understood as the realm where we can satisfy our preferences and maximize our own utility. This, naturally, gives way to consumerism (the belief that our well-being is closely attached to fulfilling our various desires through marketplace purchases).[21]

Among other things, this narrative advances an image of humans detached from any prior commitments or social identity. Sandel refers to such a conception as the *unencumbered self*, or "a self understood prior to and independent of its purposes and ends."[22] We may note that this conception undermines two important aspects of the Christian faith narrative: first, the idea that we are relational beings; and second, that we have a distinct identity conferred upon us by our Creator.

Under the humanist narrative, our individuality supersedes our relational commitments. One famous philosopher even went so far as to refer to communal, other-oriented attributes as a weakness, since they are antithetical to autonomy.[23] In contrast, the Christian narrative is clear: we have a distinct relational dimension. John Wesley, for example, points out that our relational capacity is not merely an attribute we possess, but the very blueprint of human nature: "Let us always remember the kindred between man and man, and cultivate that happy instinct whereby, in the original constitution of our nature, God has strongly bound us to each other."[24] A significant part of being human is to commune: communion with God and communion with others.

Being "relationally constituted" has implications for our identity and for establishing our sense of personhood. Specifically, our relationships and the communities in which we develop our relationships serve as formative mechanisms in shaping our sense of who we are. Or, as one theologian puts it, "Identity and fulfillment are inextricably bound up with relations and communities."[25]

This line of thinking reaches back several centuries, but it was given a clear social articulation in the work of George Herbert Mead (1863–1931), who claimed that individuals experience themselves only by means of reflection in a social context[26]—a position respected and held by many social theorists today.[27]

By suggesting that relationships shape our identity, Mead "reversed the traditional assumptions underlying philosophical, psychological, and sociological thought to the effect that human beings possess minds and consciousness as original 'givens.'"[28] In contrast, Mead maintained that interaction with others allows us to understand ourselves within the world, not merely respond to it. The shift here is that being an individual requires the presence, not absence, of others. Theologian Stanley Hauerwas provides a helpful summary of Mead's influence: "We are not 'I's' who decide to identify with certain 'we's'; we are first of all 'we's' who discover our 'I's' through learning to recognize the other as similar and different from ourselves."[29] By virtue of knowing others, I can actually know myself. That is, because others are, *I am*.[30]

Why is this even important? Because, if true, this means that relational commitments are not an encumbrance upon me, but a pathway toward freedom to experience fulfillment, meaning, and identity with others. It is through affiliation, not isolated self-appraisal, that my identity inevitably surfaces. Personhood, here, can only be defined relationally. To speak of personhood independent of other persons is a helplessly incoherent expression.

There is an important qualification to this. The problems we've identified with using the "particularities" of the individual as a reference point for truth and goodness are not necessarily overcome by appealing to the "particularities" of the community. For example, the identities of young men and women growing up in Nazi Germany were, no doubt, well-formed and commonly understood in the late 1930s and early 1940s. This, however, does not mean that that identity was true or healthy.

The point to be made is this: eventually we must implicitly or explicitly judge the *truthfulness* of the story. Alasdair MacIntyre has defined truth as balancing "the mind's judgment of a thing to the reality of that thing."[31] It is not simply the story, but the truthful story, that accurately reflects reality and transcends the otherwise relative nature of our various narratives. Courtroom judges and juries are constantly assessing the claims of competing narratives. Of course, they are hardly satisfied to simply hear these narratives. Rather, they ideally want to determine which depiction of events best coheres with reality.

For those within the faith tradition, the aforementioned Christian metanarrative does not simply exist as "one other story" to make sense of the world. Rather, we believe and affirm it to be the true story. It is the story that qualifies all other stories. To paraphrase Ravi Zacharias, our hope as Christians is not necessarily true simply because it is livable, but rather, it is livable because it is true.

This has implications for restoring humans to a proper conception of self. As we know, behind every story is a storyteller. In contrast to the humanist narrative, we cannot simply define virtue or pursue our own conception of "good" based upon our preferences, but only in relation to our purpose as humans. Understood within the creation narrative, this naturally draws us to the Creator. Hauerwas writes:

> Not only is knowledge of self tied to knowledge of God, but we know ourselves truthfully only when we know ourselves in relation to God. We know who we are only when we can place our selves—locate our stories—within God's story.[32]

It is in relationship with our Creator that we can understand ourselves, or perhaps more accurately, our "pre-fig leaf" selves (in Christopher West's terms). It was after the fall, in Genesis 3, that man and woman became fragmented—cut off and alienated from their source of fulfillment. Freedom in communion with one another was replaced by shame, fear, and distrust. Our reason became contaminated by an impulse toward self-indulgence. Self-preservation steered our will toward self-serving action. The innocent became insidious, authenticity was traded for deceit, and discord threatened the promise of unified relationships. We became "divided selves," constituted by gaps between our intentions and our actual performance. This is not simply what we do; it is who we are. Our *nature*.

This is why identity in God and the Christian narrative is so important. The story offers us a picture of an alternative reality: "*But it was not this way from the beginning.*" It speaks to humans as being deliberately designed by a loving Designer—made to commune with God and others and to find deep and lasting fulfillment in those relationships. Because we know who he is, we can truly know and understand who we are.

What God Does for Us: A New Attitude toward Others

Some time ago I attended a workshop at a faith-based institution related to peace and conflict transformation. They kicked off the event by defining *peace*: "Not the absence of conflict, but the presence of goodwill toward another." I loved the definition. It spoke to peacefulness as *shalom*, or harmony with one's self and others—which is consonant with the orthodox faith tradition.

After a rich discussion about peace and goodwill, the workshop transitioned into the topic of "peace-building." That is, thinking carefully about the conditions necessary for peace to occur. According to the presenter, these conditions include education, commerce, democracy, investment, infrastructure, and a skilled and diversified labor force.

After a while, I asked the facilitator whether the program was religiously motivated, or at the very least, offered a religious application—or whether the presence of the so-called "peace-building" conditions was sufficient to create peacefulness. The response was not what I had expected. In essence, I was told that the program had a mild religious context, but that in many ways they were trying to distance themselves from it.

I was perplexed. For one, the workshop was organized by a faith-based institution, so I found it curious that they were dismissive of their faith roots when it came to peace-building. Second, and more to the point, I was skeptical that the peace-building conditions described could actually achieve what they hoped they could.

Here is what I mean. There is little doubt that features such as education and commerce make for a peaceful social arrangement. Further, any discussion of the "common good" must necessarily consider the social, political, and economic characteristics that best allow for human flourishing. However, it is questionable whether the cocktail of attributes described at the workshop can bring about the peace the presenters so eloquently defined as "presence of good-will toward another." Can democratic governance make me love my neighbor? Can economic prosperity force me to evaluate the violence in my own heart? Does education inevitably lead to *shalom*? Will outside investment make me selfless? I suspect that I am not alone in my skepticism when I suggest that the answer is "no."

So while peace-building attributes may help to minimize conflict, they cannot create goodwill. Human effort, ingenuity, and industriousness naturally provide conditions that make our lives easier, but we cannot simply manufacture love toward another. We were designed to commune with others, but something in the design is broken.

What, in our fall, has fractured our relational capacity? Recall that humans are "relationally constituted." Like all dimensions of sin, the fall did not remove this distinctive feature from humanity, but it did have a corrupting effect upon it. Humans are still relational, but those relationships are marred. Therefore, we are marked with a human tendency to objectify others as a means to an end and to perceive them as a threat to our own autonomous existence.

As the Acton Institute's Michael Miller points out, the "objectification" of the other is a product of the fall.[33] After the fall we risk
classifying the other not as a subject like ourselves, but as *non habens
personam*—that is, a person who lacks personhood, a "no person."
Moreover, some of our ugliest blights on historical record can be
traced to the objectification of those who were different than us.
This became particularly evident to me when I visited the Holocaust Museum in Washington, DC, where I found myself before
an exhibit related to Nazi propaganda. The exhibit was described as
revealing "how the Nazi Party used modern techniques as well as
new technologies and carefully crafted messages to sway millions
with its vision for a new Germany."[34]

It was not what was in these "carefully crafted messages" that
piqued my interest, but rather what was left out. There were no
inflammatory letters, signs, or posters aimed at Jewish society. Absent was any violent imagery of their necessary demise as a people.
There were no calls for Jews to be expunged. No blueprint for wide-
scale genocide. In no document was the expression "final solution"
found. Instead, the message was far more subtle: *Jews are different.*
Propaganda included messages not to date Jews, patronize their
stores, or socialize with them in general.

How could this somewhat innocuous language inspire the justification of the century's most heinous act of violence toward a
single group of people? Because it began by objectifying them. This,
I submit, is far more insidious and devilish than we might imagine.
The impetus to annihilate the Jewish people did not originate with
violent imagery, but rather, with the simple suggestion that Jews
were a distinct *other* not to be included. They did not belong. They
were not members. It is difficult to commit violence against another
human being; less difficult, however, is an attack upon "no persons."
Whether it is Nazi-inspired violence against Jews or other minor-
ity groups, Jim Crowe-era segregation and exploitation of African
Americans, or twentieth-century marginalization of women, the
pathway toward harming another is most efficiently drawn through
their dehumanization.

Objectifying others not only strips them of their essence (allowing for acts of violence), but risks instrumentalizing them as

well. In this sense, the other person's goodness is measured by their usefulness to us. Indeed, it is when we see others as less than human that they become most eligible, in our minds, for exploitation to serve our own needs. For example, a recent article from a popular news outlet praised the potential of pornography to provide more "variety and stimulation" for adults.[35] These are "exciting times," the article reads, because now adults can better explore the variety of sexual fantasies that "get them off." Such logic no longer encourages the expression of self-giving love with one's partner. In its place, the "other" person is merely a means to an erotic end—and with the "benefits" of pornography, an increasingly unnecessary one at that.

Not only does our fallen nature lead us to objectify others, it also casts suspicion upon others as an inherent threat to our individuality. Consider the opening passage from Reinhold Niebuhr's famous book *Moral Man and Immoral Society*:

> Though human society has roots which lie deeper in history than the beginning of human life, men have made comparatively but little progress in solving the problem of their aggregate existence. Each century originates a new complexity and each new generation faces a new vexation in it. For all the centuries of experience, men have not yet learned how to live together without compounding their vices and covering each other "with mud and with blood." The society in which each man lives is at once the basis for, and the nemesis of, that fulness [sic] of life which each man seeks.[36]

Of course, the "problem of aggregate existence" is nothing new. Genesis 4 documents the well-known story of Cain and Abel. After being shown up by his brother before God, Cain's anger quickly cascades into violence, leading him to murder Abel.

It is clear that Cain's rage got the best of him, but it is what he says to God after being kicked out of the garden that gives curious insight into his state of mind: "Today you are driving me from the land, and I will be hidden from your presence; I will be a restless wanderer on the earth, *and whoever finds me will kill me*" (v. 14 NIV; italics mine). Cain recognizes that the mix of fear, distrust, and hostility he finds in himself is likely present in others. If others are a threat to him—even his own family members—then it stands to reason that he is equally a threat to others. Being driven out of God's land now means being thrust into unfamiliar and hostile territory. Ever since, the human tendency toward fear, distrust, and violence—covering each other with "mud and blood"—has been one of the more predictable patterns in human history.

In addition to this, the perception that "others" are a threat underlies a considerable portion of our modern sociopolitical arrangements. As discussed in chapter 2, "social contract" arrangements assume that we must give up some of our rights as a means to achieve "order." For, without order, life would be—according to Thomas Hobbes—"solitary, poor, nasty, brutish, and short."[37] That is, humanity in a "state of nature" (a state without rules or governance) would be characterized by violence, discord, and disunity.

Nearly a century after Hobbes provided his ominous picture of humanity, the Rector Reverend Elisha Williams addressed the 1744 graduating class of Yale with the following thoughts:

> Thus every man having a natural right to (or being proprietor of) his own person and his own actions and labour, which we call property, it certainly follows, that no man can have a right to the person or property of another: And if every man has a right to his person and property; he has also a right to defend them . . . and so has a right of punishing all insults upon his person and property.[38]

Williams suggests that certain rights are not only due to individuals, but that they should be defended *against* other individuals. Thus, the very presence of rights-based language presupposes a certain degree of conflict within society. Regarding the "rights-based" society, Sandel writes: "It is a striking feature of the welfare state that it offers a powerful promise of individual rights, and also demands of its citizens a high measure of mutual engagement. But the self-image that attends to rights cannot sustain that engagement."[39]

"For Thine Is the Kingdom"

So, to summarize: humans have a relational blueprint. Indeed, we bear the image of a relational Creator. However, our fallen nature has polluted our relational capacity, leaving us to objectify others or perceive them as threats.

Recall from the earlier section that living within God's meta-narrative provides another window for conceptualizing ourselves and our relationship to others. Our story does not end in the fall. Through God's redeeming act, our final chapter is restoration. Our destiny, and thus our current trajectory, is communion. Hauerwas writes:

> To be "at peace with ourselves" means we have the confidence, gained through participation in the adventure we call God's kingdom, to trust ourselves and others. Such confidence becomes the source of our character and our freedom as we are loosed from a debilitating preoccupation with ourselves. Moreover, by learning to be at peace with ourselves, we find we can live at peace with one another. And this freedom, after all, is the only freedom worth having.[40]

Living into God's story allows us to properly see ourselves as the subjects of his creative love. As Hauerwas reminds us, there is freedom in this—a restored conception of self and the liberty to "re-subjectify" one another.

How does one simply go about "living" into God's story? How do we recognize and participate in the overarching kingdom narrative? Jesus, in John 3, speaks of being "born again" in order to "see the Kingdom of God" (v. 3). This, according to Jesus, is not birth as we think of it, but a spiritual rebirth—being born from above. *The Message* translation of John 3:5–6 reads:

> Unless a person submits to this original creation—the 'wind-hovering-over-the-water' creation, the invisible moving the visible, a baptism into a new life—it's not possible to enter God's kingdom. When you look at a baby, it's just that: a body you can look at and touch. But the person who takes shape within is formed by something you can't see and touch—the Spirit—and becomes a living spirit.

A fleshly birth means we resemble our earthly parents; a spiritual birth means that we resemble our Creator. This "baptism into new life" not only provides us with a different grid upon which to understand reality, but empowers us for outward expressions of self-giving love toward others. We have "air in the tires," that is, new capacities—not least of which is the capacity for righteousness, or "right relationship" with others. We can now appreciate others for their inherent qualities. Our autonomy need not become a reflex for doing what we want, but rather, it can serve as a freedom to do what we know is right. Our rights can be governed by our concern for the other. Right relationships mean that love becomes an overture originating out of our love for others, not necessarily reciprocity (what we get in return). This unconditional, or *agape*, love has no competitor in the realm of human excellence and virtue. In the words of Shakespeare: "Love sought is good, but given unsought is better."[41]

The fear, distrust, and objectification that marked our conception of others need not govern us. Rather, those attributes that characterize the fall are replaced with love. Not only is there no fear in love—we have been the recipients of such self-giving love, and therefore we are free to "love because he first loved us" (1 John 4:18–19).

An illustration may help to make this clear. Years ago, I had the fortune of meeting a chaplain associated with Kairos Prison Ministry. Kairos is an international faith initiative that aims to "bring Christ's love and forgiveness to incarcerated individuals and to their families."[42] The program is unique in that it allows teams to enter into prison facilities and share fellowship with inmates over a multi-day period.

During our conversation, the chaplain described an unforgettable story about a recent visit to a maximum-security facility. Prior to their team's arrival, he asked the warden for the opportunity to invite various gang leaders to their initial gathering. The rationale was simple: influence the leaders, and you will inevitably influence their followers. The warden was understandably horrified at the idea. Assembling rival gangs and their leaders in one space was a risky venture at best. Despite his concerns, though, the warden agreed.

On the first day of their visit, the atmosphere was tense. The room was filled with an odd assortment of inmates who, in essence, were everyday threats to one another. This was not simply about a lack of harmony or trust. It was about hate. One particularly nasty conflict in the room related to race. The battleground of black versus white had long been established within the prison, and the Kairos ministry program had put these opposing gangs within dangerous proximity of one another.

Despite the tension, the opening day would go without incident. Moreover, between their initial meeting Thursday and their closing on Sunday, the ministry had been an amazing success. "God showed up," the chaplain said, "It was very powerful." Perhaps the greatest evidence of change came on Sunday. A young African American who was otherwise considered a black gang leader came to the front to give his testimony to other inmates. He had reconciled with one of his former white adversaries—an individual referred to as "Robber." While brief, his testimony left a compelling witness: "You all would have never believed that *Robber* and I would reconcile with one another." He paused. "By the way, his name is Dennis." After this beautiful display of humanizing another by giving voice to his real name, the two men met on stage and exchanged a loving embrace in front of all other inmates.

The story is powerful. But there was an additional detail in the chaplain's recounting that gave me great pause. Unbeknownst to the prisoners, an armed SWAT team stood outside the doors of the room where they met. Organized in advance by the nervous warden, the team was prepared to burst through the doors at any moment should the meeting have escalated into violence.

This presents quite a contrast, does it not? The actions of the SWAT team—armed with guns, clubs, shields, and other combative gear—would have undoubtedly exerted an influential force. Yet for all of their power, the reach of that force is limited.

No doubt the SWAT team could have penetrated the room and immediately brought any violent overtures to an equally violent halt. But they could not have broken down the barriers of gang affiliation and hatred already present in the prison. The guards could have tactically subdued the men within moments. But they could not have made the inmates see the humanity in each other ("His name is Dennis"). The team could have imposed order within the room. But they could not have made two men who on a normal day would have chosen to kill each other embrace in a public display of charity, kindness, and goodwill.

Here is the larger point: we can create the conditions for peace, security, and order. With the right resources, these things are technically within our realm of control. But we cannot impose love. We cannot muster up goodwill toward another by force. We cannot simply trade in malevolence for benevolence. Simply put, we don't have the constitution for it. We are not wired that way. Moreover, we cannot "rewire" ourselves. Our tainted relational capacity, and the problems that it breeds, are a function of our fallen nature. Yet Christ's atoning death on the cross did not simply justify us before God, but restored us toward others. Moreover, as the next section will aim to make clear, it restored our communion with God.

What God Does for Us: A Restored Relationship with the Creator

A story is told about an exchange between the famous author Henry David Thoreau and a family member while Thoreau was on his deathbed. "Have you made your peace with God?" the family member asked the sick and frail man. Thoreau's response, while cynical, was characteristic of his wit: "I did not know we had ever quarreled."

If we were to describe Christianity as a long journey, then recognizing that there is a "quarrel" between ourselves and God would represent the first step. Indeed, Paul describes the mind that is governed by the flesh as being "hostile" to God (Rom. 8:7). This is the nature of our fallen selves: we have been cut off from communion with our Creator, Designer, and Lover.

As mentioned above, the Christian metanarrative begins with communion. Therefore, to understand the restoration God is inviting us into, we must take stock of the relational attributes between God and humanity that were lost as a function of the fall. Communion connotes an idea of love, or more specifically, self-giving love. Moreover, love must be freely given. It would be absurd to propose marriage to someone while holding a gun to their head,

and then to subsequently call it "love" should they agree. Therefore, for love to be love, it must be necessarily preceded by *agency*.
To have agency is to have free will. So, while God did not create
us with a fallen nature, he did create us to love and to commune.
However, our exercise of free will for our own sakes, and not for
the sake of others (neighbor and God), corrupted our agency and
made us, in C. S. Lewis's terms, "a horror to God and ill-adapted
to the universe."[43] Moreover, Lewis goes on to suggest that the fall
did not "deprave our knowledge of the law in the same degree as
it depraved our power to fulfill it."[44]

This is consistent with Paul's description of humanity in his
letter to the Romans.[45] While writing to "God's beloved in Rome,"
Paul is clear that while we were sinners, Christ died for us (Rom.
5:8). Moreover, where sin rises up in our lives, grace rises up all
the more to cover it (Rom. 5:20). In other words, there is no sinful
state or action that we can experience that is not completely and
exhaustively met with God's own favor.

Paul anticipates the questions this might raise, and opens the
next chapter of Romans with one of them: "Shall we continue to
sin since our sins are always met with grace?" (v. 2 NIV). "Absolutely not!" he responds. We have moved away from sin; why
would we return to it? In fact, Paul tells the believers to consider
themselves "dead" to the life of sin. So this raises a new question
which is brought up in Romans 7, which, in essence, says, "If I am
to leave the sin life, am I therefore expected to make myself flawless by perfectly adhering to the law?" Wrong again. Living by the
law, writes Paul, while alienated from God (the "flesh"), simply reveals our insufficiency. We fail to do the good we desire, and we do
the evil we do not desire. The self-giving communion God had in
mind is replaced with blame, shame, fear, isolation, and hostility—
all attributes that embody the very idea of alienation from God. In
unison with Paul, we are left to cry out: "Wretched man that I am!
Who will rescue me from this body of death?" (v. 24).

Thankfully, in Romans 8, Paul spells out the remedy—being
"in" Christ Jesus (v. 1). More specifically, he writes, "For God has
done what the law, weakened by the flesh, could not do" (v. 3 NIV).
Here is the shift: the move from life in the flesh to life in the spirit

(v. 9) reflects the transition from being alienated *from* God to being connected and empowered *through* God. As the end of the last section mentioned, God's atoning act not only justifies us before him, but restores our relational capacity toward others and toward him. This is grace—God's "unmerited" gift to us. Yet we don't simply receive grace; we are renewed by it. In fact, this is the very purpose of grace—that we may change. In Romans 2, Paul writes, "Do you not realize that God's kindness is meant for your repentance?" (v. 4). In other words, God's free exercise of grace exists so that his people will have a change of mind, heart, and character. Moreover, the same grace that encourages change also serves to empower that change. Consider Paul's words in his letter to Titus:

> For the grace of God has appeared that offers salvation to all people. It teaches us to say "no" to ungodliness and worldly passions, and to live self-controlled, upright and godly lives in this present age, while we wait for the blessed hope—the appearing of the glory of our great God and Savior, Jesus Christ, who gave himself for us to redeem us from all wickedness and to purify for himself a people that are his very own, eager to do what is good. (Titus 2:11–15 NIV)

The purpose of grace as described by Paul is twofold. First, grace "teaches" or trains us to exercise the kind of holy living characteristic of God's people. This is what makes us different as people of faith. In contrast to the theology that "Christians are just like you, but forgiven" (a popular U.S. bumper sticker), Hauerwas reminds us that being set apart in the life of faith is "sacrifice and service that cannot be accounted for on the world's terms."[46] In other words, the life of faith facilitates new impulses that we cannot muster up on our own.[47]

Second, grace "purifies" us as a people who belong to God and his kingdom. Where the fall alienated us from God, grace reunites us. Grace allows us to live in the present "by the rule of what will be the case in the ultimate future."[48] That is, our virtue—empowered through faith—becomes a testimony to inhabiting God's overarching narrative for humanity.

In his book *Mere Discipleship*, Lee Camp encourages Christian practice as an alternative to modern apologetics. Camp describes the skeptics of the early church, who openly criticized the faith community, or "the way," for not delivering the prophecies of peace that the Messiah would supposedly usher in with his coming. Justin Martyr, who lived during the second century AD, offered a powerful response in his famous work *First Apology*. Camp writes:

> The fulfillment of God's purposes has already begun, [Justin] claimed, and the evidence of this fact lies in the very ethic and lifestyle of the church. Yes, there are portions of the prophetic proclamations yet to be fulfilled, which await the coming advent of Christ. But in the meanwhile, the church lives and exists as a community that bears witness to the reality of the kingdom of God having already invaded human history.[49]

Jesus' lordship is demonstrated, not with biblical proof-texting or silver-tongued speech, but with authentic Christian living by the authentic church following the authentic God. To see the manifestation of peace prophesied, we are encouraged to look at the church. The picture of unconditional love espoused by Christ himself should be evident in God's followers. This "apologetic" moves far beyond a philosophical defense and into the practice of Christian virtue, or God's kingdom "having already invaded human history."

Wholeness through Emptiness

Sin is being *incurvatus in se*—or having a heart turned inward. This idea, referenced in earlier chapters, was likely first expressed by St. Augustine of Hippo. Augustine suggests that our loves are disordered because our self is disordered. We love the wrong things. Yet Augustine could not simply clench his fists and grit his teeth to make himself love the right things. A disordered self can only be rightly ordered by the Creator through faith.

David Brooks writes, "Augustine suddenly came to realize that the solution to his problem would come only after a transformation more fundamental than any he had previously entertained, a renunciation of the very idea that he could be the source of his own solution."[50] This relates to Augustine's famous address to God, "our hearts are restless until we rest in thee." This is wholeness—being complete, not in ourselves, but in another. Given this, wholeness, ironically, comes through the emptying of one's self. This is very helpfully illustrated in a short piece written over a century ago by G. K. Chesterton. In "A Piece of Chalk," Chesterton praises the beauty of white chalk. All colors reveal a kind of beauty, but white is special. "White," he writes, "is a colour. It is not a mere absence of colour; it is a shining and affirmative thing, as fierce as red, as definite as black."[51]

In other words, most assume that the color white is neutral: it is devoid of shade, absent of expression; blank. However, Chesterton asserts that white is not the absence of color, but rather, it is the fullness of all color—expressive, vibrant, positive, and demonstrative. Indeed, we are told that white light itself represents the full spectrum of color.

But the essay was not about the color scale. Rather, Chesterton's point is that God's most beautiful paint is *white*. Just as white is not the absence of color, but the full presence of all colors; virtue is not the absence of vice, but the full presence of godliness: holy love and ordered desire. It is living in the way we were meant to live. Wholeness is arranging, managing, and navigating our lives in a unified manner, or what Ezekiel 11:19 describes as having an "undivided heart." The fullness of God leaves little room within us for alternative commitments and other worldly allegiances.

This Christian irony is worth repeating again: *Having a whole self requires us to empty ourselves wholly.* Moreover, it is here that we find our fullest, most significant expression of self in a relationship with our Creator. The atoning act of Christ has settled the "quarrel." This restores us, not to ourselves, but to communion with God.

Conclusion

In chapter 5, we looked at various disciplines that can serve to cultivate or shape our character. Here, virtue is developed by what we repeatedly do so that, in the words of Iris Murdoch, "in critical moments of choice, most of the business of choosing is already done." Yet as mentioned, the term "discipline" implies activity that is within our realm of control. I can discipline myself toward better time management; I cannot (unfortunately) discipline myself to grow more hair. Therefore, in this chapter, we considered the dimensions of virtue that we cannot simply "discipline" ourselves into. Specifically, the fall fractured us—that is, we are born into an inherited disharmony with ourselves, with others, and with God. The nature of this disharmony is intricately linked with the human bent toward self-supremacy. As we might imagine, if we are the source of the problem, then we are not the source of the solution. Rather, the answer is found in submission to God. Submission means no longer enslaving ourselves to our own self-destructive behavior. Instead, we are encouraged to "offer yourselves as slaves to righteousness leading to holiness" (Rom. 6:19). Thus it is submission, the emptying of ourselves, that paves the trail for us to be restored to our "pre-fig leaf" state of humanity.

So, how do we reconcile what we do for ourselves (disciplines) and what God must do for us (submission to God)? As a first step, it is important to recognize that the ideas of self-discipline and submission are not antithetical to one another. Rather, they are complements. Second, it is helpful to borrow familiar New Testament language to understand these ideas: works and faith. Our "works" are the spiritual acts of communal worship, piety, and mercy that we can reasonably undertake. "Faith," in Scripture, is not simply belief, but trust. Moreover, it is an overture or a distinct and deliberate movement toward God.

Paul was very clear in his theology that salvation comes from grace through faith—not by our own doing. Yet there is more to this story. James also makes it clear that the exercise of faith without the presence of works is an impoverished faith. Quite similarly, it was Martin Luther who scribbled *Sola Fide* in the margins of his Bible: *Faith Alone*. Yet Luther was also quoted as saying, "Faith alone will save you. But if your faith is alone, then it isn't faith." Why? Because, as the famous hymnist Isaac Watts points out, Christ's life-giving act of atonement is an expression of love that is so amazing and divine that it "demands my soul, my life, my all." Similarly, Will Willimon writes that faith, embodied in Scripture, "Is not only forming us but also reforming us, making us over, over and over again, into people who more closely resemble the family whom *God's righteousness demands.*"[52]

Recall from chapter 5 that who we are (people of faith) and what we do (actions, disciplines) do not necessarily exist as a cause and effect relationship. Rather, they are mutually causal. They are continually reinforcing each other. Godly habits will naturally lead us to submission, but submission inevitably leads us to godly habits.

There is a final point to be made when looking at the practice of virtue. The description of a fully virtuous self may appear, on the surface, to offer a picture of some kind of a superhuman. Indeed, modern day saints such as Mother Teresa are characterized in a way that suggests they are something other than human. They are "super saints"—icons to be shelved and admired, but certainly not a height that "normal" humans could ascend to. "To err is human," we say. In other words, our humanity is best captured or reflected in our incomplete selves. We believe that it is our greed, our fear, and our failures that define what it means to be human.

Yet our apprehension, pursuit, and embodiment of virtue does not make us superhuman; it simply makes us human. In other words, we are subhuman now—we're driving on flat tires. The incomplete nature of our fallen selves was never meant to be the picture of humanity. Rather, our fullest expression of being a human being is realized in a restored harmony with self, with others, and with God. Spirituality means becoming more like Jesus, writes Jill Carattini, and subsequently, "to become more like ourselves."[53] Similarly, the Colson Center's John Stonestreet points out that Christianity is not is not simply a way to be religious, "but a distinct vision for being fully and truly human in God's world."[54]

Full humanity is the purpose of our lives. We were meant to have "air in the tires." This future trajectory has obvious significance for our present—or what N. T. Wright calls the "vocation to holiness":

> Enfolded in this vocation to build now, with gold, silver, and precious stones, the things that will last into God's new age, is the vocation to holiness: to the fully human life, reflecting the image of God, that is

180   DESIGNED FOR GOOD

made possible by Jesus' victory on the cross and that is energized by the Spirit of the risen Jesus present within communities and persons.[55]

God's overture of love toward us in the person of Jesus did not occur so that we could live some kind of a superhuman life. Jesus died so that we could be made whole and experience "the fully human life"—to be everything we were designed to be.

Humanity proper is rightly expressed in the embodiment of our design, which is our life purpose. Moreover, this insight is the key to answering the question: "Why be moral?" Our attention will now be given over to this age-old inquiry in the final chapter.

DISCUSSION QUESTIONS
FOR GROUP STUDY

1. The chapter discusses areas of our lives that are ruptured by the fall, suggesting that some dimensions of our lives cannot simply be fixed through a disciplined regimen of practices. Can you think of examples from your own life?

2. In the early 1990s the grunge band Nirvana, led by the gifted singer/songwriter Kurt Cobain, was one of the most popular alternative bands in the world. In constant pain due to a stomach ailment, and frequently espousing various nihilistic and hedonistic views of life, it was little surprise that Cobain took his life in April 1994.

   Years after his death, the movie "About a Son" was released, and documented a running conversation between Cobain and interviewer Michael Azerrad. While the singer could hardly be described as religious, one particular expression offers fascinating insight into his mind:

   > I used to think when I was young that I was adopted by my Mother because they found me in a spaceship [from a] different planet . . . and every night I used to talk to my real parents and my real family in the sky. I knew that there were thousands of other alien babies dropped off and they're all over the place and I've met quite a few of them. It's just something I like to toy with in my mind; it's really fun to pretend that. There's some special reason for me to be here. I feel really homesick all the time and so do all of the other aliens. Not only have I had the chance to come across a handful of other aliens throughout the rest of my life, eventually one day we'll find out what we're supposed to do.

   How would you make sense of Cobain's description based upon the humanist narrative described in the chapter? What about based upon the Christian narrative?

3. What are the risks to our faith if we do not recognize a "quarrel" or, more accurately, a divide between ourselves and God?

4. Where, in society, have we objectified or instrumentalized others? What would it look like to "re-subjectify" them?

5. The chapter ends by describing the relationship between our disciplines (works) and our submission to God (faith) as being mutually causal, as discussed in chapter 5. Do you think this is a good description? Why or why not?

7

WHY BE MORAL?

Rules in our society, therefore, are not derived from some
fundamental conception of the human good. They are the
basis of morality only insofar as they represent a consensus
about what is necessary to ensure societal peace and survival.

—Stanley Hauerwas

*Oderunt peccare boni, virtutis amore; Oderunt
peccare mali, formidine poenae.*
[Good men avoid sin from the love of virtue; Wicked
men avoid sin from a fear of punishment]

—John Wesley, quoting a popular Latin expression

" 'Love the Lord your God with all your heart, and with all
your soul, and with all your mind, and with all your strength.'
The second is this, 'You shall love your neighbor as yourself.'
There is no other commandment greater than these."

—Mark 12:30–31

A Final Appeal to Virtue

Let us return to the question raised by Thrasymachus and Glaucon in the introduction. Recall their conviction that the virtuous
life is not necessarily the best life. Prosperity and fulfillment, they
argue, cannot properly be derived from moral excellence. By their
calculations, it is vice, not virtue, that best allows us to secure the
things in life that make us happy. To address this, we must adequately get underneath their argument, where we find a larger
philosophical question looming: Why be moral?

The assertions made by Thrasymachus and Glaucon were penned thousands of years ago in approximately 380 BC. Amazingly, though, they are relevant today. To be clear, the question is not whether we are moral beings. Moral judgments and values are inescapable for all persons across place, space, and time. We are *morum hominum*—moral humans. Rather, the question is why we should pursue virtue in our lives. My hope is that certain themes throughout this book have surfaced that implicitly or explicitly speak to this timeless matter. So, with the book's previous chapters in mind, I want to now end by specifically addressing this question: Why should a person be moral?

A Rationale for Moral Excellence?

At the close of 2009 and in the wake of the worst financial crisis in the United States since the Depression era, the otherwise self-proclaimed free market authors writing for *The Economist* reflected on the idea of "progress."[1] On the heels of the financial meltdown, one might have expected them to give a defense of the existing free market structure.[2] After all, we still live within the most prosperous century on historical record. One need only survey past periods of economic, scientific, and technological prosperity to see that they have no parallel when compared to the present. This alone is reason enough, it might be argued, for pause when considering the distribution of blame in the wake of the financial crisis.

However, in their article "Onwards and Upwards," a different conclusion was reached.[3] Indeed, the authors conclude, after centuries of increased efficiency in producing food, enhanced scientific capacity, industrial growth, technological innovation, and gains in overall wealth among both rich and poor nations, our "material progress" has failed to deliver emotional satisfaction, overall happiness, and social solidarity. According to the article, progressing *materially* is different from progressing *morally*. In other words, we may have more possessions than previous generations, but are we better people?

The article goes on to suggest that our behavior should not be shaped by power, innovation, or material wealth, but rather by what is "right," despite the inconveniences that sometimes come with trying to be a good person. The collective pursuit of finely tuned moral sensibilities, the article contends, is a more appropriate measurement of progress and prosperity.

Many are likely to resonate with this idea, myself included. A world abundant with stuff but lacking in character still seems like an impoverished world. But there is a problem. The article fails to answer what morality, in itself, actually brings to the table. Why should the realization of virtue be considered a measure of progress? That is, why should I be moral in the first place?

Not only is this an important question, we might say that it is a foundational question, or the question underlying all the questions in this book. There are numerous attempts to answer this important issue, but I want to focus on three streams of reasoning that seem most relevant to the question: "Why be moral?" Moreover, I want to suggest that it is the third rationale that most comprehensively and compellingly links faith to virtue. Let's explore each.

Rationale #1: Goodness Works

The first answer to the question "Why be moral?" relates to the usefulness of virtue and morality. It is pragmatic. Many believe that obeying standards of goodness is necessary to achieve some desirable, practical outcome. This can take on a variety of different forms.

For example, many arguments challenge us to cohere to "good" standards because, we are told, it will improve our life outcomes. Whether we're encouraging children to eat vegetables so they can grow up strong or obeying rules because they will keep us safe, the impetus for moral and ethical action is motivated by the promise of a fruitful reward.

Another variation in the pragmatic paradigm relates to reciprocity. According to evolutionary biologist Richard Dawkins, reciprocity is a compelling "Darwinian" incentive to cloak oneself in morality.[4] Another author writes, "Reciprocity is the most logical reason for morality."⁵ That is, we should concern ourselves with the rightness, justness, and fairness of our actions toward others, because in doing so, we can reasonably expect others to concern themselves with the rightness, justness, and fairness of their actions toward us. This is evident in the way we encourage one another ("You pat my back and I'll pat yours"), or even the way we warn one another ("What goes around comes around"). Notice, here, that it is not charity toward others that motivates virtuous action, but rather a kind of *karma* that loosely promises that my good thoughts, intentions, and actions will boomerang back to me. Tit for tat.

One of the more compelling and commonly referenced pragmatic arguments for moral action relates to output. Here, virtuous behavior leads to desirable consequences in the marketplace of personal, or corporate, productivity. This argument is particularly evident in the field of "business ethics" (see chapter 2). Managers consistently extol the value of the virtues because they best clear the path toward performance and profit. If immorality in the marketplace is problematic, then more ethics, so goes the reasoning, must be good for business. One can find no shortage of evidence to support this belief. For example, one author opens his ethics book with the following: "This book takes the view that ethical behavior is the best long-term business strategy for a company—a view that has become increasingly accepted during the last few years."⁶ Similarly, Harvard's Lynn Sharp Paine points out that many companies turn to ethics for its positive benefits. Moral behavior, she says, is not a cost. To be virtuous is to benefit the company. Many leaders, Paine contends, believe that an enhanced ethical awareness "is essential to building a high-performing company that is going to survive and thrive over the long term."⁷

Finally, yet another variation of the pragmatic argument for morality is deterrence. That is, being good (or obeying the rules) prevents me from suffering the consequences that tend to accompany rule breaking. I may want to cheat on my taxes, but the penalty may be so severe (e.g., jail time) as to *deter* me from action. Therefore, the advantages of being good (freedom, avoiding punishment or penalty, etc.) far outweigh any advantages that may come from being bad, since there is a reasonable threat of punishment associated with unjust activity. Here, being good and staying out of trouble are nearly interchangeable.

To summarize, whether it is life quality, reciprocity, desirable outcomes (such as profit), or simply avoiding punishment, we often find ourselves compelled to adopt a posture of virtue and moral integrity for pragmatic reasons.

Rationale #2: Divine Command Theory

Though often appealed to, many find the pragmatic rationale for morality to be insufficient. As we saw in chapter 2, one need only reorient the equation in order to weaken the logic of this approach. In other words, what if virtue did not produce desirable outcomes? What if following rules was actually unsafe or harmed me in some way? What if my concern for others was not returned in a reciprocal fashion? In contrast to virtue, what if conniving, cutthroat selfishness produced greater profit? Given this, we might say that the pragmatic rationale for acting virtuous is built on "sinking sand."

This leads us to consider a different rationale for virtuous action, one that relies less on achieving practical outcomes and more on following the orders and dictates of a divine lawgiver. Here, the moral status of our actions is based on whether or not God has commanded them. For example, why should I "love my neighbor as myself?" Because God, through Scripture, tells us to. Further, if an action is good because God commands it, it follows that an action is bad if God forbids it. In other words, stealing should be avoided because God condemns it. In this sense, doing good is motivated by following a kind of law. Not necessarily the law of the land (e.g., speed limits or IRS tax rates), but the laws of a divine lawgiver.

This rationale for virtuous activity is referred to as "Divine Command Theory." Divine Command Theory provides a more transcendent rationale for why human beings should be moral. The theory has two primary dimensions. One dimension, similar to what was discussed above, points to practical benefits associated with morality. However, this is a form of spiritual pragmatism. For example, just as people are compelled to obey rules of good living because they want to avoid the consequences of punishment, many people of faith adhere to the rules dictated by God because, they determine, the eternal consequences of doing otherwise would be too unpleasant.

For example, consider the "fire and brimstone" sermons thundered out by revival preachers like Jonathan Edwards, which effectively left the masses too afraid to go against God's orders and rules. Under the threat of punishment, virtue and goodness are more or less forms of "fire insurance" to avoid eternal suffering. We even find this dimension evident in "Pascal's wager." Here, the seventeenth-century mathematical genius suggests that humans should adopt belief in God and follow his decrees because the benefits of heaven would far outweigh the cost of hell should they be wrong. Therefore, it is in one's rational best interest to do what God tells one to do, even if one doesn't believe in God, in order to avoid an otherwise unpleasant eternal penalty (if, indeed, such a thing as eternity exists).

The second, more common dimension of Divine Command Theory relates to rules—not necessarily to consequences or "what works." Here, our rationale for morality more or less relies upon adherence to the laws of a cosmic judge. The logic is summarized in the oft-quoted phrase: "God said it. I believe it. That settles it." Put differently, God gives us rules to follow. Following a rule is good; breaking a rule is bad. For example, not far from where I live, a small town county clerk recently found herself in the national spotlight for refusing to issue marriage licenses to same-sex couples. As she was sentenced for contempt of court, she justified her actions before the judge: "God's moral law conflicts with my job duties."[8] In other words, she was prohibited from carrying out her duties as a public official because it would violate God's preordained rules.

Obviously, the appeal to Divine Command Theory will be less than compelling to individuals who do not believe in a divine lawgiver, for if there is no divine lawgiver, there is no divine law. Yet even for members of the faith community who do believe in God, Divine Command Theory may not be as helpful as we think. This leads us to consider a more robust rationale for why we should be moral.

Rationale #3: Teleological Morality

The gaps in Divine Command Theory raise a dilemma that can point us to a more holistic solution: teleological morality. This dilemma was best articulated by Plato. In Plato's famous dialogue *Euthyphro*, Socrates is confronted with an early version of Divine Command Theory, where "holiness is what the gods all love, and its opposite is what the gods all hate, unholiness."[9] He responds (as classical philosophers often do) with a question: "Is what is holy [only] holy because the gods approve it, or do they approve it because it is holy?"[10] In other words, is something good because God commands it, or does he command it because it is good?

Put in these terms, Socrates serves up a philosophical "fork in the road." Furthermore, supporters of Divine Command Theory are likely to find both paths dissatisfying. For example, if something is only good because a god commands it, then this means that goodness is arbitrary and based only upon the whims of the god(s). If, therefore, a god said that murder, rape, and theft were "good," we would be forced to follow these patterns of behavior if we wanted to be good ourselves (contradicting our otherwise innate moral sensibilities). In fact, such a god might even create humans with the innate idea that murder, rape, and theft are virtuous. Here, morality is subject to the nature of the gods. While they might be benevolent, they may also be tyrannical despots.

Conversely, if a god were to command something because it is good, then goodness must be external to god. That is, god does not author goodness so much as he identifies or discovers what goodness is. In this picture, goodness is outside god, so that he apprehends it much the way we do. This route, of course, does not make god seem very "godlike." When he is thus stripped of sovereignty, we can only describe the divine overseer as a kind of judge at best, but not a god (and certainly not the Judeo-Christian God).

This leads us to consider a third answer for the question "Why be moral?" However, prior to describing this, we must first answer two antecedent questions. I use the term "antecedent" because the question "Why be moral?" cannot be sufficiently, or correctly, answered without first answering these questions. In order to answer this question, we must first deliberate about God. That is, "What is the nature of God?" Next, we can consider the nature of humans. That is, "What is the essence of a human?"

Let's begin with the nature of God. Recall Hegel's question raised in chapter 6: "If God is all-sufficient, and lacking in nothing, then why did he need to create a world and, moreover, people to inhabit that world?" In other words, God, by definition, doesn't need anything—so why did he create the cosmos, the planets, the earth, and people?

As discussed, among other things, this tells us that God is creative, productive, and relational. Creation, and relating to creation, is an overflow of God's nature; it is in his essence to create and relate. To go a step further, God relates to his creation (humankind) in a loving way. It is here that we find an important caveat. God doesn't simply show love—God *is* love (1 John 4:8). In other words, in relating love to God, we are not simply saying something about what he *does*. We are making a statement about who he *is*. God is love. God is goodness. God is excellence. God is compassion.

Understanding the nature of God has direct implications for understanding our own nature as humans. We are told in Genesis that man was created in God's image, the *imago Dei* (Gen. 1:26–27). In other words, we are reflections of God's character in many ways. God constituted our humanity in the beginning. If we accept this line of thinking, there are several important implications for how we should understand the *essence* of a human being.

First, every human being has an inherent dignity because they were deliberately created and bear God's image. We often implicitly ascribe artificial values to human life through political institutions, science, technology, or market mechanisms. While these forces can justify life as being important or valuable for various reasons, they cannot, on their own terms, affirm life as *sacred*. In contrast, orthodox faith tells us that each life is supremely valuable because that life was created by God and bears his image.

Second, we have attributes of our Creator inherent in our being. This, of course, does not mean we are like God or we are God, but it does mean that we bear his thumbprint. *Imago Dei* literally means an "image" or likeness of God. That is, we have a Godlike resemblance. Therefore, we might say that when we produce, create, and relate, we are co-producing, co-creating, and co-relating with God. We are exercising these image-reflecting attributes.

To better understand this, it might be helpful to use the example of a historical apprentice. If a trade craftsman had effectively apprenticed their subject (carpentry, silversmithing, etc.), then outsiders would be able to identify that craftsman through the apprentice's work. In other words, their work would bear the instructor's image. The teacher can be seen through the student. Similarly, when we create, relate, love, and so forth, we are bearing the image of the one whose characteristics are inherent in our DNA. As Jesus says in Matthew 5, the purpose of productive human activity and creativity is not to draw attention to ourselves, but to point others to God (and "glorify your Father in heaven"). As Peterson puts it, "Let me tell you why you are here. You're here to be salt-seasoning that brings out the God-flavors of this earth" (Matt. 5:13, *The Message*).

Third, this means that humans have an elevated status in God's created order. Though all of creation originates from the Creator, it is only human beings, we are told, that bear his likeness. In distinction to other creatures, humans can exercise both reason and will upon the world. We can consider our circumstances, reflect on the past, and intuit the future. We have *agency*.

Finally, the *imago Dei* means that we are spiritual beings. We are not simply the sum of our biological components. Nor does our value merely rise to the level of our economic productivity. We have a spirit—a soul. Because a lover created us, we are inherently valuable and loved. Moreover, the intrinsic quality of this sacred value is shared across all humanity.

So, given this understanding of God, and the subsequent understanding of ourselves, we are now better equipped to explore the implications for morality, and specifically the question, "Why be moral?"

Notice that this understanding of God, and ourselves, bypasses the more practical reasons for morality (rationale #1). The practical justification for virtue does not account for our nature as humans who bear God's image. Rather, it depicts humans as rational, utility-seeking automatons who only respond to practical incentives because they "work." Moving on, what about Divine Command Theory (rationale #2), which says we should act moral because God told us to? This may sound orthodox, or even faithful, but upon closer inspection it is found wanting.[11]

We can do better.

Let's return to the *Euthyphro* Dilemma. If we begin with the aforementioned understanding of God, then the *Euthyphro* Dilemma loses its teeth. Here's why. We can agree that God does not command something simply because it is good (goodness outside of God). Furthermore, we can agree that something is not necessarily good because God commands it (goodness arbitrarily decided by God). Rather, as mentioned above, God commands something because *he is good, he is loving,* and *he is relational*. As Aquinas argued long ago, God's will is consistent with the truth of who he is—the integrity of his being, self, and nature. Because God doesn't merely show love, but is love, this love is an overflow into his created order. So, God does not arbitrarily decide what is good—God is good. That is, goodness is his nature; goodness is derived from his unchanging character.

So what are the implications of this for us? Moreover, how does this answer the question, "Why be moral?" Because being moral, in short, is what we were designed to do by our good Creator. It is our best, most fulfilling, complete, and undivided expression of humanity. Dick Staub writes, "To be fully human is to fully reflect God's creative, spiritual, intelligent, communicative, relational, moral and purposeful capacities, and to do so holistically and synergistically."[12] This is what it means to flourish as a human. As John Paul II wrote in his *Theology of the Body*, the creation account gives us an important anthropological picture of humankind where "being and good are convertible"—that is, they are the same.[13] In God's original creation plan, goodness is synonymous with existence. As John Paul II reminds us, this is our foundation for human anthropology (who we are) and ethics (what we do).[14]

To summarize: God is goodness. We are an overflow of his nature. Reflecting his character is, we might say, our intended destiny. Our souls long for goodness. We were designed for virtue. What I am describing here is different from Divine Command Theory: it is teleological morality. It is virtue motivated by design.

Revisiting Progress and Prosperity

Recall C. S. Lewis's list, discussed in chapter 4, of the questions that must be answered when a fleet of ships goes out to sea: (1) How to avoid colliding with other ships, (2) How to avoid sinking, and (3) Why the ship is even out there in the first place. The first question is a question of social interaction: How do I balance my own interests with that of society? What is the most appropriate arrangement for a given social situation? The second question relates to individuality: How can I take care of myself? How do I manage my own life? However, and of most importance, the third question is a foundational one: Who am I? Why am I here? What is my purpose? What is meaningful? What does it mean to live well?

As Lewis's example makes clear, it seems foolish to devote our attention to questions 1 and 2 if we have not first given careful examination and thought to why we do what we do in the first place. In other words, if we have not settled questions about who we are as humans (our origins, our nature, our purpose), which is necessarily derived from our understanding of who God is, then all other questions risk losing their coherence. It is for this reason that Ravi Zacharias, when asked "Can man live without God?" responded by saying that we can, indeed, live without God pragmatically, but we cannot live without God coherently.

Recall the discussion of the flute in chapter 3. If we ask, what makes a good flute? we must first answer by explaining what a flute is. What is its purpose? What is it for? That is, what is the *teleology* of a flute? If a flute exists, as most can agree, to make beautiful music, we now have a basis to determine whether or not a given flute is "good." Indeed, there is no other measure by which to ordain the "goodness" or "badness" of a flute outside of its intended purpose, nature, design, and aim.

The logic follows for humanity. To speak of goodness for a human, we must first determine human teleology: why a human exists. For the naturalist, human existence is random, a mere product of chance and time. For the existentialist, human existence is relative; we effectively create the essence of the world around us. But within the Judeo-Christian narrative, human existence is deliberate: individuals exist through the creative and communal expression of God. Moreover, deliberate design implies teleology. We were made on purpose, therefore we have a purpose. Furthermore, if humans were made on purpose, it follows that we are not autonomous. As a flute exists to produce beautiful music, we exist for the purpose of loving communion with our Creator and with our neighbor. Goodness is not, and cannot be, choosing to live however I want; goodness is fulfilling who I was created to be.

To summarize, this chapter began with the suggestion that our moral climate—that is, the identification, pursuit, and realization of virtue—might be a better measure of progress and prosperity than calculations of material development. I agree. Yet, as mentioned, the *Economist* article failed to establish why morality was a necessary attribute in our development, and flourishing, as human beings.

As outlined, we could make a case that morality is good because, simply put, it works. The problem, though, is that many times it doesn't "work" the way we want. In other words, if this is our only justification for why we should act virtuous, it is a thin one at best.

We could also make a case that we should be moral because God tells us to, what is referred to as Divine Command Theory. Yet the theory isn't likely to win over too many people who don't identify closely with religion. Furthermore, it provides a rigid rationale for moral action based upon the arbitrary whims of a totalitarian god-figure, or worse, suggests that God is simply a third party who helps to adjudicate—not determine—what is right and wrong for people.

But there is a third rationale. What if the best justification for our moral action is because that is what we were designed for? In other words, we realize—we *actualize*—ourselves as humans when we embody the virtuous life. As this book has argued, this embodiment occurs in our minds, our language, and our practices. Chapter 3 discussed the idea of virtue—reorienting how we think so as to "educate the sentiments." In contrast to reigning meta-values of preference and choice, virtue invites us to deny ourselves, connect our desire to its true object, and to desire well. The big questions of life were explored in chapter 4. What is valuable? What is morality? Who is God? In answering these questions, the language of virtue cultivates responses that are essentialist rather than instrumentalist, consistent rather than incoherent, and communal rather than individualistic. But virtue is not relegated to the realm of ideas and language alone—we are invited to weave virtuous practices into the fabric of our everyday lives. In chapter 5, we learned that "what is good" can be summarized in the practices of justice, mercy, and humility, and specifically in practices that cultivate generosity, charitable judgment ("double vision"), steadfast love, and humility (confession and works of mercy). Finally, in chapter 6, we were reminded that our practices can only take us so far. Embodying virtue necessarily requires God's grace, which restores our capacity to be at harmony with ourselves, with our neighbor, and with God.

The idea, language, and practice of virtue are not pursued because they "work," or even because God said they should be pursued. They require that we embrace the good because God *is* goodness, and as his image bearers, we become more of who God designed us to be when we reflect his goodness. We become the perfect version of ourselves.

This is our best life. This is our "happy" life—*eudaemonia*. This is how we experience fulfillment. This is what it means to be blessed. This is righteousness—or "right relationship" with creation, with others, with ourselves.

We were designed for good.

Conclusion: Two Stories

Chapter 1 began with two stories suggesting that we possess an impulse toward order. Therefore, it seems fitting that two stories should end this book.

An enjoyable pastime for me is simply talking to my father over coffee. Several years ago, while walking and talking, we were

discussing an incident in his church involving an elderly congre-
gant who was the victim of a scam. She needed money. While the
details cannot be laid out here, she found herself in a unique and
unfortunate situation where receiving financial support from others would only complicate matters. As we walked, we discussed
why giving can sometimes create more harm than help. But after a
reflective pause, my father said: "My dad would have given it to her.
His criterion for generosity was pretty simple."

"What was it?" I asked.

He smiled. "All someone had to do was ask."

My grandfather passed away long before I ever had the chance
to meet him, but the stories of his unconditional giving to those in
his community are powerful. My father described him as "one of
the most generous persons I have ever known."

One of our family friends will forever be wheelchair bound. Decades ago, while on summer break from college, she found herself
working alone in her small hometown souvenir shop. A stranger
entered the store, pulled out a gun, and shot her twice. After he fled,
leaving her for dead, she tried to move and quickly realized that she
was paralyzed from the waist down. "In that very moment, I had
a very important choice to make," she later said. "The choice was
either to allow despair, hurt, unforgiveness, and bitterness to take
root in my heart, or choose to give myself over to the God I had
professed to believe in all of my life." She chose the latter. "I decided,
in that moment, to *choose God over my circumstances.*"

The stories are very different, but both illustrate what I believe
to be mature expressions of virtue. The subjects in each story, my
grandfather and our friend, displayed a default setting. If sin is the
heart curved inward, this setting is a heart bowed outward. For my
grandfather, his default was to help those in need: family, neighbor,
friends, and strangers. For our friend, in the very abyss of tragedy,
she defaulted to God.

To be clear, I am not suggesting that naked generosity without
consideration of the circumstances is good (indeed, in the case
of the scam victim, giving would have been harmful). Nor am I
suggesting that unqualified loyalty to any force or figure is praiseworthy. Indeed, as we've learned, it's quite the opposite. We were

endowed with reason as humans in order to deliberate upon the good. "Test everything," writes Paul, and "hold fast to what is good" (1 Thess. 5:21).

Reason aside, these stories represent the most significant dimension of virtue: a reflex toward others and toward our Creator. My grandfather's life was characterized by generosity toward neighbor; our friend's life can be characterized by goodwill toward God. Virtue.

For where virtue begins with an impulse toward order, it ends with a reflex toward other: God and neighbor. This is goodness. This is excellence. This is life at its best.

DISCUSSION QUESTIONS
FOR GROUP STUDY

1. The chapter began by discussing "Progress and Prosperity" through human history. Why should morality be a measure of our progress and prosperity? How would you articulate that to someone else?

2. Where do you see appeals to morality because it *works*? Where do you see appeals to morality based upon Divine Command Theory?

3. The chapter describes what it means to flourish as a human. How is this picture of happiness (*eudaemonia*) different from some of our modern conceptions of being happy?

4. Consider the quote: "We were made on purpose, therefore we have a purpose." Can you think of other examples of this (e.g., a hammer, car, stapler, etc.)?

5. What are some concrete examples of how your life would be different if you possessed a "reflex toward other: God and neighbor"?

6. If you found yourself on the news or being interviewed by a major newspaper outlet, and you were asked "Why should we be moral?," what would you say?

NOTES

Introduction

1. Plato, *The Republic of Plato*, ed. Allan Bloom (New York: Basic Books, 1991), 15.
2. Ibid., 36.
3. Ibid., 38.
4. Ibid.
5. Steven J. Jensen, *Living the Good Life: A Beginner's Thomistic Ethics* (Washington, DC: The Catholic University of America Press, 2013), 184.
6. Eric Schwitzgebel, "The Moral Behavior of Ethics Professors and the Role of the Philosopher," *The Splintered Mind* (blog), September 3, 2013, http://schwitzsplinters.blogspot.com/2013/09/the-moral-behavior-of-ethics-professors.html.
7. Cohen, cited in Schwitzgebel, "The Moral Behavior of Ethics Professors."
8. See Nigel Warburton, "G. A. Cohen on Inequality of Wealth," *Philosophy Bites*, podcast audio, December 23, 2007, http://philosophybites.com/2007/12/ga-cohen-on-ine.html.
9. David Gill, *Becoming Good: Building Moral Character* (Downers Grove, IL: InterVarsity Press, 2000), 30.
10. Skye Jethani, "Media and the Mind of Christ: How We See the World Precedes What We Do," *Q Ideas* (blog), December 2013, http://www.qideas.org/blog/media-and-the-mind-of-christ.aspx; italics his.
11. Alasdair MacIntyre, *After Virtue*, 3rd ed. (Notre Dame, IN: University of Notre Dame Press, 2008), 204.
12. C. S. Lewis, *Mere Christianity* (San Francisco: Harper Collins, 2001), 92.
13. Julia Annas, *Ancient Philosophy: A Very Short Introduction* (Oxford: Oxford University Press, 2000), 49.
14. Jonathan Haidt, *The Righteous Mind: Why Good People Are Divided by Politics and Religion* (New York: Pantheon Books, 2012), 97.

15. Robert Nozick, "The Experience Machine," in *Ethical Theory: An Anthology*, ed. Russ Shafer Landau, 2nd ed. (Malden, MA: Wiley-Blackwell, 2013), 264.

16. Jonathan Phillips, Luke Misenheimer, and Joshua Knobe, "The Ordinary Concept of Happiness (And Others Like It)," *Emotion Review* 3, no. 3 (2011): 320–22.

17. Kelvin Knight, *Aristotelian Philosophy: Ethics and Politics from Aristotle to MacIntyre* (Cambridge: Polity Press, 2007), 14.

18. John Paul II, *Veritatis splendor* (Libreria Editrice Vaticana, 1993), http://w2.vatican.va/content/john-paul-ii/en/encyclicals/documents/hf_jp-ii_enc_06081993_veritatis-splendor.html.

Chapter 1

1. Daniel Goleman, *Emotional Intelligence: Why It Can Matter More than IQ*, tenth anniversary ed. (New York: Bantam Books, 2005), 3–4. See also "'Miracle Child' Is Survivor," *New York Times*, September 25, 1993, http://www.nytimes.com/1993/09/25/us/miracle-child-is-survivor.html.

2. Rick Bragg, "Psychiatrist for Susan Smith's Defense Tells of a Woman Desperate to Be Liked," *New York Times*, July 22, 1995, http://www.nytimes.com/1995/07/22/us/psychiatrist-for-susan-smith-s-defense-tells-of-a-woman-desperate-to-be-liked.html.

3. *Merriam-Webster OnLine*, s.v. "intuitive," n.d., http://www.merriam-webster.com/dictionary/intuitive.

4. Jonathan Haidt, *The Righteous Mind: Why Good People Are Divided by Politics and Religion* (New York: Pantheon, 2012), 28.

5. Ibid., 37.

6. Ibid., 38.

7. Ibid., 50.

8. From the podcast *Rationally Speaking: Exploring the Borderlands between Reason and Nonsense*. The commenter, one of the show's hosts, was Massimo Pigliucci. The show is referred to as the "Official Podcast of New York City Skeptics." See *Rationally Speaking*, "Joshua Knobe on Experimental Philosophy," November 7, 2010, http://rationallyspeaking-podcast.org/show/rs21-joshua-knobe-on-experimental-philosophy.html.

9. C. S. Lewis, *The Abolition of Man* (New York: HarperCollins Publishers, 1971), 43.

10. Antoine de Saint-Exupéry, *The Little Prince*, trans. Irene Testot-Ferry (Hertfordshire: Wordsworth Classics, 1995), 82.

11. Eugene Peterson, *Life at Its Best: A Guidebook for the Pilgrim Life* (Grand Rapids, MI: Zondervan, 2002), 403.

12. Note here that this is the very definition of empiricism. An empiricist values experience apprehended through one's senses.

13. Thomas Williams, introduction to *On Free Choice of the Will* by Augustine, trans. and ed. Thomas Williams (Indianapolis: Hackett, 1993).

14. Joshua Knobe, "In Search of the True Self," *The Stone* (blog), *New York Times*, June 5, 2011, http://opinionator.blogs.nytimes.com/2011/06/05/in-search-of-the-true-self/?_php=true&_type=blogs&_r=2.

15. Ibid. Knobe arrives upon this conclusion based upon his research. Specifically relating to Pierpont, he found that those who frown upon the homosexual lifestyle claimed that Pierpont's true self was the evangelical activist, while those who support and celebrate the homosexual lifestyle saw his true self as being the suppressed, closet homosexual. In other words, each seemingly objective determination about Pierpont's true self was closely tied to an underlying value judgment about what it means to live well.

16. "Mosquito-net fishing threatens Lake Tanganyika," IRIN, October 13, 2009, http://www.irinnews.org/report/86565/zambia-mosquito-net-fishing-threatens-lake-tanganyika.

17. "Moral Issues," Gallup, 2015, http://www.gallup.com/poll/1681/moral-issues.aspx.

18. Lewis, *The Abolition of Man*, 26.

19. "Is College Worth It?" Pew Research Center: Social and Demographic Trends, May 15, 2011, http://www.pewsocialtrends.org/2011/05/15/is-college-worth-it.

20. "Teaching the Children: Sharp Ideological Differences, Some Common Ground," Pew Research Center: US Politics and Policy, September 18, 2014, http://www.people-press.org/2014/09/18/teaching-the-children-sharp-ideological-differences-some-common-ground.

21. "Young Adults and Liberals Struggle with Morality," The Barna Research Group, August 25, 2008, https://www.barna.org/barna-update/millennials/25-young-adults-and-liberals-struggle-with-morality.

22. "Americans Are Most Likely to Base Truth on Feelings," The Barna Research Group, February 12, 2002, https://barna.org/component/content/article/5-barna-update/45-barna-update-sp-657/67-americans-are-most-likely-to-base-truth-on-feelings#.V1Hy8DUrK70.

23. Hagop Sarkissian et al., "Folk Moral Relativism," *Mind and Language* 26, no. 4 (2011): 486.

24. Ibid., 488.

25. "Barna Survey Examines Changes in Worldview among Christians over the Past 13 Years," The Barna Research Group, 2010, https://www.barna.org/barna-update/21-transformation/252-barna-survey-examines-changes-in-worldview-among-christians-over-the-past-13-years#.VFjyKDTF98E.

26. "Religion (Trends)," Gallup, 2014, http://www.gallup.com/poll/1690/religion.aspx.

27. Rodney Clapp, *A Peculiar People: The Church as Culture in a Post-Christian Society* (Downers Grove, IL: InterVarsity Press, 1996), 19.

28. Corydon Ireland, "Getting Justice Right," September 9, 2009, http://news.harvard.edu/gazette/story/2009/09/getting-justice-right.

29. This can be found in Isaiah Berlin's *Four Essays on Liberty.*

30. Eugene Peterson, *The Quest for Life at Its Best* (Grand Rapids, MI: Zondervan, 1995), 202.

Chapter 2

1. Richard Shears, "New Zealand student sells virginity for £20,000 on the web," *Daily Mail*, February 3, 2010, http://www.dailymail.co.uk/news/article-1248209/New-Zealand-student-offers-virginity-sale-web.html.

2. Robert Skidelsky and Edward Skidelsky, *How Much is Enough? Money and the Good Life* (New York: Other Press, 2012), 86.

3. This dilemma has taken on a variety of forms. Most recently, Michael Sandel posed something quite similar in his 2009 book *Justice*, 21–24, as well as Bazerman and Tenbrunsel in their 2011 book *Blind Spots*, 25–26. See Michael Sandel, *Justice: What's the Right Thing to Do?* (New York: Farrar, Straus and Giroux, 2009), and Max H. Bazerman and Ann E. Tenbrunsel, *Blind Spots: Why We Fail to Do What's Right and What to Do about It* (Princeton, NJ: Princeton University Press, 2011).

4. David Edmonds, *Would You Kill the Fat Man? The Trolley Problem and What Your Answer Tells Us about Right and Wrong* (Princeton, NJ: Princeton University Press, 2013).

5. As a rebuttal, the philosopher would likely say that "Trolley Puzzles" reveal how we process hypothetical ethical quandaries (and some of our own inconsistencies in moral deliberation)—they were never meant to reflect potential real-life scenarios.

6. Told in Glenn M. Stein, "An Arctic Execution: Private Charles B. Henry of the United States Lady Franklin Bay Expedition 1881–84," *Arctic* 64, no. 4 (2011): 401.

7. "The Greely Expedition," *Papers Past,* ed. The National Library of New Zealand., n.d., http://paperspast.natlib.govt.nz.

8. *Merriam-Webster OnLine*, s.v. "efficiency," n.d, http://www.merriam-webster.com/dictionary/efficiency.

9. Manuel G. Velasquez, *Business Ethics: Concepts and Cases* (Upper Saddle River, NJ: Prentice Hall, 2002), 74.

10. The numbers I use here are from Velasquez, 74–75.

11. Jessica Bennett and Jesse Ellison, "The Case against Marriage," *Newsweek Online*, June 11, 2010, http://www.newsweek.com/case-against -marriage-73045.

12. It is important to point out that the same consequentialist mentality can be used to argue against the bank employee's actions. That argument might say that if all of society lied and cheated in this way, then our social landscape would be a chaotic wreck. However, I would argue that we should not lie, not because it produces bad social consequences, but because it is degrading to our nature as human beings.

13. David J. Fritzsche, *Business Ethics: A Global and Managerial Perspective* (New York: McGraw Hill, 1997), 18; italics mine.

14. "About the Center for Christian Business Ethics Today," The Center for Christian Business Ethics Today, n.d., http://www.cfcbe.com/about; italics mine.

15. Larry Ruddell, *Business Ethics, Faith That Works: Leading Your Company to Long-Term Success* (Houston: Halcyon, 2004), 19.

16. John Maxwell, *There's No Such Thing as "Business" Ethics: There's Only One Rule for Making Decisions* (New York: Center Street, 2003), 15; italics his.

17. Coleman McCarthy, "'I'm a Pacifist Because I'm a Violent Son of a Bitch:' A Profile of Stanley Hauerwas," *The Progressive* 67, no. 4 (2003).

18. While in language the Scriptures and the Christian faith tradition in general make a distinction between 'best' and 'faithful,' this practice is not universally held by the church. Biblical manipulations creating "prosperity gospel" and other "heretical" manifestations (Ross Douthat's term) of the faith tradition take a clear line of departure from this aforementioned thought.

19. Amartya Sen, *The Idea of Justice* (Cambridge, MA: Harvard University Press, 2009), 16.

20. Stein, "An Arctic Execution," 402.

21. Penelope Wang, "Cutting the High Cost of End-of-Life Care," *CNN Money*, December 12, 2012, http://money.cnn.com/2012/12/11/pf/ end-of-life-care-duplicate-2.moneymag.

22. Jonathan Swift, "A Modest Proposal," *The Art Bin*, n.d., http://art-bin.com/art/omodest.html.

23. Sandel, *Justice*, 103.

24. It is important to note that the tradition of "rights" was at one time very closely aligned with the Christian faith. Rights were understood to be universal endowments by the Creator. However, post-Enlightenment rights began to take a much different form. Today, in liberal society, the rights-based tradition is justified apart from the Christianity that it was once so closely linked with.

25. Some reading this might point out that Rawls may better be used as an example for social contract theory (discussed in the "enforceability" section). True as this may be, I chose to discuss Rawls in the equity section based upon his appeal to fairness, rights, and impartiality.

26. Daniel Bell, *The Coming of Post Industrial Society: A Venture in Social Forecasting* (New York: Basic Books, 1973), 425; italics his.

27. Michael Sandel, "America's Search for a New Public Philosophy," *The Atlantic Monthly* (1996): 58.

28. John Rawls, *A Theory of Justice* (Delhi: Universal Law Publishing, 1971), 191.

29. Richard Hays, *The Moral Vision of the New Testament* (New York: HarperCollins, 1996), 35; italics his.

30. Rawls famously writes, "In justice as fairness, men agree to share in one another's fate." *Theory of Justice*, 102.

31. Daniel M. Bell Jr., "Deliberating: Justice and Liberation," in *Blackwell Companion to Christian Ethics*, ed. Samuel Wells and Stanley Hauerwas (Malden, MA: Blackwell Publishing, 2006), 183.

32. Ibid., 183.

33. Amy Gutmann and Dennis Thompson, *Why Deliberative Democracy?* (Princeton, NJ: Princeton University Press, 2004), 64.

34. Obviously, questions as to what one should do about international labor issues and supply chain ethics is a highly complex issue in itself, and addressing our appropriate action as people of faith is far beyond the scope of this book. I offer this story to illustrate the limits of individuals navigating moral complexities on the basis of their own personal beliefs and values.

35. Debra Satz, "The Egalitarian Intuition," *Boston Review*, May–June 2012, http://new.bostonreview.net/BR37.3/ndf_debra_satz_markets_morals.php.

36. Skidelsky and Skidelsky, *How Much is Enough?*, 160–61.

37. Haidt, *The Righteous Mind*, 104.

38. "Banned Books Awareness: *Lord of the Flies*," Banned Books Awareness, November 10, 2013, http://bannedbooks.world.edu/2013/11/10/banned-books-awareness-lord-of-the-flies.

39. Thomas Hobbes, *Leviathan* (London: Routledge, 1894), 64.

40. Eric Noe, "Scammers Target Katrina, Rita Survivors," *ABC News Online*, November 8, 2005, http://abcnews.go.com/Business/story?id=1281692.

41. I should point out, however, that there is a strong counterargument against this line of thinking that can be presented in moral terms. In other words, natural equilibrium price—even if it seems exploitative—can actually bring the most resources to an area. This, certainly, is the efficiency argument. Nevertheless, as mentioned earlier in the chapter, this does not necessarily bracket out its moral dimension.

42. LaRue Tome Hosmer, *The Ethics of Management* (New York: McGraw Hill, 2011), 64–68.

43. F. F. Bruce, *International Bible Commentary with the New International Version* (Basingstoke: Marshall Pickering, 1979), 1205.

44. Ibid.

45. Alexander Solzhenitsyn, "A World Split Apart," *American Rhetoric*, June 8, 1978, http://www.americanrhetoric.com/speeches/alexander solzhenitsynharvard.htm.

46. Federal Document Clearing House: Text of Clinton's Statement, *Washington Post Online*, August 18,1998, http://www.washingtonpost.com /wp-srv/politics/special/clinton/stories/text081898.htm.

47. Richard Lacayo, "When Is Sex Not 'Sexual Relations'?" *CNN*, August 24, 1998, http://www.cnn.com/ALLPOLITICS/1998/08/17/time/clinton .html.

48. Robert Shapiro in Ravi Zacharias, "The Disoriented Self," chap. 8 in *Deliver Us from Evil* (Nashville: Thomas Nelson, 1998).

49. Bruce Weinstein, "If It's Legal, It's Ethical . . . Right?" *Bloomberg Business*, October 15, 2007, http://www.bloomberg.com/bw/stories/2007 -10-15/if-its-legal-its-ethical-right-businessweek-business-news-stock-market-and-financial-advice.

50. *Post* Staff Reporter, "New Zealand virgin auctions herself for tuition," *New York Post Online*, February 3, 2010, http://nypost.com/2010 /02/03/new-zealand-virgin-auctions-herself-for-tuition.

Chapter 3

1. Jonathan Wolff, "Jonathan Wolff on John Rawls' *A Theory of Justice*," *Philosophy Bites*, podcast audio, February 28, 2010, http://philosophybites. com/2010/02/jonathan-wolff-on-john-rawls-a-theory-of-justice.html.

2. Glenn Sunshine, *Why You Think the Way You Do: The Story of Western Worldviews from Rome to Home* (Grand Rapids, MI: Zondervan, 2009), 16.

3. John Stuart Mill, *Utilitarianism*, ed. George Sher, 2nd ed. (Indianapolis, Indiana: Hackett, 2001), 7.

4. Carolyn Gregoire, "Happiness Index: Only 1 in 3 Americans Are Very Happy, According to Harris Poll," *The Huffington Post*, June 1, 2013, http://www.huffingtonpost.com/2013/06/01/happiness-index-only-1-in_n_3354524.html.

5. Frances Rhodes et al., *Aristotle De Anima: Ensouled Body* (Cambridge: Cambridge University Press, 1993), xxvii-xxviii.

6. Debra Satz, *Why Some Things Should Not Be for Sale: The Moral Limits of Markets* (New York: Oxford University Press, 2010), 59–60.

7. Daniel M. Hausman and Michael S. McPherson, "Preference Satisfaction and Welfare Economics," *Economics and Philosophy* 25, no. 1 (2009): 1–25; see esp. 7–8.

8. Murray N. Rothbard, *Economic Controversies* (Auburn, AL: Mises Institute, 2011), 289. Austrian economists, in particular, stress the individual subjective theory of value as it helps to describe human activity, or praxeology. Ludwig Von Mises writes: "No treatment of economic problems proper can avoid starting from acts of choice; economics becomes a part, although hitherto the best elaborated part, of a more universal science, praxeology." *Human Action: A Treatise on Economics* (Auburn, AL: Ludwig Von Mises Institute, 1998), 3.

9. Robert Skidelsky and Edward Skidelsky, *How Much Is Enough? Money and the Good Life* (New York: Other Press, 2012), 88. They go on to write: "It does not matter, from the economic point of view, whether people are altruists, egoists, hedonists, masochists or anything else; all that matters is that they have certain preferences and act on them," 101.

10. Jodi Beggs, "My Imagined Yet Realistic Debate between Michael Sandel and the Economics World," *Economists Do It with Models*, November 24, 2012 (blog), http://www.economistsdoitwithmodels.com/2012/11/24 /my-imagined-yet-realistic-debate-between-michael-sandel-and-the -economics-world.

11. Michael Sandel, *Liberalism and the Limits of Justice*, 2nd ed. (Cambridge: Cambridge University Press, 1998), 1.

12. Alasdair MacIntyre, *Whose Justice? Which Rationality?* (Notre Dame, IN: University of Notre Dame Press, 1998), 377.

13. Rawls, cited in MacIntyre, 337.

14. Ibid.

15. Michael Sandel, "The Procedural Republic and the Unencumbered Self," *Political Theory* 12, no. 1 (1984): 81–96; see also 157.

16. Michael Philips, "Preference Satisfaction and the Good," *PhilosophyNow.org*, July–August 2001, http://philosophynow.org/issues/31/ Preference_Satisfaction_and_the_Good.

17. MacIntyre, *Whose Justice?*, 344.

18. Daniel M. Bell Jr., "Deliberating: Justice and Liberation," in Samuel Wells and Stanley Hauerwas, eds., *Blackwell Companion to Christian Ethics* (Malden, MA: Wiley-Blackwell, 2006), 182–95; see esp. 183.

19. Steve Jobs, " 'You've got to find what you love,' Jobs says," *Stanford Report*, June 14, 2005, http://news.stanford.edu/news/2005/june15/ jobs-061505.html. Interestingly, shortly after writing this chapter, I heard a prominent faith-based radio station extol Jobs' "great advice" that any graduate would do well to follow.

20. Tennyson's *Maud*, lines 396–397.

21. Steven J. Jensen, *Living the Good Life: A Beginner's Thomistic Ethics* (Washington, DC: The Catholic University of America Press, 2013), 20–21.
22. "And now on to polygamy," *The Economist Online*, April 8, 2013, http://www.economist.com/blogs/democracyinamerica/2013/04/gay -marriage. After highlighting the quote, the author from *The Economist* responds, "Right on."
23. Laurie Segall, "I have a fiancé, a girlfriend and two boyfriends," *CNN Money*, 2015, http://money.cnn.com/2015/01/25/technology/polyamory -silicon-valley/.
24. Chris Messina, "Why I Choose Non-Monogamy," *CNN Money*, January 29, 2015, http://money.cnn.com/2015/01/29/technology/chris -messina-non-monogamy/index.html.
25. Michael Harris, *The End of Absence* (New York: Current Press, 2014), 169.
26. Ibid., 176.
27. Ibid.
28. David Brooks, *The Road to Character* (New York: Random House, 2015), 249.
29. Frederick C. Copleston and Bertrand Russell, "A Debate on the Existence of God," BBC, 1948; audio recording and transcript at http:// www.biblicalcatholic.com/apologetics/p20.htm.
30. Chris Chase, "Lance Armstrong and Oprah Winfrey: Live Updates," *USA Today Online*, January 17, 2013, http://www.usatoday.com /story/gameon/2013/01/17/lance-armstrong-oprah-interview-updates-live/1843235; italics mine.
31. Lewis, *The Abolition of Man* (New York: HarperCollins, 1971), 2; italics his.
32. Skidelsky and Skidelsky, *How Much Is Enough?*, 161.
33. Ibid., 72–73.
34. Mark Buchanan, *Your God Is Too Safe* (Colorado Springs: Multnomah Books, 2001), 72–73.
35. Ibid.
36. Dennis Kinlaw, *Let's Start with Jesus: A New Way of Doing Theology* (Grand Rapids, MI: Zondervan, 2005), 112.
37. From the song "Good Intentions" by Toad the Wet Sprocket.
38. Lewis, *Abolition of Man*, 15.
39. Peter Kreeft, "Good, True, and Beautiful: C. S. Lewis" (lecture, Acton University, Grand Rapids, MI, June 19, 2015).
40. Montague Brown, "Augustine on Freedom and God," *The Saint Anselm Journal* 2, no. 2 (2005): 52.
41. Brooks, *Road to Character*, 197.
42. Rodney Clapp, *Tortured Wonders: Christian Spirituality for People, Not Angels* (Grand Rapids, MI: Brazos Press, 2004), 80.

43. Parker Palmer and Arthur Zajonc, *The Heart of Higher Education: A Call to Renewal* (San Francisco: Jossey-Bass, 2010), 103.

44. Patricia M. King and Marcia B. Baxter Magolda, "A Developmental Perspective on Learning," *Journal of College Student Development* 37 (1996): 163–73, quoted in Parker and Zajonc, *Heart of Higher Education*, 103.

45. Lewis, *Abolition of Man*, 16.

46. Clapp, *Tortured Wonders*, 78.

47. Augustine, *The City of God: Modern Library Paperback Edition*, trans. Marcus Dods (New York: Random House, 2000), 511.

48. Stuart McAllister, "Slice of Infinity," *Ravi Zacharias International Ministries*, September 4, 2014.

Chapter 4

1. I borrow this expression from philosopher Nick Phillipson. See Nick Phillipson, "Nick Phillipson on Adam Smith on What Human Beings Are Like," *Philosophy Bites*, podcast audio, November 20, 2010, http://philosophybites.com/2010/11/nick-phillipson-on-adam-smith-on-what-human-beings-are-like.html.

2. Elizabeth Anderson, *Value in Ethics and Economics* (Cambridge, MA: Harvard University Press, 1993).

3. Immanuel Kant, *Groundwork for the Metaphysics of Morals*, ed. Lara Denis (Ontario, Canada: Broadview Press, 2005), 93; italics his.

4. Baruch Fischhoff and Lita Furby, "Measuring Values: A Conceptual Framework for Interpreting Transactions with Special Reference to Contingent Valuation of Visibility," *Journal of Risk and Uncertainty* 1, no. 2 (1988): 147–84.

5. For example, an Ivy League education in the U.S. would cost substantially more than, say, a basic community college. Yet a degree from the former would produce greater earning power in the workforce, as opposed to the latter; it has more "value."

6. For clarity, I feel compelled to point out that my friend in the story would agree with my line of thinking. In other words, while he may use cost-benefit analysis to determine whether he should mow his grass, he would not likely use the same analysis when assessing time with family or other "higher goods."

7. Bennett and Ellison, "The Case Against Marriage," *Newsweek*, June 11, 2010; web October 28, 2010, http://www.newsweek.com/2010/06/11/i-don-t.html.

8. Other research suggests that finding the right person to marry may actually increase your wealth opportunities. The point, however, is that this remains an impoverished definition of marriage. For a trivial example, see

Jeff Haden, "Want to Make More Money? Marry the Right Person, Science Says," *Linkedin Pulse*, January 19, 2015, https://www.linkedin.com/pulse /make-more-money-marry-right-person-science-says-so-jeff-haden.

9. Jonathan Sacks offered a similar description of marital ends in his 1990 Reith Lectures in the UK. In his lectures, he describes the marital norms of "loyalty and trust." See Sacks in David Fergusson, *Community, Liberalism and Christian Ethics* (Cambridge: Cambridge University Press, 1998), 142.

10. Abhijit V. Banerjee and Esther Duflo, *Poor Economics* (New York: PublicAffairs, 2010), 121.

11. Michael Sandel, *Justice: What Is the Right Thing to Do?* (New York: Farrar, Straus and Giroux, 2009), 48–49.

12. Ibid., 49.

13. Glenn Sunshine, "The Image of God and Human Dignity," *The Christian Worldview Journal*, n.d., http://www.colsoncenter.org/the-center /columns/call-response/15270-the-image-of-god-and-human-dignity; italics his.

14. Term used in Psalm 51.

15. Worse, political structures may even be hostile to such a conception of human essence. Philosopher J. Budziszewski, for example, has suggested that "social contract theory is an implicit rejection of human teleology." See J. Budziszewski, "How to Talk about Natural Law" (lecture, Acton University, Grand Rapids, MI, June 19, 2015).

16. Kathleen Norris, *The Cloister Walk* (New York: Riverhead Books, 1996), 22.

17. David Edmonds and Nigel Warburton, *Philosophy Bites: 25 Philosophers on 25 Intriguing Subjects* (Oxford: Oxford University Press, 2010), 17.

18. Lewis, *Abolition of Man*, 26.

19. Erika Rawes, "Is It Okay to Cheat on Your Taxes? Some Americans Say Yes," *Money and Career CheatSheet*, 31 January 2015, http://www .cheatsheet.com/personal-finance/is-it-ok-to-cheat-on-your-taxes-some -americans-say-yes.html/?a=viewall.

20. Alan Fram, "IRS Estimate: 17 Percent of Taxes Owed Went Unpaid," *Yahoo Finance*, 6 January 2012, http://finance.yahoo.com/news/irs -estimate-17-percent-taxes-204637410.html.

21. David Brooks, "What Is Your Purpose?" *New York Times*, May 5, 2015, http://www.nytimes.com/2015/05/05/opinion/david-brooks-what -is-your-purpose.html?_r=0.

22. Richard Hays, *The Moral Vision of the New Testament* (New York: HarperCollins, 1996), 20–21.

23. C. S. Lewis, *The Joyful Christian: 127 Readings* (New York: Touchstone, 1977), 13.

24. Jill Carattini, "Life Embodied," *A Slice of Infinity* (journal of Ravi Zacharias International Ministries), November 22, 2013, http://ca.rzim.org/a-slice-of-infinity/life-embodied/.

25. Deborah Evans Price in Megan Livengood and Connie Ledoux Book, "Watering Down Christianity? An Examination of the Use of Theological Words in Christian Music," *Journal of Media and Religion* 3, no. 2 (2004): 119.

26. For an example, see Gesa Hartje, "Keeping in Tune with the Times: Praise and Worship Music as Today's Evangelical Hymnody in North America," *Dialog: A Journal of Theology* 48, no. 4 (2009): 364–73.

27. Or, as a statistician might put it, there is not enough evidence to conclude they are different.

28. The study was conducted using linguistic technology from Linguistic Inquiry and Word Count technology (LIWC—found at http://www.liwc.net/). Sample sizes for each category were between 80 and 100 songs. The mean proportion of self-referencing language for classical hymns was 7.84 (that is, 7.84% of all words in the songs were comprised of self-referencing language). For contemporary worship, the mean was 10.86. For pop radio, the mean was 10.8. A 95% Confidence Level or higher constituted statistical significance.

29. See Elizabeth Bernstein, "A Tiny Pronoun Says a Lot about You: How Often You Say 'I' Says More Than You Realize," *Wall Street Journal*, October 7, 2013, http://www.wsj.com/articles/SB10001424052702304626104579121371885556170.

30. For a good summary, see Christian Smith, "On 'Moralistic Therapeutic Deism' as U.S. Teenagers' Actual, Tacit, De Facto Religious Faith," *The 2005 Princeton Lectures on Youth, Church, and Culture* (2005): 46–57, https://www.ptsem.edu/uploadedFiles/School_of_Christian_Vocation_and_Mission/Institute_for_Youth_Ministry/Princeton_Lectures/Smith-Moralistic.pdf.

31. Ross Douthat, *Bad Religion: How We Became a Nation of Heretics* (New York: Free Press, 2012), 233.

32. Ibid., 53.

33. Katelyn Beaty and Christian Smith, "Lost in Transition," *Christianity Today*, October 9, 2009, http://www.christianitytoday.com/ct/2009/october/21.34.html.

34. Christian Smith, in Douthat, *Bad Religion*, 235.

35. Melinda Lundquist Denton and Christian Smith, *Soul Searching: The Religious and Social Lives of American Teenagers* (New York: Oxford University Press, 2005), 170.

36. Ibid., 171.

37. A. W. Tozer, *The Knowledge of the Holy: The Attributes of God; Their Meaning in the Christian Life* (New York: Harper and Row, 1961), 7.

38. Laurie Fendrich, "I Could Believe in God," *The Chronicle of Higher Education*, September 21, 2011, http://chronicle.com/blogs/brainstorm/i-could-believe-in-god/39443?sid=cr&utm_source=cr&utm_medium=en.

39. Skye Jethani, *With: Reimagining the Way You Relate to God* (Nashville: Thomas Nelson, 2011), 61.

40. Christopher Wright, "Living as the People of God," in *New Dictionary of Christian Ethics and Pastoral Theology*, ed. David J. Atkinson (Downers Grove, IL: IVP, 1995), 113, 117–24.

41. Ibid.

42. Term used by Michael Harris. See Michael Harris, *The End of Absence* (New York: Current Press, 2014), 15.

43. David Brooks, "What Is Your Purpose?" New York Times, May 5, 2015, http://www.nytimes.com/2015/05/05/opinion/david-brooks-whatis-your-purpose.html?_r=0.

44. Ibid.

Chapter 5

1. Jonathan Stock, "The Penitent Warlord: Atoning for 20,000 War Crimes," *ABC News Online*, November 2, 2013, http://abcnews.go.com/International/penitent-warlord-atoning-20000-war-crimes/story?id=20749940.

2. Aristotle, *Nichomachean Ethics*, trans. Terrence Irwin, 2nd ed. (Indianapolis, IN: Hackett, 1999), 2.1103a.

3. Timothy Keller, *Generous Justice: How God's Grace Makes Us Just* (New York: Riverhead Books, 2010), 3.

4. Daniel J. Simundson, *Abingdon Old Testament Commentary: Hosea, Joel, Amos, Obadiah, Jonah, Micah* (Nashville: Abingdon Press, 2005), 338.

5. Helen Fox, *Their Highest Vocation: Social Justice and the Millennial Generation* (New York: Peter Lang Publishing, 2012).

6. It is important to note here that this description of justice is used in the context of distributive justice, which is defined as being "concerned with the fair distribution of society's benefits and burdens," in Velasquez, 76. However, the dictum "each their due" is also present in forms of retributive justice (punishments and penalties) and compensatory justice (compensation for being wronged by others). See Manuel G. Velasquez, *Business Ethics: Concepts and Cases* (Upper Saddle River, NJ: Prentice Hall, 2002).

7. Plato, *The Republic of Plato*, ed. Allan Bloom (New York: Basic, 1991), 1.331e, 7. Note here that Simonides is quoted by Polemarchus when defining justice as giving "each what is owed."

8. Marx cited in Velasquez, *Business Ethics*, 81.

9. Jennifer L. Hochschild, *What's Fair? American Beliefs about Distributive Justice* (Cambridge, MA: Harvard University Press, 1981), 46.

10. Keller, *Generous Justice*, 3.

11. Ibid.

12. OT Scholar Dennis Kinlaw describes *chesedh* in Micah 6:8 as "the attitude and disposition of your being that determines how you act." In *Lectures in Old Testament Theology* (Wilmore, KY: Francis Asbury Society, 2010), 182.

13. Ibid., 23.

14. Gordon Graham, *The Idea of Christian Charity: A Critique of Some Contemporary Conceptions* (Notre Dame, IN: University of Notre Dame Press, 1990), 158.

15. Daniel Bell Jr., "Deliberating: Justice and Liberation," in Samuel Wells and Stanley Hauerwas, eds., *Blackwell Companion to Christian Ethics* (Malden, MA: Blackwell Publishing, 2006), 182–95.

16. Daniel Bell Jr., "Forgiveness and the End of Economy," *Studies in Christian Ethics* 20, no. 325 (2007): 333, 340.

17. Richard N. Longenecker, *New Testament Social Ethics for Today* (Grand Rapids, MI: Eerdmans, 1984), 52.

18. Miroslav Volf, *Exclusion & Embrace: A Theological Exploration of Identity, Otherness, and Reconciliation* (Nashville: Abingdon Press, 1996), 208; italics his.

19. Ibid., 213–14.

20. Ibid., 215.

21. Ibid., 221; italics mine.

22. See Matthew 20:1–16.

23. More specifically, it was a rabbinical story preserved in the Jerusalem Talmud according to Jeremias. See Joachim Jeremias, in Jan Lambrecht, *Out of the Treasure: The Parables in the Gospel of Matthew* (Louvain: Peeters Press/W. B. Eerdmans, 1998), 75.

24. Ibid.

25. Volf, *Exclusion & Embrace*, 214.

26. Timothy Gorringe, *Capital and the Kingdom:Theological Ethics and Economic Order* (New York: Orbis Books, 1994), 10; italics his.

27. Ibid., 24.

28. Gorringe often cites Levinas, whose famous work *Totality and Infinity* (1969) concerns itself with this very issue. Gorringe, however, outlines the implications within the context of the Christian faith tradition.

29. David Fillingim, *Extreme Virtues* (Scottdale, PA: Herald Press, 2003), 66.

30. Statistic found at Zach Epstein, "Horrifying Chart Reveals How Much Time We Spend Staring at Screens Each Day," *BGR*, May 29, 2014, http://bgr.com/2014/05/29/smartphone-computer-usage-study-chart/.

31. Dallas Willard, "Spiritual Disciplines, Spiritual Formation and the Restoration of the Soul," *Journal of Psychology and Theology* 26, no. 1 (1998): 101–09, http://www.dwillard.org/articles/artview.asp?artID=57.

32. Wyndy Corbin Reuschling, *Desire for God and the Things of God* (Eugene, OR: Cascade Books/Wipf and Stock, 2012), 34.

33. Caitlin Johnson, "Cutting through Advertising Clutter" *CBS Sunday Morning*, September 17, 2006, http://www.cbsnews.com/news/cutting -through-advertising-clutter/.

34. Tim Urban, "Why Generation Y Yuppies Are Unhappy," *Huffington Post*, November 15, 2013, http://www.huffingtonpost.com/wait-but-why /generation-y-unhappy_b_3930620.html.

35. Roger Ebert, "Review: Chariots of Fire," RogerEbert.com, January 1, 1981, http://www.rogerebert.com/reviews/chariots-of-fire-1981.

36. Kathleen Norris, John D. Witvliet, and Enuma Okoro, "Three Views: Why Confess Sins in Worship When It Seems So Rote?" *Christianity Today*, November 22, 2013, http://www.christianitytoday.com/ct/2013/december /why-confess-sins-inworship-when-it-seems-so-rote.html.

37. See Joel Green and Will Willimon, *The Wesley Study Bible New Revised Standard Version* (Nashville: Abingdon Press, 2009).

38. Paul Woodruff, *Reverence: Renewing a Forgotten Virtue*, 2nd ed. (New York: Oxford University Press, 2014), 1; italics mine.

39. In this text, the authors argue that their study (2000) was one of the first to actually address evangelicalism and contemporary racial division in the United States. See Michael O. Emerson and Christian Smith, *Divided by Faith: Evangelical Religion and the Problem of Race in America* (New York: Oxford University Press), 2000.

40. They write: "We argue that religion, as structured in America, is unable to make a great impact on the racialized society. In fact, far from knocking down racial barriers, religion generally serves to maintain these historical divides, and helps to develop new ones." See Emerson and Smith, *Divided by Faith*, 18.

41. Individual-level problems might include education, lack of work motivation and effort, proclivities toward crime, etc. See Emerson and Smith, *Divided by Faith*, 40, 89.

42. Ibid., 80.

43. Ibid., 106.

44. Ibid., 107.

45. James Loder, *The Logic of the Spirit: Human Development in Theological Perspective* (San Francisco: Jossey-Bass Publishers, 1998), 4.

Chapter 6

1. Robin Lovin, *Christian Ethics: An Essential Guide* (Nashville: Abingdon Press, 2000), 63.

2. Kelvin Knight, *Aristotelian Philosophy*, 45.

3. Ibid., 43.

4. Christopher West, *Theology of the Body for Beginners* (West Chester, PA: Ascension Press, 2009), 19.

5. Ibid., 20.

6. Ibid.

7. Friedrich Hegel in Gerry A. Cohen, *If You're an Egalitarian, How Come You're So Rich?* (Cambridge, MA: Harvard University Press, 2000), 83.

8. Ibid.

9. West, *Theology of the Body for Beginners*, 8.

10. Skye Jethani, *With: Reimagining the Way You Relate to God* (Nashville: Thomas Nelson, 2011), 15–16.

11. Ibid., 16

12. Stanley Hauerwas, *Christian Existence Today: Essays on Church, World, and Living in Between* (Durham, NC: The Labyrinth Press, 1988), 245.

13. Dallas Willard points out that we should not equate "flesh" with "fallen human nature." In other words, Paul calls us to take off the "flesh"— which we cannot do in a literal sense. So, a "fleshly body" is not the problem; it is the nature of sin that resides in the fleshly body. Willard writes: "The true effect of the Fall was to lead us to trust in the flesh alone." See *The Spirit of the Disciplines: Understanding How God Changes Lives* (San Francisco: HarperSanFrancisco, 1990), 90–91.

14. Ross Douthat, interview by Bill Maher, *Real Time*, episode 245, April 20, 2012.

15. These certainly aren't the only stories to explain ourselves and the world around us—but they are dominant in our culture, and moreover, they contrast sharply.

16. "Margaret Thatcher's famous proclamation that 'There is no such thing as society,'" Margaret Thatcher Foundation, September 23, 1987, http://www.margaretthatcher.org/document/106689.

17. From Rand's book *Anthem* (Claremont, CA: Coyote Canyon Press, 2008), 104.

18. Amy Gutmann and Dennis Thompson, *Why Deliberative Democracy?* (Princeton, NJ: Princeton University Press, 2004), 64.

19. This finds its clearest expression in John Stuart Mill's famous "Liberty Principle." He says, "The liberty of the individual . . . must not make himself a nuisance to other people. But if he refrains from molesting others in what concerns them, and merely acts according to his own inclination and judgment in things which concern himself, the same reasons which show that opinion should be free, prove also that he should be allowed, without molestation, to carry his opinions into practice at his own cost." In other words, people are free to do what they want, so long as it

does not prohibit others from doing what they want. See Mill in Michael Curtis, *The Great Political Theories* (New York: Avon, 1981), 197.

20. Michael Sandel, "America's Search for a New Public Philosophy," *The Atlantic Monthly* (1996): 57–74.

21. In his book introduction on consumer culture entitled "Christ and Consumerism," Craig Bartholomew describes three major differences between simple commerce and consumerism. First, he notes that consumerism is a culture in which the core values are derived from consumption, and not where consumption is derived from a predefined set of core values. Second, freedom is equated with individual choice and private life. A postmodern culture exalts choice over what is chosen, and this, somehow, equates to true freedom. Finally, Bartholomew describes consumer culture as one in which needs are unlimited and insatiable. See "Christ and Consumerism: An Introduction," in *Christ and Consumerism: Critical Reflections on the Spirit of Our Age*, ed. Craig Bartholomew and Thorsten Moritz (Carlisle: Paternoster Press, 2000), 1–11.

22. Michael Sandel, *Public Philosophy: Essays on Morality in Politics* (Cambridge, MA: Harvard University Press, 2005), 162.

23. The philosopher John Rawls went on to refer to communal affections as "lower-order impulses." See Samuel R. Freeman and John Rawls, *Collected Papers* (Cambridge, MA: Harvard University Press, 2001), 315.

24. John Wesley, *Explanatory Notes upon the New Testament* (New York: J. Soule and T. Mason for the Methodist Episcopal Church in the United States, 1818), 174.

25. David Fergusson, *Community, Liberalism and Christian Ethics* (Cambridge: Cambridge University Press, 1998), 143.

26. Herbert Blumer, "Sociological Implications of the Thought of George Herbert Mead," *American Journal of Sociology* 71, no. 5 (1966): 535–44.

27. Indeed, Fergusson (1998) writes that this assumption underlines much of communitarian thinking: "The communitarian . . . is more impressed by the essentially social nature of the human being. The self is formed by its roles, attachments, and relationships with other people, institutions, communities, and traditions." See *Community, Liberalism, and Christian Ethics*, 139.

28. Blumer, "Sociological Implications," 535.

29. Stanley Hauerwas, *The Peaceable Kingdom: A Primer in Christian Ethics* (Notre Dame, IN: University of Notre Dame Press, 1983), 96–97.

30. In South Africa, this concept is referred to as *Ubuntu*. The term reflects the shared humanity that we all inevitably participate in; that is, one human is *no* human. We are who we are because of our engagement and involvement in the lives of others.

31. Alasdair MacIntyre, in Christopher Stephen Lutz, *Tradition in the Ethics of Alasdair MacIntyre: Relativism, Thomism, and Philosophy* (Lanham, MD: Lexington, 2004), 9.

32. Hauerwas, *The Peaceable Kingdom*, 27.

33. Michael Matheson Miller, "Moral Imagination" (lecture, Acton University, Grand Rapids, MI, June 19, 2015).

34. *History*, United States Holocaust Memorial Museum, Fall 2011, http://www.ushmm.org/information/exhibitions.

35. Ben Tinker, "The Pros and Cons of Porn: It Just Isn't What It Used to Be," *CNN.com*, October 16, 2015, http://www.cnn.com/2015/10/16/health /playboy-explicit-porn/index.html.

36. Reinhold Niebuhr, *Moral Man and Immoral Society: A Study of Ethics and Politics* (Louisville, KY: Westminster John Knox Press, 2002), 1.

37. Thomas Hobbes, *Leviathan* (London: Routledge, 1894), 64.

38. Murray N. Rothbard, *The Ethics of Liberty* (New York: New York University Press, 1998), viiii.

39. Ibid., 172.

40. Hauerwas, *The Peaceable Kingdom*, 49.

41. Olivia, in William Shakespeare, "Twelfth Night" Act 3, Scene 1.

42. Kairos Prison Ministry International, "Kairos Frequently Asked Questions," n.d., http://www.mykairos.org/faq.html.

43. C. S. Lewis, *The Problem of Pain* (New York: Harper One, 1996), 63.

44. Lewis in P. H. Brazier, *C. S. Lewis—On the Christ of a Religious Economy, I. Creation and Sub-Creation* (Eugene, OR: Pickwick/Wipf and Stock, 2013), 56.

45. I greatly owe the exposition to the work of John Oswalt. See *Called to be Holy: A Biblical Perspective* (Nappanee, IN: Francis Asbury Press of Evangel, 1999).

46. Hauerwas, *The Peaceable Kingdom*, 60.

47. I borrow this expression from Pastor Steve Deneff, College Wesleyan Church in Marion, Indiana.

48. N. T. Wright, *Evil and the Justice of God* (Downers Grove, IL: InterVarsity Press, 2006), 120.

49. Lee Camp, *Mere Discipleship: Radical Christianity in a Rebellious World* (Grand Rapids, MI: Brazos Press, 2008), 188.

50. Brooks, *The Road to Character*, 201.

51. G. K. Chesterton, *A Piece of Chalk*, The American Chesterton Society, n.d., https://www.chesterton.org/a-piece-of-chalk/.

52. Will Willimon, *Shaped by the Bible* (Nashville: Abingdon Press, 1990), 83; italics mine.

53. Jill Carattini, "Land of Likeness," *A Slice of Infinity* (journal of Ravi Zacharias International Ministries), May 2, 2014, http://ca.rzim.org/a-slice -of-infinity/land-of-likeness/.

54. John Stonestreet, "Christianity and Cultural Responsibility" (Grand Rapids, MI: Acton University, 2015).

55. Marcus Borg and N. T. Wright, *The Meaning of Jesus: Two Visions* (New York: HarperCollins, 1999), 126–27.

Chapter 7

1. On the "About Us" section of their website, *The Economist* cites a commitment to 'free trade and free markets.'

2. This defense has taken on several forms. For example, many insist that the financial crisis is just as much of a regulatory failure as it is a market failure.

3. "Onwards and Upwards," *The Economist*, December 17, 2009, http://www.economist.com/node/15108593.

4. From Dawkins's book *The God Delusion* (Boston: Houghton Mifflin, 2006).

5. LaRue Tome Hosmer, *The Ethics of Management* (New York: McGraw Hill, 2011), 113.

6. Manuel G. Velasquez, *Business Ethics: Concepts and Cases* (Upper Saddle River, NJ: Prentice Hall, 2002), 5.

7. Lynn S. Paine, "Is Ethics Good Business? Interview with Lynn Sharp Paine," *Challenge Magazine* (2003): 6–21, esp. 10, http://www.challengemagazine.com/Challenge%20interview%20pdfs/Paine.pdf.

8. WKYT Staff, "A Breakdown of the Kim Davis Same-Sex Marriage Case," WKYT, September 9, 2015, http://www.wkyt.com/home/headlines/A-breakdown-of-the-Kim-Davis-same-sex-marriage-case-325915631.html.

9. Peter Kreeft, *Philosophy 101 by Socrates: An Introduction to Philosophy via Plato's* Apology (San Francisco: Ignatius Press, 2002), 103.

10. Ibid., 109.

11. It is worth noting that the Euthyphro Dilemma is not simply a dilemma for people of faith. We could just as easily ask if someone's prescription for living or their various value judgments are made by that person because they are good, or are they good because they are made by that person. If the latter, then goodness is arbitrary to the person; if the former, then there is—at the very least—an appeal to some transcendent standard of goodness that would have to be defined.

12. Dick Staub, "What 'Made in the Image of God' Really Means: Taking a Second Look at a Very Misunderstood Part of Our Faith," *Relevant Magazine*, March 4, 2013, http://www.relevantmagazine.com/god/deeper-walk/features/23549-qmade-in-the-image-of-godq#fzELHi2Rb1szr4St.99.

13. John Paul II, *A Theology of the Body*, ed. and trans. Michael Waldstein (Boston: Pauline Books and Media, 2006), 137; 3:1.

14. Ibid.